AF482127

Cool Restaurants
Las Vegas

teNeues

Imprint

Editor: Patrice Farameh

Editorial direction: Martin Nicholas Kunz
Editorial coordination: Rosina Geiger

Photos (location): E Brands Restaurants, food (AquaKnox), Jeff Green (Boa Steakhouse 24, 25, Sushi
Roku), courtesy Chinois restaurant (Chinois, food), courtesy MGM MIRAGE (Craftsteak, food; Fiamma 48,
50, 51, 52; Mix; Fleur de Lys; Noodles 90, 91; Pearl; Restaurant rm; Sensi; Shibuya), Bill Milne for Wynn
Las Vegas (Daniel Boulud Brasserie, Okada), courtesy Eiffel Tower Restaurant: Steinkamp/Ballogg (Eiffel
Tower Restaurant 46, 47), Ricardo Ridecos (Fix), Jerry Metellus (N9NE Steakhouse), Ian Vaughn (N9NE
Steakhouse, food), Rockwell Group/Paul Warchol (Nobu), Shibata publishing Co. Ltd.: Eiichi Takahashi
(Nobu, food), courtesy Simon (Simon kitchen & bar), Warren Jagger (Tao), courtesy Wolfgang Puck Bar &
Grill (Wolfgang Puck Bar & Grill)
All other photos are by Gavin Jackson

Introduction: Patrice Farameh

Layout & Pre-press: Martin Nicholas Kunz

Imaging: Jeremy Ellington

Translations: SAW Communications, Dr. Sabine A. Werner, Mainz
Melanie Koster (German / introduction), Nina Hausberg (German, English / recipes),
Sabine Boccador (French), Silvia Gómez de Antonio (Spanish), Maria-Letizia Haas (Italian)

Produced by fusion publishing GmbH, Stuttgart . Los Angeles   www.fusion-publishing.com

Published by teNeues Publishing Group

teNeues Book Division
Kaistraße 18
40221 Düsseldorf, Germany
Tel.: 0049-(0)211-994597-0
Fax: 0049-(0)211-994597-40
E-mail: books@teneues.de

teNeues France S.A.R.L.
4, rue de Valence
75005 Paris, France
Tel.: 0033-1-55766205
Fax: 0033-1-55766419

teNeues Publishing Company
16 West 22nd Street
New York, NY 10010, USA
Tel.: 001-212-627-9090
Fax: 001-212-627-9511

teNeues Ibérica S.L.
c/Velázquez, 57 6.° izda.
28001 Madrid, Spain
Tel.: 0034-657-132133

teNeues Publishing UK Ltd.
P.O. Box 402
West Byfleet
KT14 7ZF, Great Britain
Tel.: 0044-1932-403509
Fax: 0044-1932-403514

teNeues
Representative Office Italy
Via San Vittore 36/1
20123 Milan
Tel.: 0039-(0)347-7640551

Press department: arehn@teneues.de
Phone: 0049-2152-916-202

www.teneues.com

ISBN-10: 3-8327-9116-7
ISBN-13: 978-3-8327-9116-2

© 2006 teNeues Verlag GmbH + Co. KG, Kempen

Printed in Italy

Bibliographic information published by Die Deutsche Bibliothek.
Die Deutsche Bibliothek lists this publication in the Deutsche Nationalbibliografie;
detailed bibliographic data is available in the Internet at http://dnb.ddb.de.

Average price reflects the average cost for a dinner main course without beverages. Recipes serve four.

Contents   Page

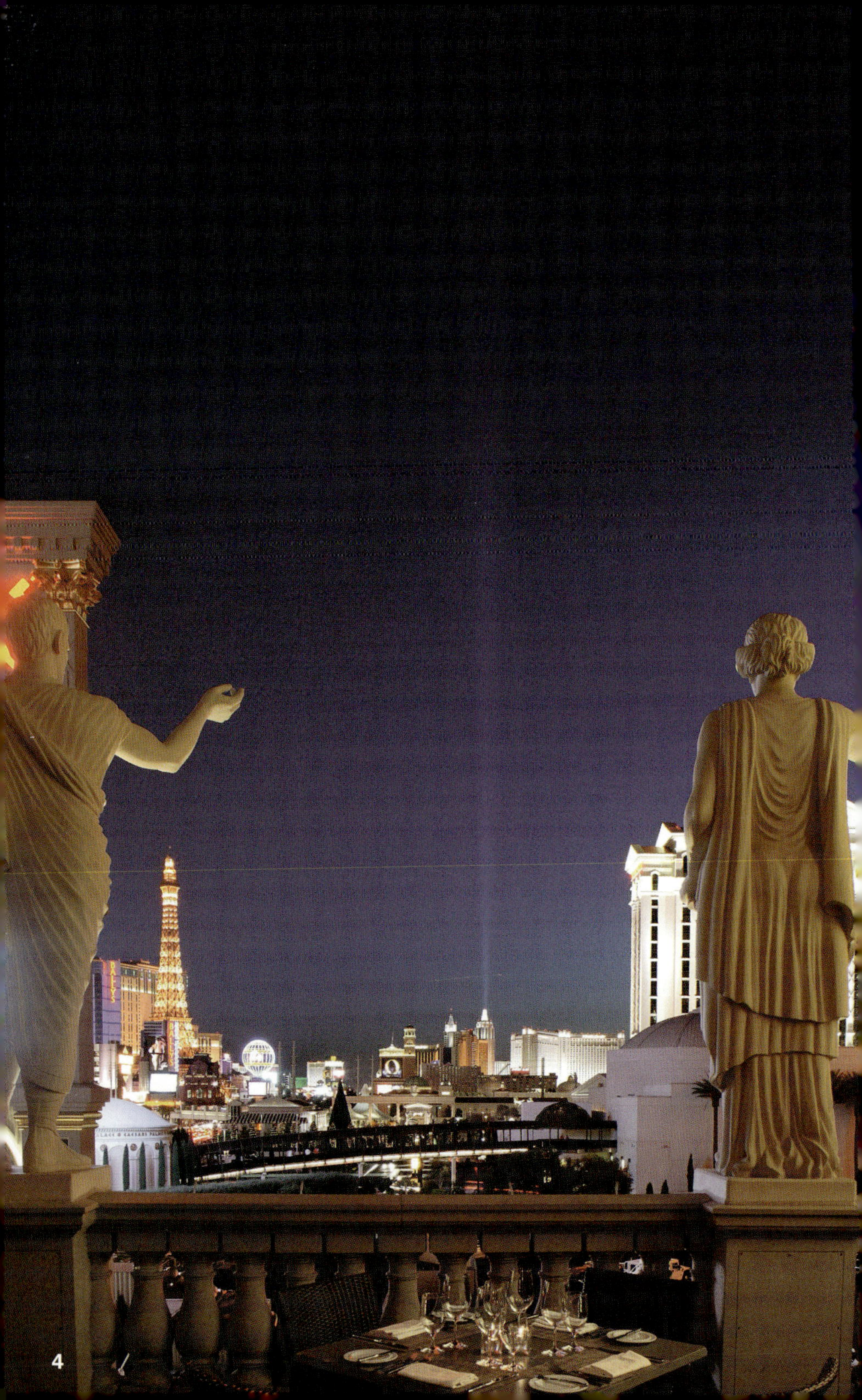

Introduction

Las Vegas, a city literally carved out of a desert and built on dreams, is America's most outrageous themed playground of extravagant pleasure palaces. The four mile artery of flashing neon that runs through Las Vegas, once infamous for enticing gamblers into their casinos with sizzling shows, big name entertainment, and $9.99 steak specials, has evolved into the nation's premiere dining Mecca. Today, casinos try to demand individual recognition by creating a dining experience to seduce even the most discerning gourmands into their restaurants with award-winning cuisines, such an $175 entree of Kobe beef at Bradley Ogden, and with uniqueness in architecture and surreal interiors, such as the four-story tower of 10,000 wine bottles at Charlie Palmer's Aureole.
Since Wolfgang Puck opened his star-studded Spago a decade ago, celebrity chefs have flocked to Las Vegas in record numbers. This Celebrity Chef Mania has created a melting pot of rare tastes from the world's best cuisines served up in ultra-upscale settings, trying to be as exotic and decadent as all the others. Chefs such as Daniel Boulud, Nobu Matsuhisa, and Bobby Flay have all set up bigger, and bolder restaurants, drawing attention and breathless praise for their designer endeavors.
In the city known for unbridled excess, visionaries are also ramping up the already lively restaurant scene by mating dining and nightclub adventure, such as the opulent, 40,000 square foot temple of Tao and the eclectic, Asian-inspired Little Buddha.
A wealth of over 100 stunning photographs celebrate these Las Vegas restaurants as aesthetic art and illustrate the best representatives of the modernized dining adventure in Sin City, including extracts of favorite recipes from internationally acclaimed chefs. Whether relaxing in elegance or energetic in party, one thing is for sure. These restaurants are stylish in every way, and you're sure to love the performance.

Patrice Farameh

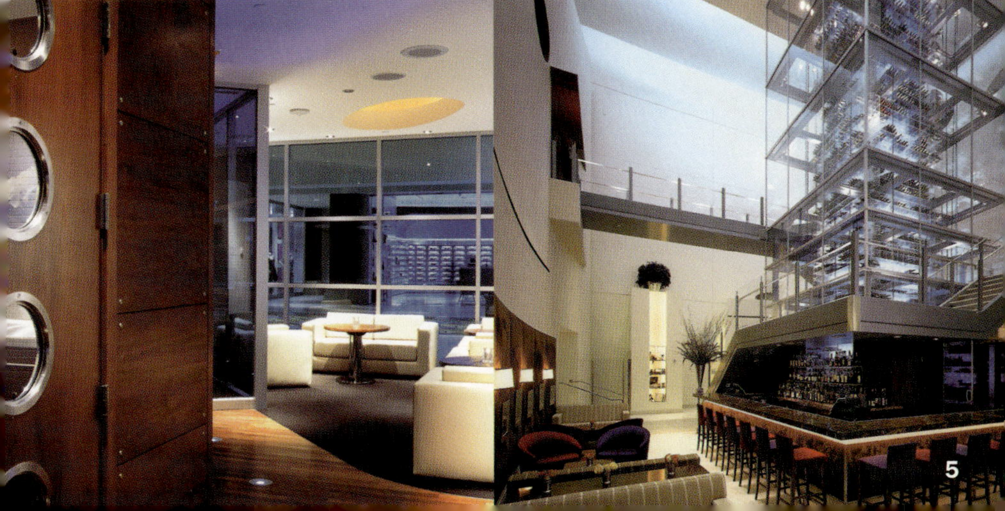

Einleitung

Las Vegas, aus der Wüste geformt und auf Träumen erbaut, ist mit seinen extra-
vaganten Vergnügungspalästen Amerikas grellster Spielplatz. Die sechseinhalb
Kilometer lange Aorta aus blinkenden Neonlichtern, die sich durch Las Vegas zieht
und einst berüchtigt dafür war, mit heißen Shows, Super-Stars und Steaks für nur
$ 9.99 Spieler in ihre Casinos zu locken, hat sich zum wichtigsten Speise-Mekka
des Landes entwickelt. Heute streben die Casinos nach Individualität, indem sie
selbst kritischste Gourmets mit kulinarischen Erlebnissen aus preisgekrönter Cuisine, wie einem Hauptgericht für $ 175 aus Kobe-Rind im Bradley Ogden, in ihre
Restaurants zu locken versuchen, oder durch einzigartige Architektur und surreale
Interieurs, wie dem vier Stockwerke hohen Turm aus 10.000 Weinflaschen in
Charlie Palmers Aureole.
Seit Wolfgang Puck vor zehn Jahren sein mit Sternen ausgezeichnetes Spago
eröffnete, kann sich Las Vegas vor Starköchen kaum noch retten. Diese Star-
koch-Manie hat einen Schmelztiegel der erlesensten und besten Küchen der Welt
entstehen lassen, an gigantischen Schauplätzen, die einander an Exotik und De-
kadenz zu übertreffen versuchen. Köche wie Daniel Boulud, Nobu Matsuhisa und
Bobby Flay ziehen mit gewaltigen und gewagten Restaurants, mit ausgefallenen
Designs Aufmerksamkeit und Bewunderung auf sich.
In der Stadt, die für ihre grenzenlosen Exzesse bekannt ist, mischen auch Visionä-
re die ohnehin schon extrem lebhafte Restaurant-Szene auf, indem sie das Erleb-
nis des Speisens mit dem Abenteuerhaften eines Nachtclubs verquicken, so wie
im opulenten 3.700 m² großen Tempel des Tao und dem eklektischen, asiatisch
angehauchten Little Buddha.
Mehr als 130 atemberaubende und ästhetische Fotografien erheben diese Restaurants in Las Vegas zur Kunst und stellen die besten Beispiele des modernen
kulinarischen Abenteuers in der Stadt der Sünde vor und gewähren Ihnen einen
Einblick in die beliebtesten Rezepte international gefeierter Köche. Ganz gleich,
ob Sie einfach nur in eleganter Umgebung entspannen wollen oder auf Party aus
sind, eines ist sicher: Stylisch sind diese Restaurants in jeder Hinsicht und Sie
werden vom dargebotenen Szenario begeistert sein.

Patrice Farameh

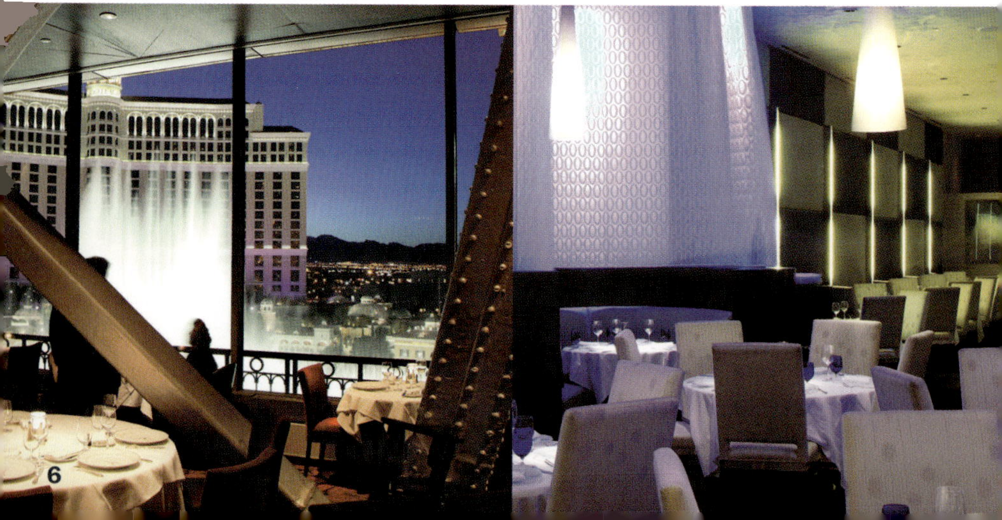

Introduction

Las Vegas, créée au beau milieu du désert et bâtie sur des rêves, est le plus éblouissant terrain de jeux de l'Amérique avec ses palais extravagants destinés à l'amusement. Parcourue de néons étincelants, l'aorte de six kilomètres et demi de long qui traverse Las Vegas était autrefois réputée pour attirer dans ses casinos les joueurs qui venaient pour ses spectacles chauds, ses « super stars » et ses steaks pour seulement 9,99 $. Las Vegas est pourtant devenue le point de rendez-vous gastronomique le plus important du pays. Aujourd'hui, les casinos aspirent à plus d'individualité et tentent même d'attirer les gourmets les plus critiques avec leur gastronomie étoilée, par exemple avec un plat de bœuf de Kobe à 175 $ au Bradley Ogden, ainsi qu'avec l'architecture singulière et les intérieurs surréalistes de leurs restaurants, comme les quatre étages de la grande tour de l'Aureole de Charlie Palmer, réalisée à partir de 10 000 bouteilles de vin.
Depuis que Wolfgang Puck a ouvert il y a dix ans le remarquable Spago étoilé, les stars gastronomiques accourent à Las Vegas. En raison de cet engouement des grands chefs cuisiniers, la ville est devenue le creuset des meilleures cuisines du monde dans des lieux gigantesques qui rivalisent d'exotisme et de décadence. Cuisiniers comme Daniel Boulud, Nobu Matsuhisa et Bobby Flay nous émerveillent et attirent également l'attention en exerçant leurs talents dans des restaurants monumentaux et osés au design original.
Dans cette ville connue pour ses excès sans limites, les visionnaires mélangent aussi la scène extrêmement vivante des restaurants avec celle des clubs nocturnes, comme dans le grand temple opulent du Tao de 3 700 m² et dans le Little Buddha éclectique et d'influence asiatique.
Plus de 130 photographies esthétiques et d'une beauté à en couper le souffle transforment ces restaurants de Las Vegas en œuvres d'art et illustrent parfaitement la gastronomie moderne de la ville des péchés. Elles vous offrent un aperçu des recettes les plus appréciées des chefs cuisiniers de renommée internationale. Peu importe que vous souhaitiez simplement vous détendre dans un environnement élégant ou que vous ayez envie de vous amuser, une chose est sûre : les restaurants sont stylés à tous points de vue et vous serez enthousiasmé par la mise en scène qu'ils proposent.

Patrice Farameh

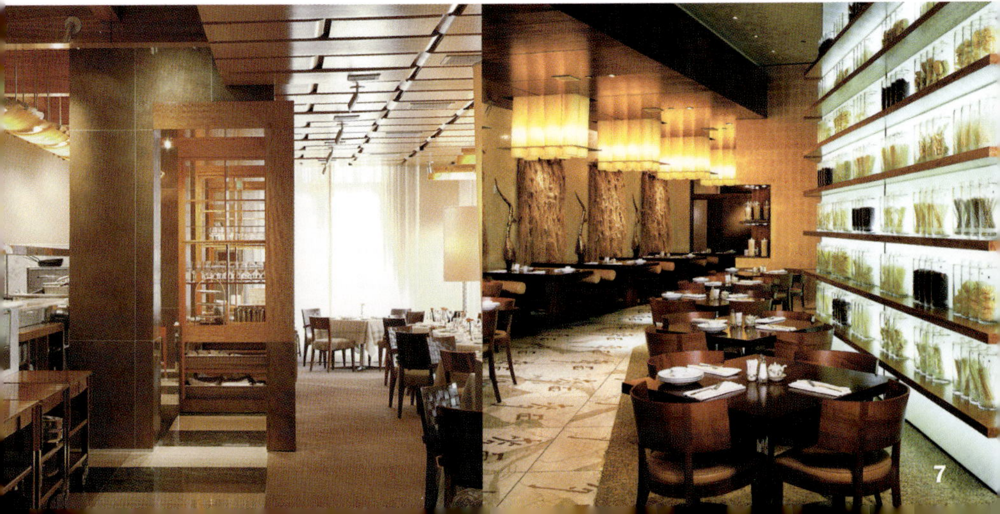

Introducción

Las Vegas, una ciudad erigida en el desierto y cimentada sobre sueños, es el patio de juegos más estridente de América donde se levantan los palacios del placer más extravagantes. La aorta de seis kilómetros y medio de luces de neón que recorre toda la ciudad, tuvo una vez la mala fama de atraer a los jugadores hasta sus casinos con espectáculos excitantes, estrellas y steaks por sólo 9,99 dólares. Hoy, esta ciudad se ha convertido en la meca culinaria más importante del país. Los casinos buscan ahora la individualidad y, para alcanzarla, intentan atraer incluso a gourmets críticos a través de aventuras culinarias de cocinas premiadas, como un plato principal de carne de vaca de Kobe por 175 dólares en Bradley Ogden, o mediante una arquitectura única e interiores surrealistas, como la torre de cuatro pisos de altura compuesta de 10.000 botellas de vino en el Aureole de Charlie Palmer.

Desde que Wolfgang Puck abriera hace diez años su Spago, premiado con estrellas, Las Vegas se ha convertido en el destino de famosos cocineros. Esta moda de cocineros estrella ha permitido la aparición de un crisol de las mejores y más selectas cocinas del mundo presentado en escenarios que intentan superarse en exotismo y decadencia. Cocineros como Daniel Boulud, Nobu Matsuhisa y Bobby Flay se inclinan por impresionantes y atrevidos restaurantes de extravagantes diseños interiores para atraer la atención y la admiración.

En esta ciudad, conocida por sus excesos sin límites, los visionarios agitan también el mundo de la restauración, ya de por sí muy animado, uniendo la experiencia culinaria con la extravagancia de los clubes nocturnos, como el opulento templo de Tao, de 3.700 m², o el Little Buddha, ecléctico y con reminiscencias asiáticas.

Las más de 130 embriagadoras fotografías de este libro elevan a los restaurantes de Las Vegas hasta la categoría de arte y presentan a los mejores representantes de la moderna experiencia culinaria de la ciudad de los pecados, al mismo tiempo que permiten al lector conocer las recetas más populares de cocineros mundialmente reconocidos. No importa si lo que desea es sólo relajarse en un ambiente elegante o si lo que más le apetece es ir de fiesta, sólo hay una cosa segura: estos restaurantes están llenos de estilo y su puesta en escena le fascinará.

Patrice Farameh

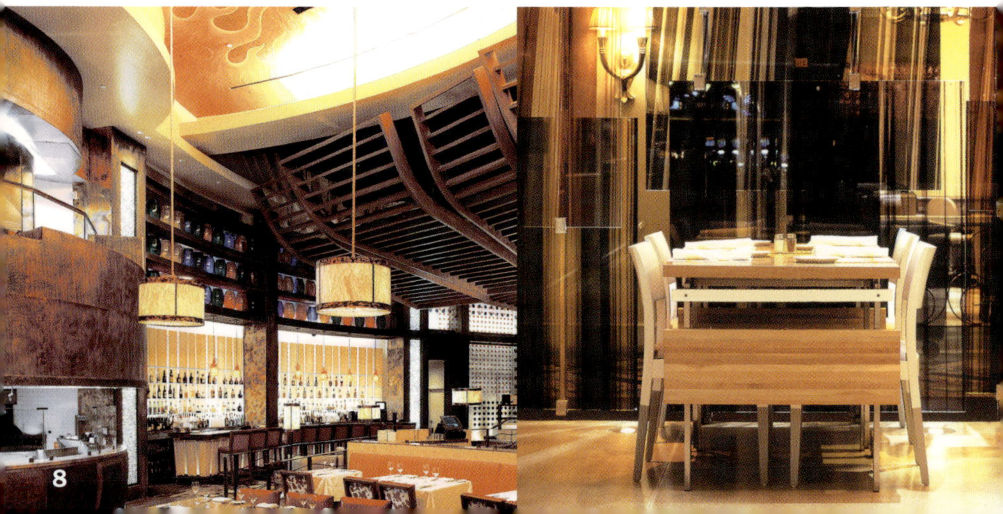

Introduzione

Las Vegas, una città sorta dal deserto e costruita sui sogni: con le sue strava-
ganti roccaforti del divertimento, essa è il parco-giochi più colorato d'America. La
via principale, pullulante di luci al neon, che si snoda per sei chilometri e mezzo
attraverso la città, e che un tempo era nota per attirare gli amanti del gioco con
show eccitanti, star di grido e bistecche a soli 9,99 dollari, si è trasformata nella
Mecca gastronomica più importante del Paese. Oggi le case da gioco aspirano ad
una individualità tutta loro, e cercano di attirare nei propri ristoranti perfino i buon-
gustai più esigenti, per mezzo di ottimi menu e della straordinaria architettura che
caratterizza i loro interni, dal carattere surreale: è il caso del Bradley Ogden, che
propone un piatto a base di manzo Kobe per la cifra di 175 dollari, o dell'Aureole
di Charlie Palmer, che richiama la clientela con la sua torre di quattro piani fatta
di 10.000 bottiglie di vino.
Da quando, dieci anni fa, Wolfgang Puck aprì il rinomato Spago, Las Vegas non si
è più salvata dall'assalto di cuochi di fama internazionale, che hanno dato origine
ad un crogiuolo delle migliori cucine del mondo, sulla scena di luoghi straordinari,
che fanno a gara tra loro per fascino esotico e decadente. Maestri come Daniel
Boulud, Nobu Matsuhisa e Bobby Flay puntano invece su ristoranti grandi e dal
carattere particolare, che attirano l'attenzione e conquistano grazie allo straordina-
rio design.
In questa città, famosa per i suoi eccessi, trovano il loro posto anche visiona-
ri che arricchiscono lo scenario gastronomico, già estremamente vivo, unendo
all'esperienza del cibo l'avventura che solo un nightclub è in grado di offrire, come
il Tempio del Tao, opulento locale di 3.700 m², o il Little Buddha, eclettico, dal
fascino orientale.
Oltre 130 splendide fotografie elevano ad arte l'essenza dei ristoranti di Las
Vegas, presentando i migliori locali in cui andare incontro a questa moderna avventura gastronomica nella "città del peccato". Cool Restaurants Las Vegas Vi
regala alcune delle ricette più note ideate da cuochi di fama internazionale, in una
cornice di stile assoluto, che convincerà sia coloro che vogliono solo rilassarsi in
un ambiente elegante, sia gli amanti delle feste: il risultato sarà in ogni caso entu-
siasmante.

Patrice Farameh

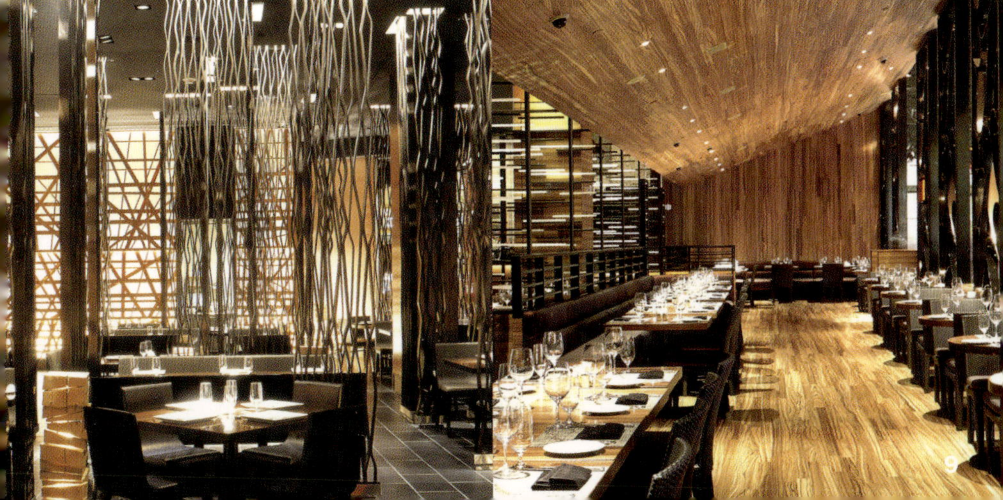

AquaKnox

Design: Gail McCleese | Chef: Tom Moloney
Owner: E Brands Restaurants

3355 Las Vegas Boulevard | Las Vegas, NV 89109 | The Venetian Resort Hotel Casino
Phone: +1 702 414 3772
www.e-brands.com
Opening hours: Daily from 5 pm
Average price: $ 75
Cuisine: Global Water Cuisine, Seafood
Special features: Water encased walk in wine tower

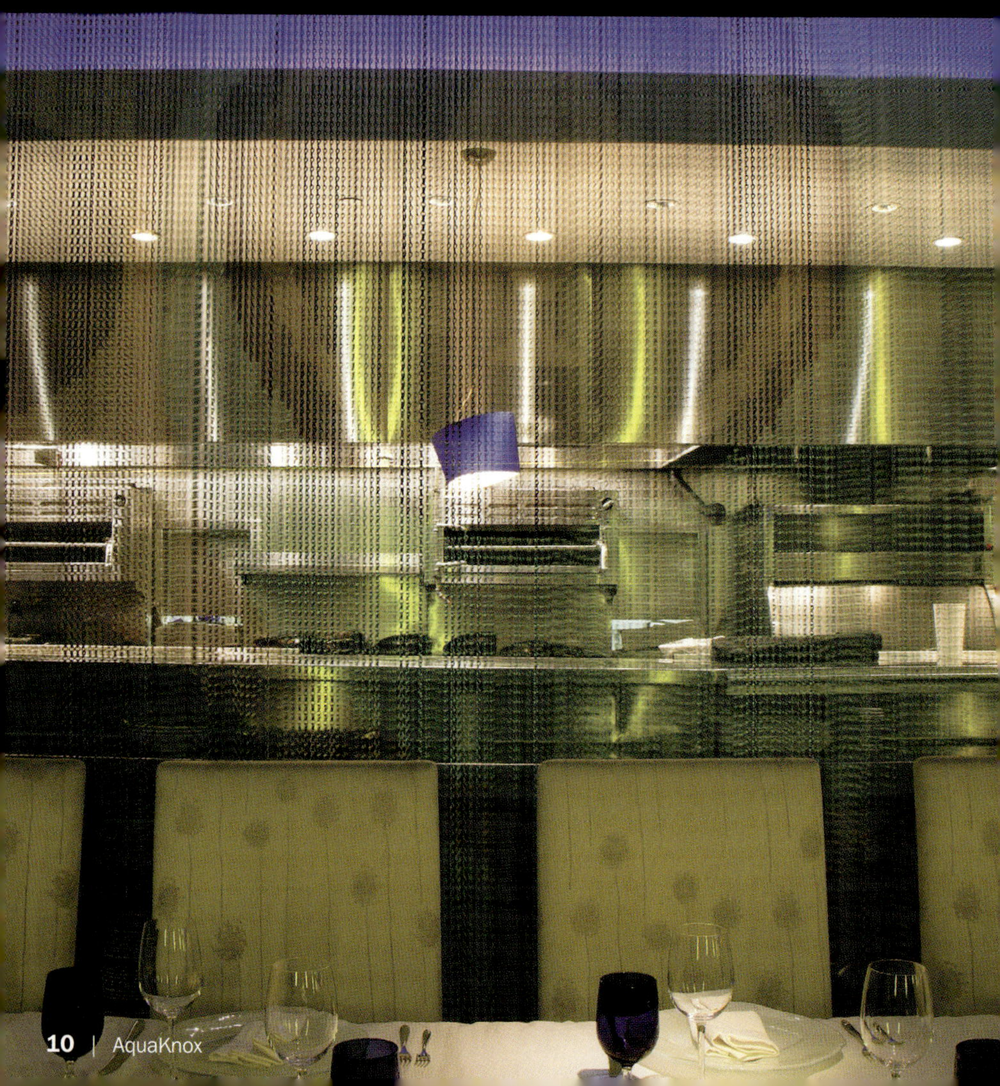

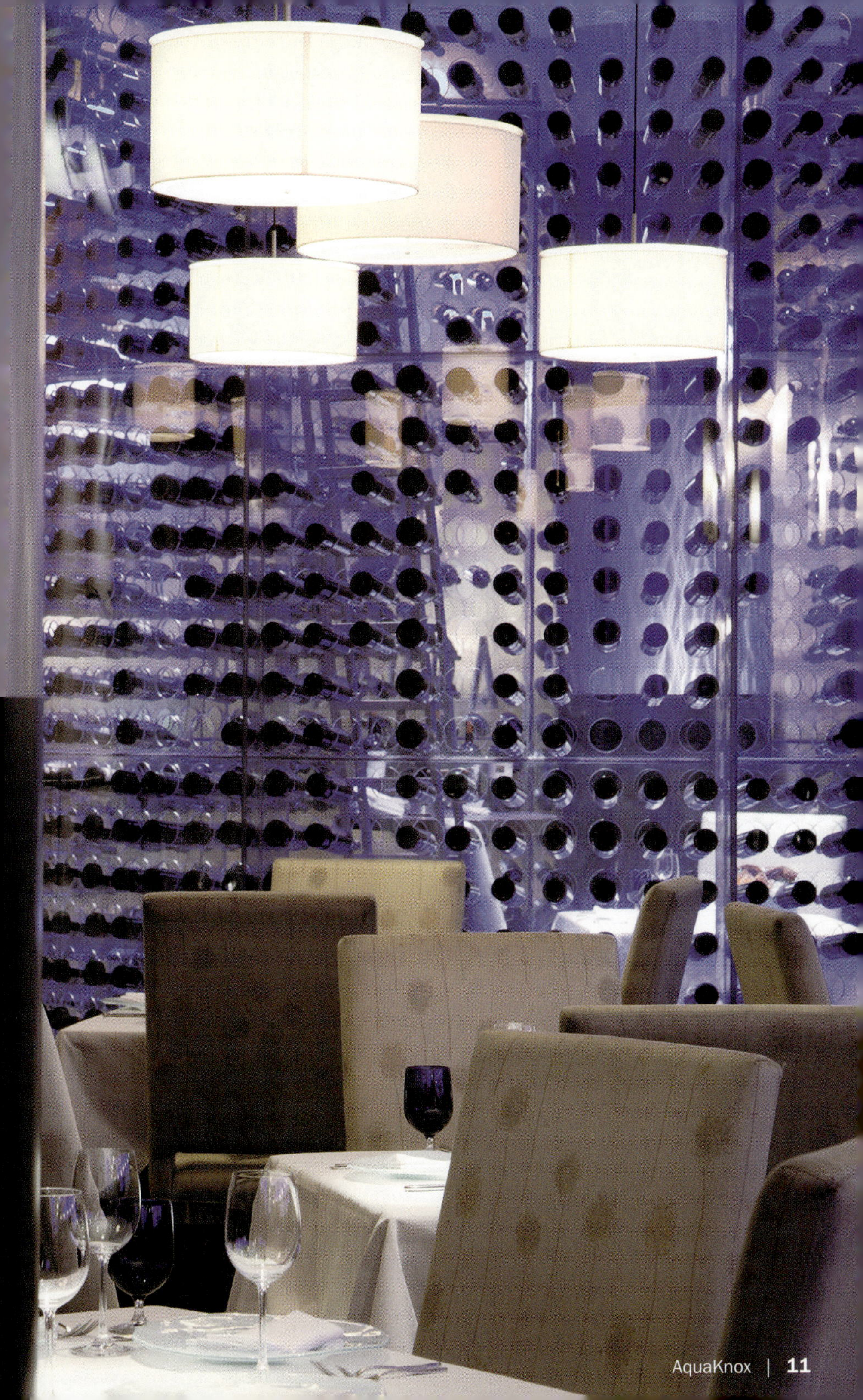

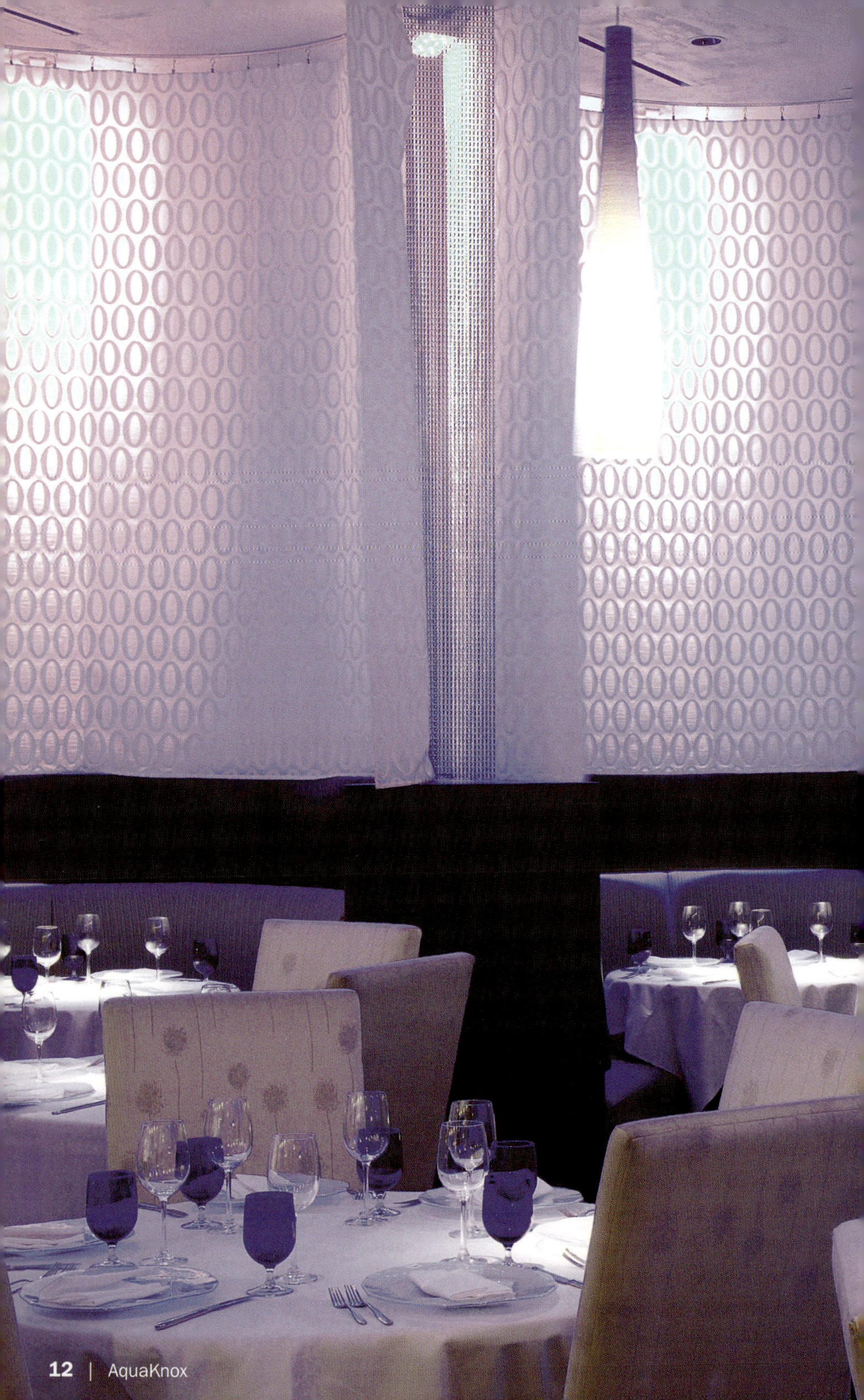

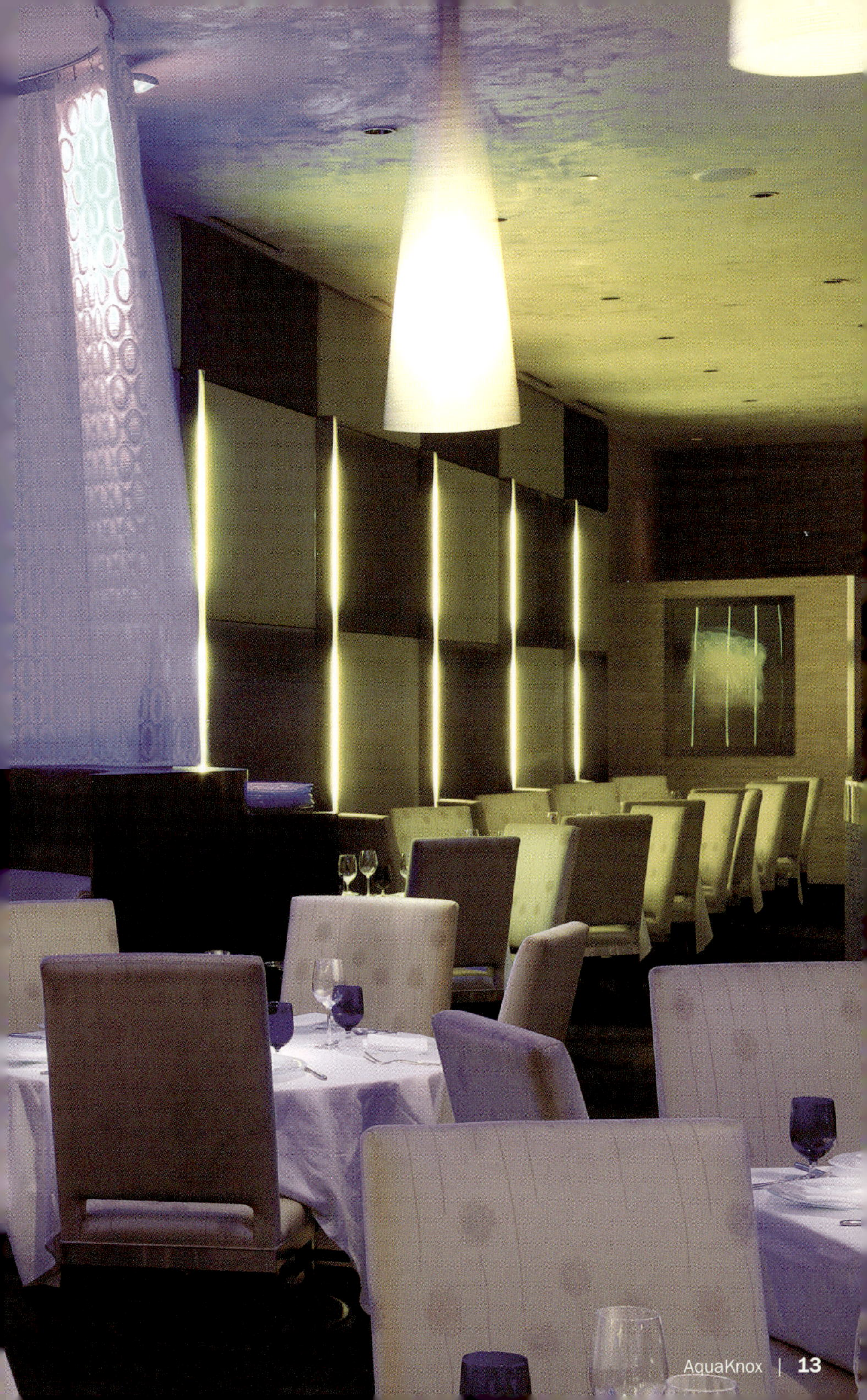

John Dory

Heringskönig

Saint-pierre

Pez de San Pedro

Pesce San Pietro

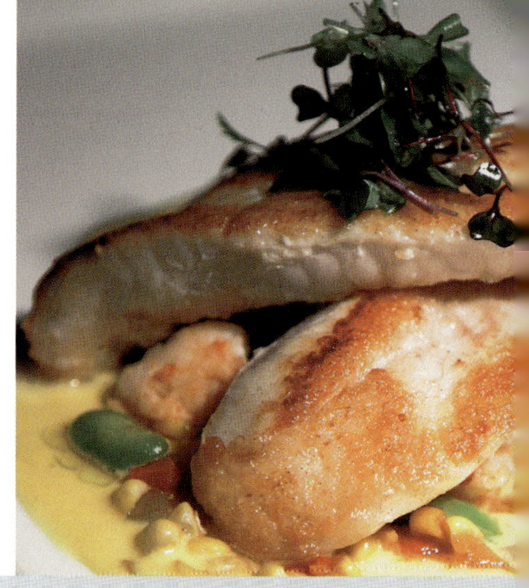

4 John Dory fillets, 6 oz each
Salt, pepper
3 tbsp vegetable oil

4 ears of corn
2 twigs of thyme
1 tbsp sugar
2 onions, diced
2 carrots, diced
8 oz green beans, blanched
8 oz lobster meat, chopped
3 tbsp butter

Cress and thyme twigs for decoration

Place the ears of corn in a large pot, cover with water, add thyme twigs and sugar and bring to a boil. Cook for 45 minutes, then remove the ears of corn from the water. Reserve 400 ml of the corn stock. Scrape the corn off the cobs, set aside approx. 4 tbsp corn. Sautée the corn with onions and carrots and fill up with corn stock. Season with salt and pepper and let simmer for 20 minutes. Mash, strain and keep warm. Season the fish with salt and pepper and sear in hot oil from both sides for 3 minutes. Combine reserved corn, green beans, lobster meat and butter with the mashed vegetables and season, if necessary. Divide the vegetable stew onto four plates, place the John Dory fillets on top and garnish with cress and thyme.

4 Heringskönig-Filets, je 170 g
Salz, Pfeffer
3 EL Pflanzenöl

4 Maiskolben
2 Thymianzweige
1 EL Zucker
2 gewürfelte Zwiebeln
2 gewürfelte Karotten
225 g blanchierte grüne Bohnen
225 g gehacktes Hummerfleisch
3 EL Butter

Kresse und Thymianzweige zur Dekoration

Maiskolben in einen großen Topf geben und mit Wasser bedecken. Thymianzweige und Zucker hinzufügen und das Ganze zum Kochen bringen. 45 Minuten lang garen lassen. Anschließend die Maiskolben herausnehmen und 400 ml der Maisbrühe beiseite stellen. Die Maiskörner aus den Kolben lösen und ca. 4 EL Maiskörner beiseite stellen. Den Mais mit den Zwiebeln und den Karotten kurz anbraten und Maisbrühe hinzu gießen. Mit Salz und Pfeffer abschmecken und 20 Minuten köcheln lassen. Pürieren, passieren und warm halten. Den Fisch mit Salz und Pfeffer würzen und in heißem Öl ca. 3 Minuten auf beiden Seiten scharf anbraten. Die übrigen Maiskörner, die grünen Bohnen, das Hummerfleisch und die Butter unter das Gemüsepüree geben und, falls nötig, nachwürzen. Den Gemüseeintopf auf vier Teller geben, die Heringskönig-Filets darauf anrichten und mit Kresse und Thymian garnieren.

4 filets de saint-pierre de 170 g
Sel, poivre
3 c. à soupe d'huile végétale

4 épis de maïs
2 branches de thym
1 c. à soupe de sucre
2 oignons coupés en dés
2 carottes coupées en dés
225 g de haricots verts blanchis
225 g de chair de homard hachée
3 c. à soupe de beurre

Cresson et branche de thym en guise de garniture

Disposer les épis de maïs dans une grande casserole et les couvrir d'eau. Ajouter les branches de thym et le sucre et porter le tout à ébullition. Laisser cuire pendant 45 minutes. Sortir ensuite les épis de maïs et réserver 400 ml de bouillon. Détacher les grains et en réserver environ 4 c. à soupe. Faire revenir légèrement le maïs, les oignons et les carottes et verser le bouillon dessus. Saler et poivrer, puis laisser mijoter 20 minutes. Écraser le mélange et le mouliner, puis le garder au chaud. Saler et poivrer le poisson et bien le saisir 3 minutes de chaque côté dans l'huile chaude. Incorporer dans la purée de légumes le reste de grains de maïs, les haricots verts, la chair de homard et le beurre, puis assaisonner de nouveau si nécessaire. Répartir le mélange sur quatre assiettes, disposer les filets de saint-pierre dessus et garnir de cresson et de thym.

4 filetes de pez de San Pedro de 170 g cada uno
Sal, pimienta
3 cucharadas de aceite vegetal

4 mazorcas
2 ramitas de tomillo
1 cucharada de azúcar
2 cebollas en dados
2 zanahorias en dados
225 g de judías verdes escalfadas
225 g de carne de langosta picada
3 cucharadas de mantequilla

Berros y ramitas de tomillo para decorar

Introduzca las mazorcas de maíz en una cazuela grande y cúbralas con agua. Añada las ramitas de tomillo y el azúcar y lleve el agua a ebullición.

Deje que cueza durante 45 minutos. Saque después las mazorcas y reserve 400 ml del caldo. Separe los granos de maíz de las mazorcas y reserve aprox. 4 cucharadas. Sofría brevemente el maíz con las cebollas y las zanahorias y vierta por encima el caldo de maíz. Salpimiente y deje que cueza a fuego lento durante 20 minutos. Machaque después las verduras, páselas por el pasapurés y mantenga el puré caliente. Salpimiente el pescado y fríalo a fuego fuerte y en aceite caliente durante aprox. 3 minutos por cada lado. Mezcle los granos de maíz que había reservado, las judías verdes, la carne de langosta y la mantequilla con el puré y sazone nuevamente si fuera necesario. Reparta la verdura entre cuatro platos, ponga encima los filetes de pescado y decore con los berros y el tomillo.

4 filetti di pesce San Pietro di 170 g ciascuno
Sale, pepe
3 cucchiai di olio vegetale

4 pannocchie di mais
2 ramoscelli di timo
1 cucchiaio di zucchero
2 cipolle tagliate a dadini
2 carote tagliate a dadini
225 g di fagiolini scottati
225 g di polpa di astice tritata
3 cucchiai di burro

Per la guarnizione: crescione e ramoscelli di timo

Mettere le pannocchie in una grossa pentola e coprirle d'acqua. Unire i ramoscelli di timo e lo zucchero e portare ad ebollizione. Lasciar cuocere per 45 minuti. Estrarre quindi le pannocchie e mettere da parte 400 ml del brodo di mais. Sgranare i chicchi di mais e metterne da parte circa 4 cucchiai. Rosolare brevemente il mais con le cipolle e le carote e bagnare con il brodo. Salare, pepare e lasciar cuocere a fuoco lento per 20 minuti. Quindi schiacciare, passare con il passaverdura e tenere in caldo. Salare e pepare il pesce e rosolarlo a fuoco vivo in olio bollente per circa 3 minuti da entrambi i lati. Aggiungere alla purea di verdure i rimanenti chicchi di mais, i fagiolini, la polpa di astice ed il burro e, se necessario, regolare il condimento. Ripartire il passato di verdure in quattro piatti, disporvi sopra i filetti di pesce e guarnire con crescione e timo.

Aureole

Design: Adam Tihany | Chef: Charlie Palmer | Owner: Mandalay Bay Resort & Casino

3950 Las Vegas Boulevard S | Las Vegas, NV 89119 | Mandalay Bay Resort & Casino
Phone: +1 702 632 7401
www.charliepalmer.com
Opening hours: Mon–Sun 6 pm to 10:30 pm
Average price: $ 95
Cuisine: Progressive American
Special features: Signature wine tower, eWinebook

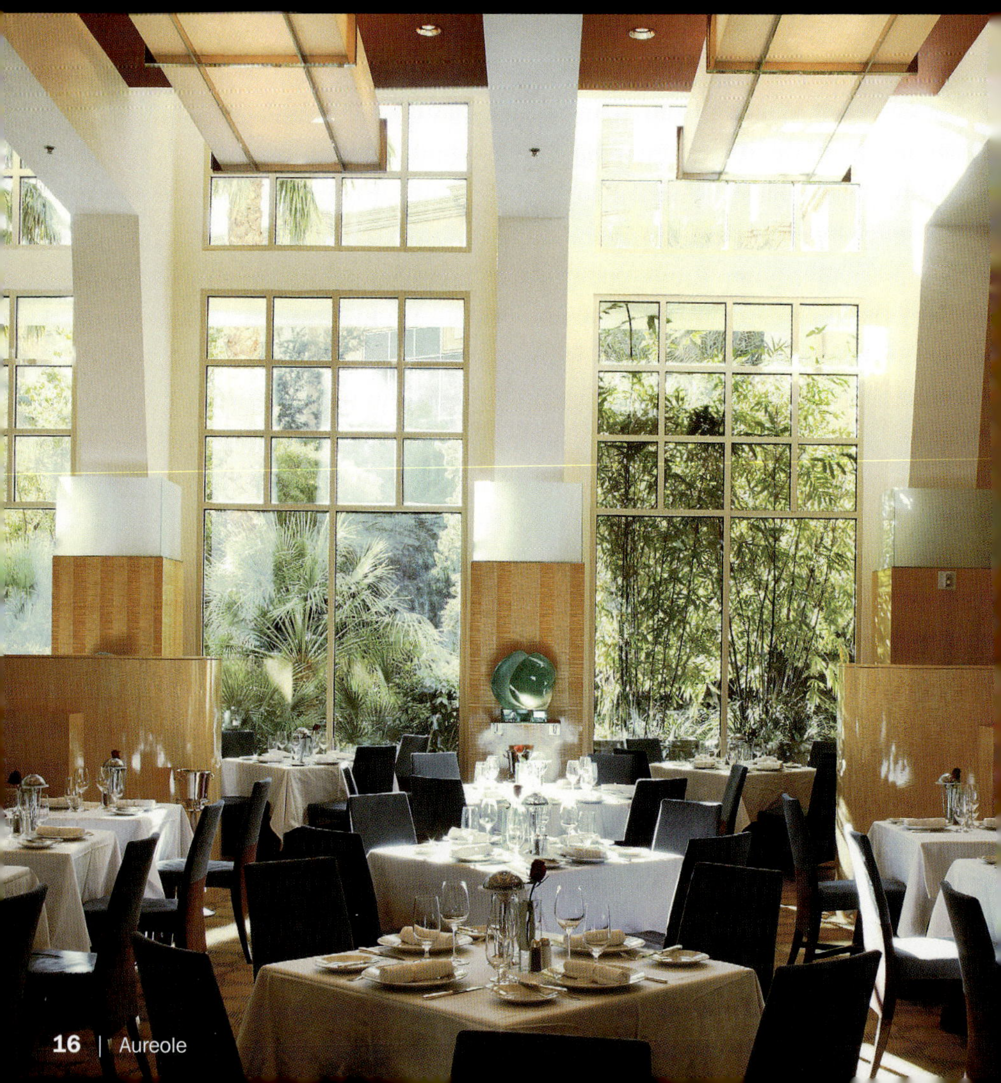

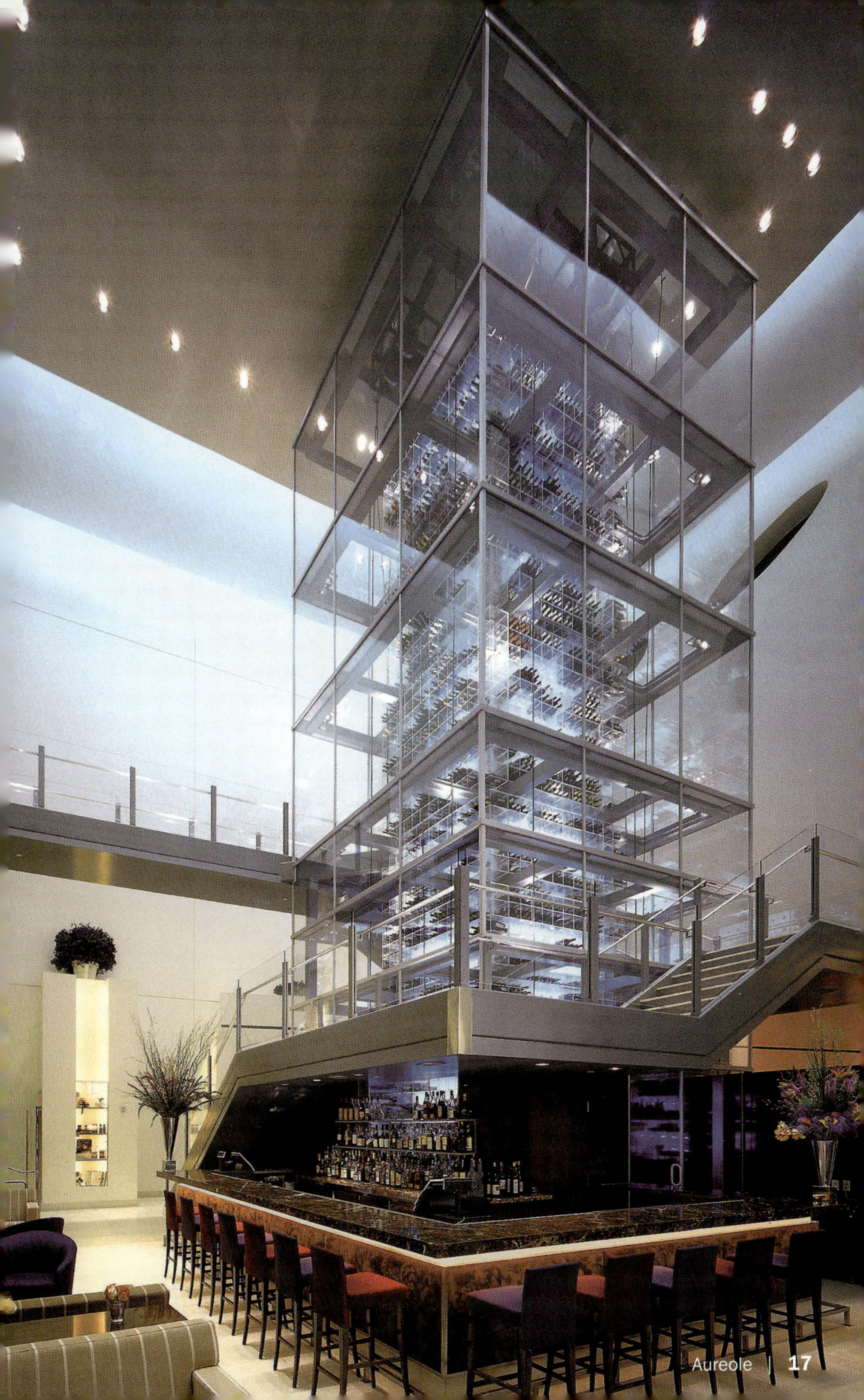

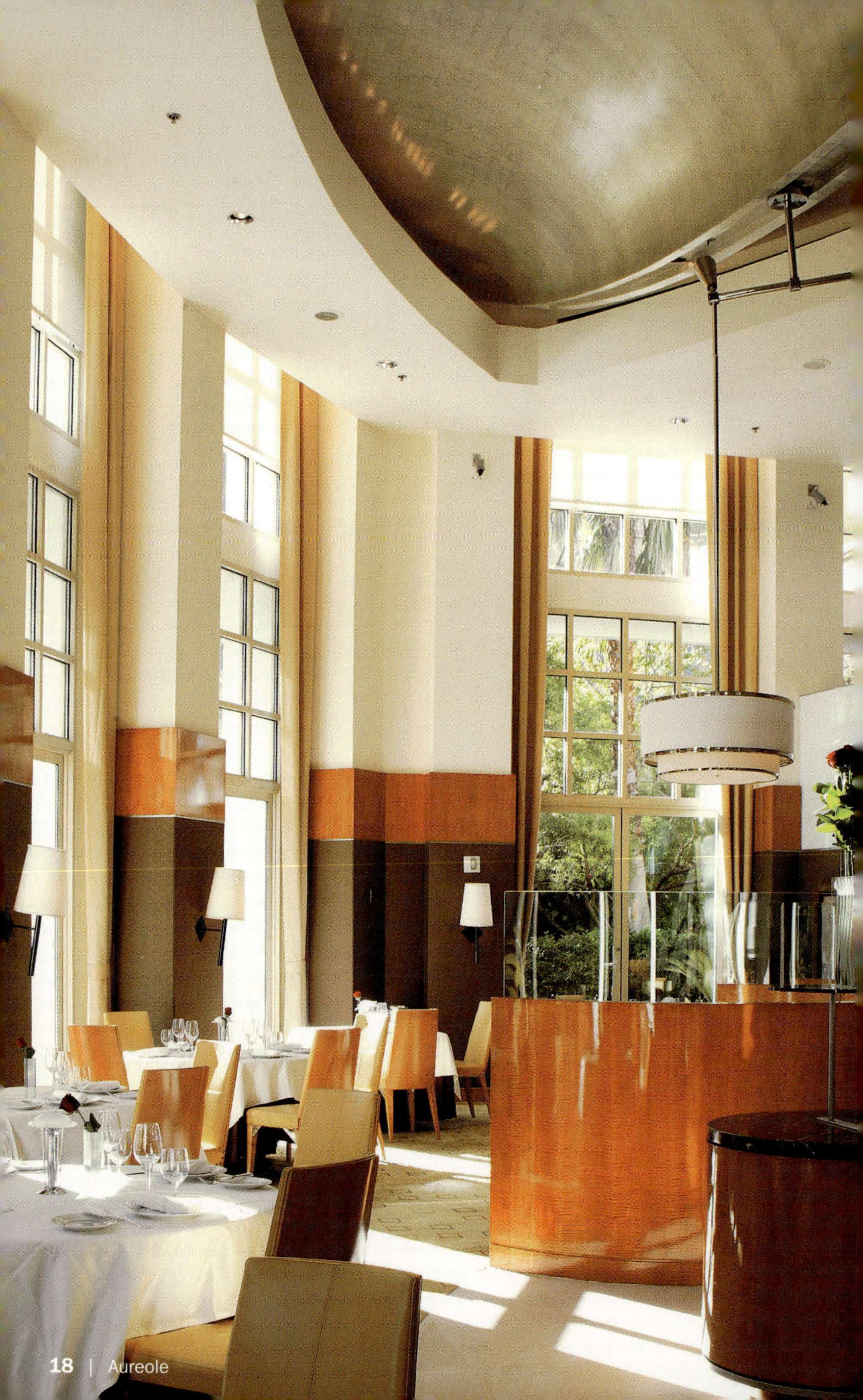

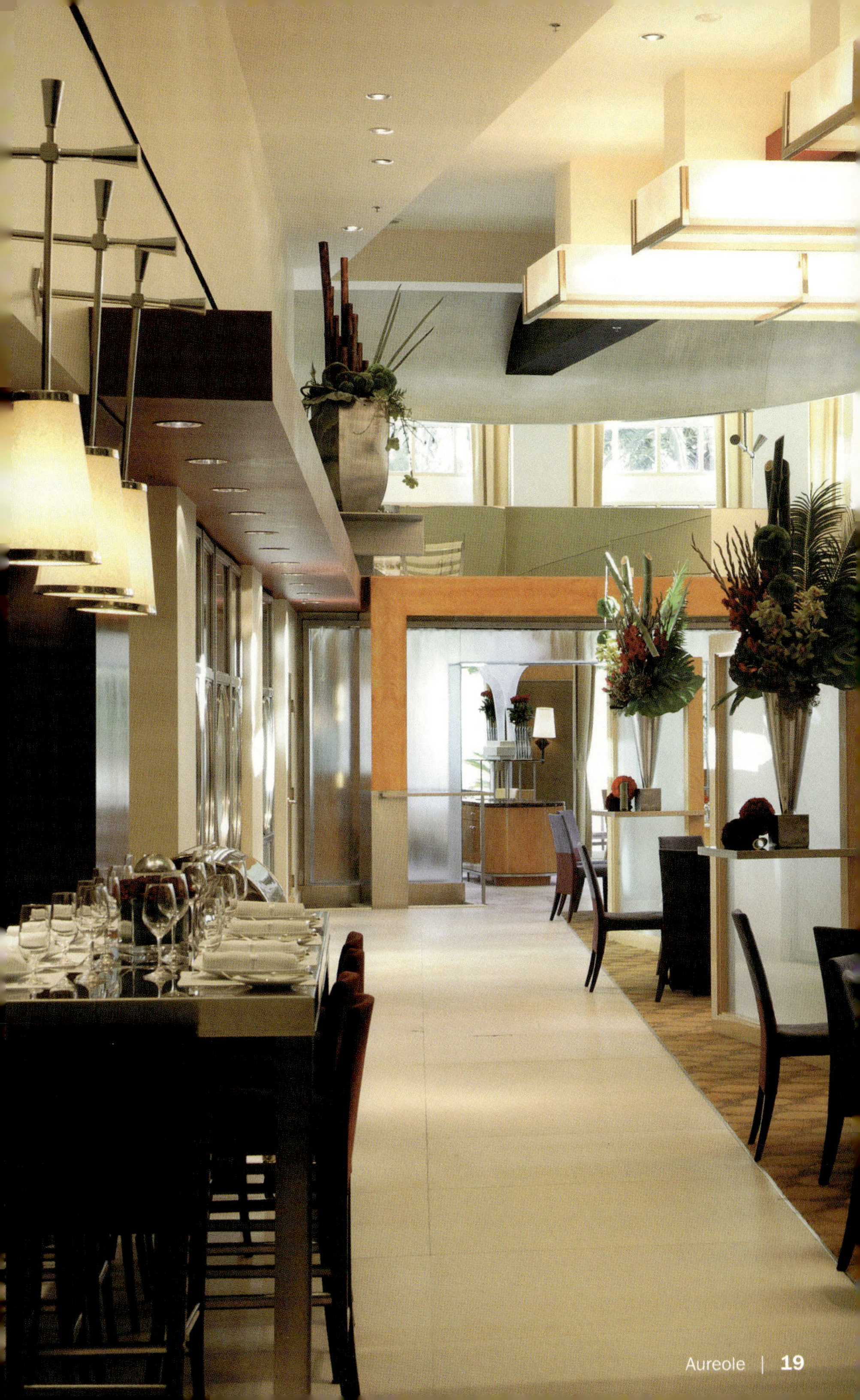

Caramelized Quail

Karamellisierte Wachtel

Caille caramélisée

Codorniz caramelizada

Quaglie caramellate

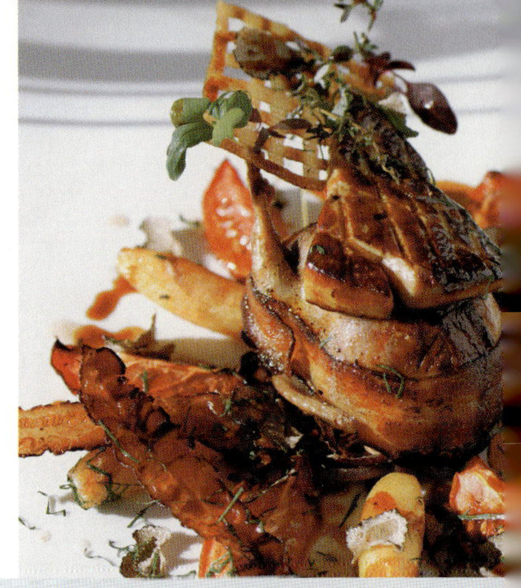

4 quails, de-boned
8 oz truffle butter
5 large potatoes, peeled, quartered and blanched
5 tomatoes, quartered
2 onions, cut in wedges
3 tbsp olive oil
½ tsp fresh thyme, chopped
½ tsp fresh rosemary, chopped
2 cloves of garlic, chopped
Salt, pepper

Stuffing:
4 oz foie gras, diced
4 pieces canned black truffles, chopped
10 oz ground pork belly
2 tbsp parsley, chopped
Salt, pepper
Combine all ingredients in a bowl and season.

4 slices foie gras
2 tbsp olive oil

White truffle and fresh herbs for decoration

Clean quails, season them from the inside and fill with stuffing. Coat the entire surface of the quails with softened truffle butter and place with potatoes, tomatoes and onions in a deep baking dish. Drizzle with olive oil and season with thyme, rosemary, garlic, salt and pepper. Bake at 400 °F for 18 minutes. Season sliced foie gras and sear in hot olive oil from both sides. Arrange vegetables on four plates, place one quail on each plate, put one slice of foie gras on top and drizzle with the pan juices. Decorate with white truffle slices and fresh herbs.

4 Wachteln ohne Knochen
225 g Trüffelbutter
5 große geschälte, geviertelte und blanchierte Kartoffeln
5 geviertelte Tomaten
2 in Spalten geschnittene Zwiebeln
3 EL Olivenöl
½ TL frischer gehackter Thymian
½ TL frischer gehackter Rosmarin
2 gehackte Knoblauchzehen
Salz, Pfeffer

Für die Füllung:
115 g gewürfelte Gänsestopfleber
4 gehackte schwarze Trüffel aus der Dose
285 g gehackter Schweinebauch
2 EL gehackte Petersilie
Salz, Pfeffer
Alle Zutaten in eine Schüssel geben und abschmecken.

4 Scheiben Gänsestopfleber
2 EL Olivenöl

Weißer Trüffel und frische Kräuter zur Dekoration

Die Wachteln putzen, von innen würzen und mit der Füllung ausstopfen. Rundum mit geschmolzener Trüffelbutter einstreichen und mit den Kartoffeln, Tomaten und Zwiebeln in eine tiefe Backform geben. Mit Olivenöl beträufeln und mit Thymian, Rosmarin, Knoblauch, Salz und Pfeffer würzen. Bei 200 °C 18 Minuten schmoren. Die Gänsestopfleber-Scheiben würzen und in heißem Olivenöl von beiden Seiten scharf anbraten. Das Gemüse auf vier Tellern anrichten, je eine Wachtel darauf geben, zuoberst eine Scheibe Gänsestopfleber legen und das Ganze mit dem Bratensaft beträufeln. Mit Scheiben vom weißen Trüffel und frischen Kräutern garnieren.

4 cailles désossées
225 g de beurre de truffe
5 grosses pommes de terre épluchées, coupées en quatre et blanchies
5 tomates coupées en quatre
2 oignons coupés en quatre
3 c. à soupe d'huile d'olive
½ c. à café de thym frais haché
½ c. à café de romarin frais haché
2 gousses d'ail hachées
Sel, poivre

Pour la farce :
115 g de foie gras d'oie coupé en dés
4 truffes noires hachées en boite
285 g de poitrine de porc hachée
2 c. à soupe de persil haché
Sel, poivre
Mélanger tous les ingrédients dans un plat creux et assaisonner.

4 tranches de foie gras d'oie
2 c. à soupe d'huile d'olive

Truffe blanche et herbes fraîches pour la garniture

Nettoyer les cailles, les assaisonner à l'intérieur et les farcir. Les badigeonner complètement de beurre de truffe fondu et les disposer dans un plat à four creux avec les pommes de terre, les tomates et les oignons. Arroser d'huile d'olive, ajouter le thym, le romarin, l'ail, saler et poivrer. Laisser braiser pendant 18 minutes à 200 °C. Assaisonner les tranches de foie gras d'oie et les faire bien revenir de chaque côté dans l'huile d'olive chaude. Dresser les légumes sur quatre assiettes et disposer les cailles dessus. Couronner le tout d'une tranche de foie gras et arroser de jus de cuisson. Garnir de tranches de truffe blanche et d'herbes fraîches.

4 codornices deshuesadas
225 g de mantequilla de trufa
5 patatas grandes, peladas, en cuartos y escaldadas
5 tomates en cuartos
2 cebollas en rodajas
3 cucharadas de aceite de oliva
½ de cucharadita de tomillo fresco picado
½ de cucharadita de romero fresco picado
2 dientes de ajo picados
Sal, pimienta

Para el relleno:
115 g de foie gras en dados
4 trufas negras picadas de lata
285 g de vientre de cerdo picado
2 cucharadas de perejil picado
Sal, pimienta
Ponga todos los ingredientes en un cuenco y sazone.

4 rodajas de foie gras
2 cucharadas de aceite de oliva

Trufa blanca y hierbas frescas para decorar

Limpie las codornices, sazónelas por dentro y rellénelas con el relleno. Úntelas por todos los lados con mantequilla de trufa derretida y póngalas en una bandeja de horno profunda junto con las patatas, los tomates y las cebollas. Vierta por encima el aceite de oliva y sazone con el tomillo, el romero, el ajo, la sal y la pimienta. Deje que se asen a 200 °C durante 18 minutos. Sazone las rodajas de foie gras y fríalas bien por ambos lados en aceite de oliva. Reparta la verdura en cuatro platos, coloque sobre ella una codorniz y ponga después encima una rodaja de foie gras. Vierta por encima el jugo del asado. Decore con lonchas de trufa blanca y hierbas frescas.

4 quaglie disossate
225 g di burro al tartufo
5 patate grosse sbucciate, tagliate in 4 e scottate
5 pomodori tagliati in 4
2 cipolle tagliate a spicchi
3 cucchiai di olio di oliva
½ cucchiaino di timo fresco tritato
½ cucchiaino di rosmarino fresco tritato
2 spicchi d'aglio tritati
Sale, pepe

Per il ripieno:
115 g di foie gras tagliato a dadini
4 tartufi neri in scatola tritati
285 g di pancetta di maiale
2 cucchiai di prezzemolo tritato
Sale, pepe
Mettere tutti gli ingredienti in una ciotola, assaggiare e regolare il condimento.

4 fette di foie gras
2 cucchiai di olio di oliva

Per la guarnizione: tartufo bianco ed erbe fresche

Pulire le quaglie, condirle internamente e farcirle con il ripieno. Spalmarle esternamente con il burro al tartufo fuso e disporle in una pirofila alta con le patate, i pomodori e le cipolle. Pillottarle con l'olio di oliva e condire con il timo, il rosmarino, l'aglio, il sale e il pepe. Cuocere in forno a 200 °C per 18 minuti. Condire le fette di foie gras e rosolarle a fuoco vivo nell'olio bollente da entrambi i lati. Mettere le verdure in quattro piatti, disporre una quaglia su ciascun piatto, poggiarvi sopra una fetta di foie gras e versare sul tutto il sugo d'arrosto. Guarnire con fettine di tartufo bianco ed erbe fresche.

Boa Steakhouse

Design: Tag Front | Chef: Jose Aleman
Owner: Innovative Dining Group

3500 Las Vegas Boulevard | Las Vegas, NV 89109 | The Forum Shops of Caesars
Phone: +1 702 733 7373
www.boasteak.com
Opening hours: Sun–Thu noon to 10 pm, Fri and Sat noon to midnight
Average price: $ 35
Cuisine: Steakhouse
Special features: Views of the strip, patio dining

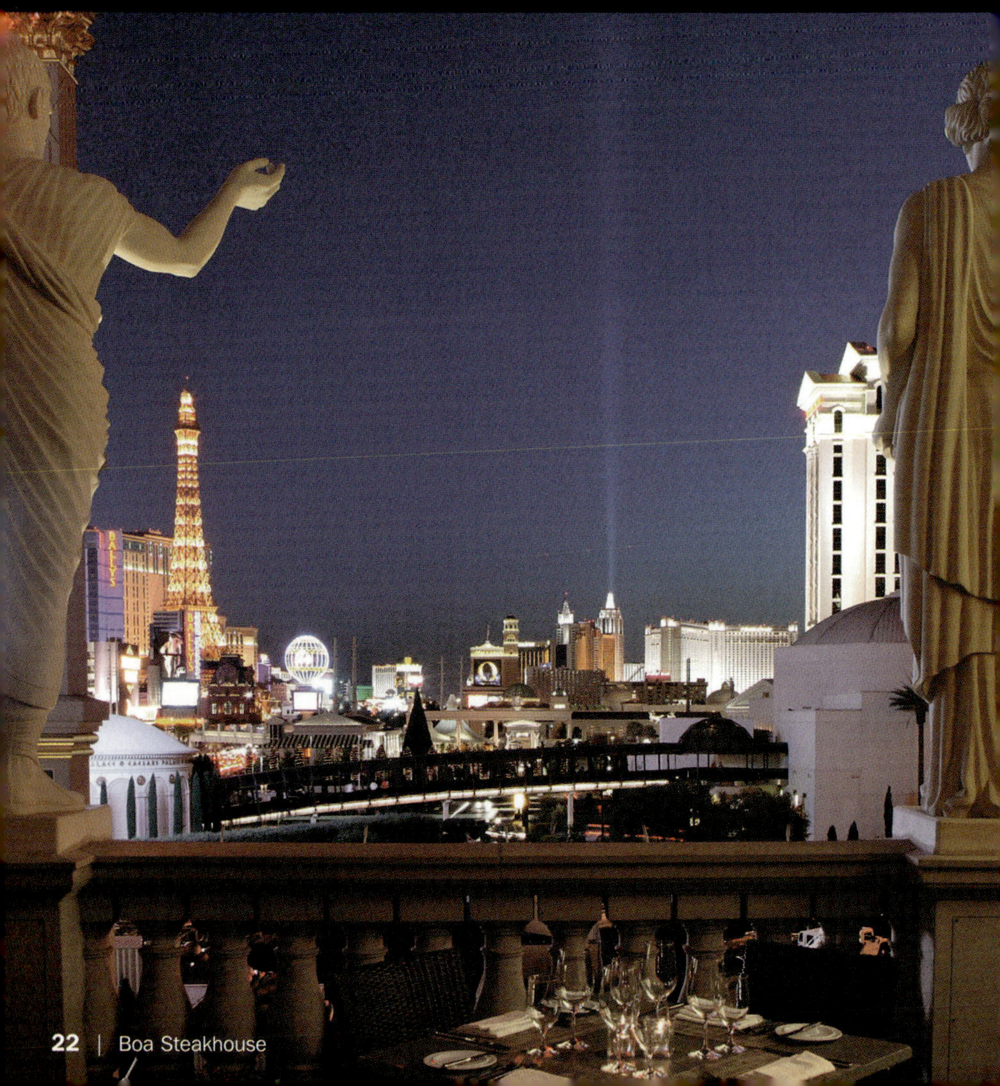

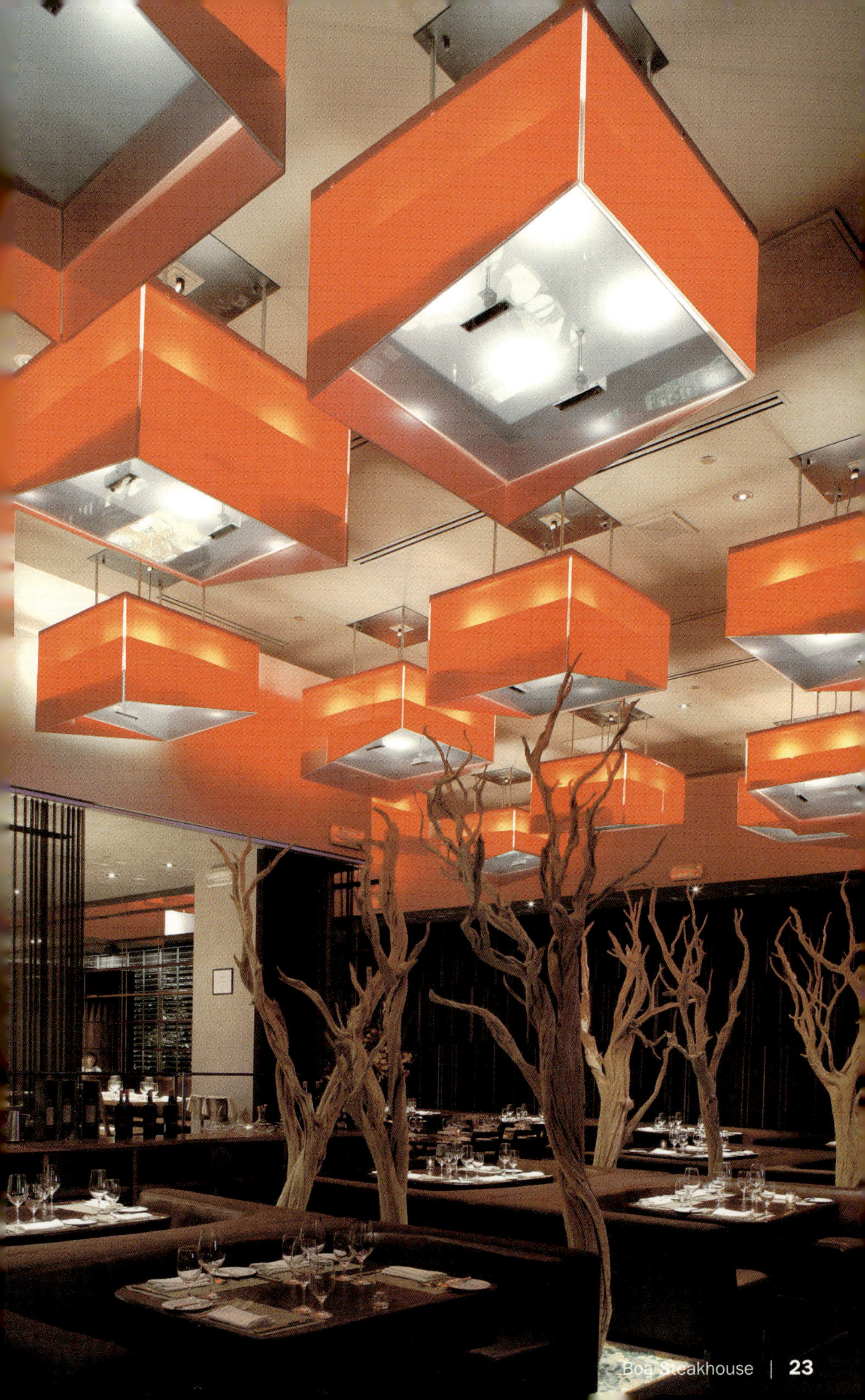

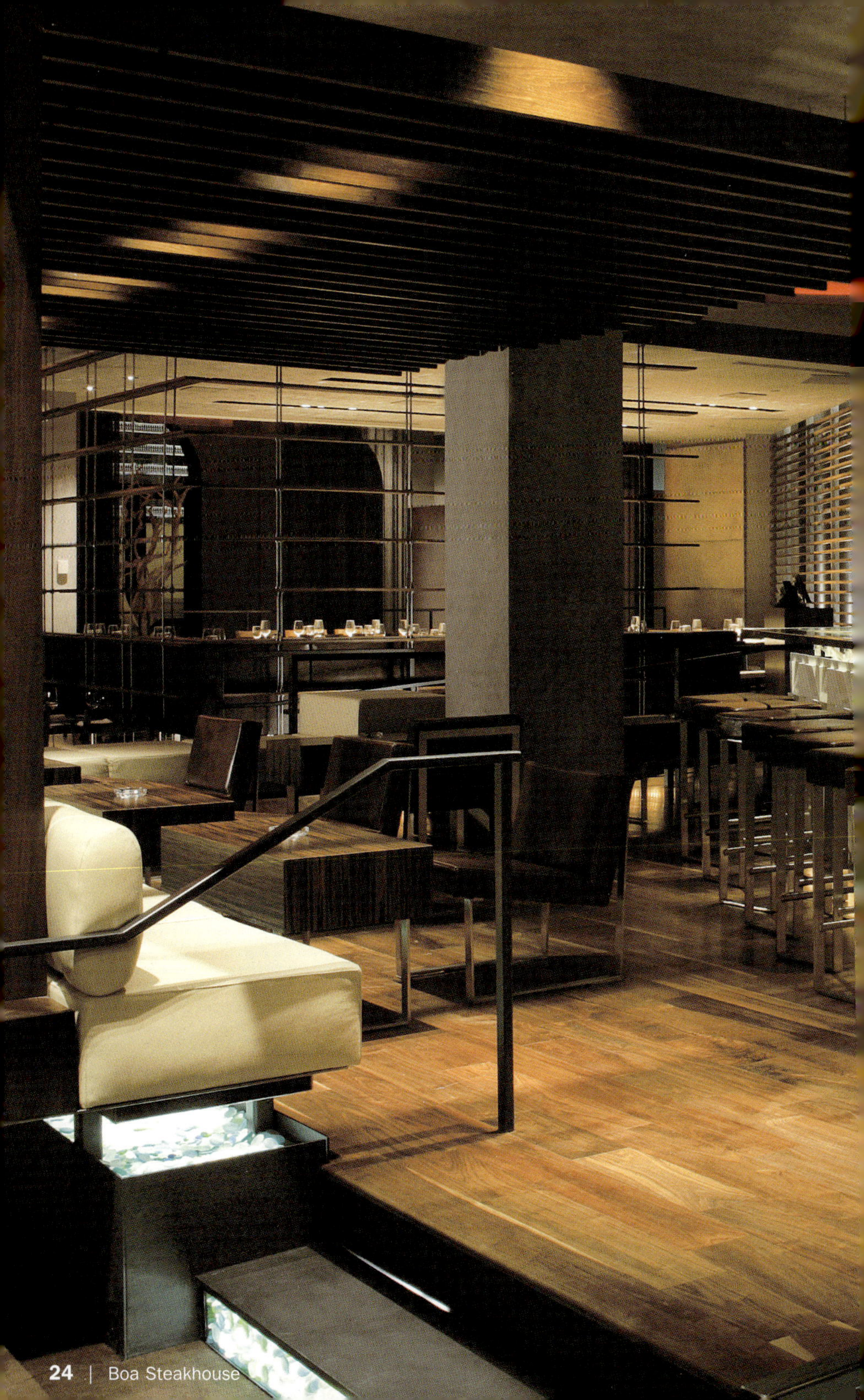

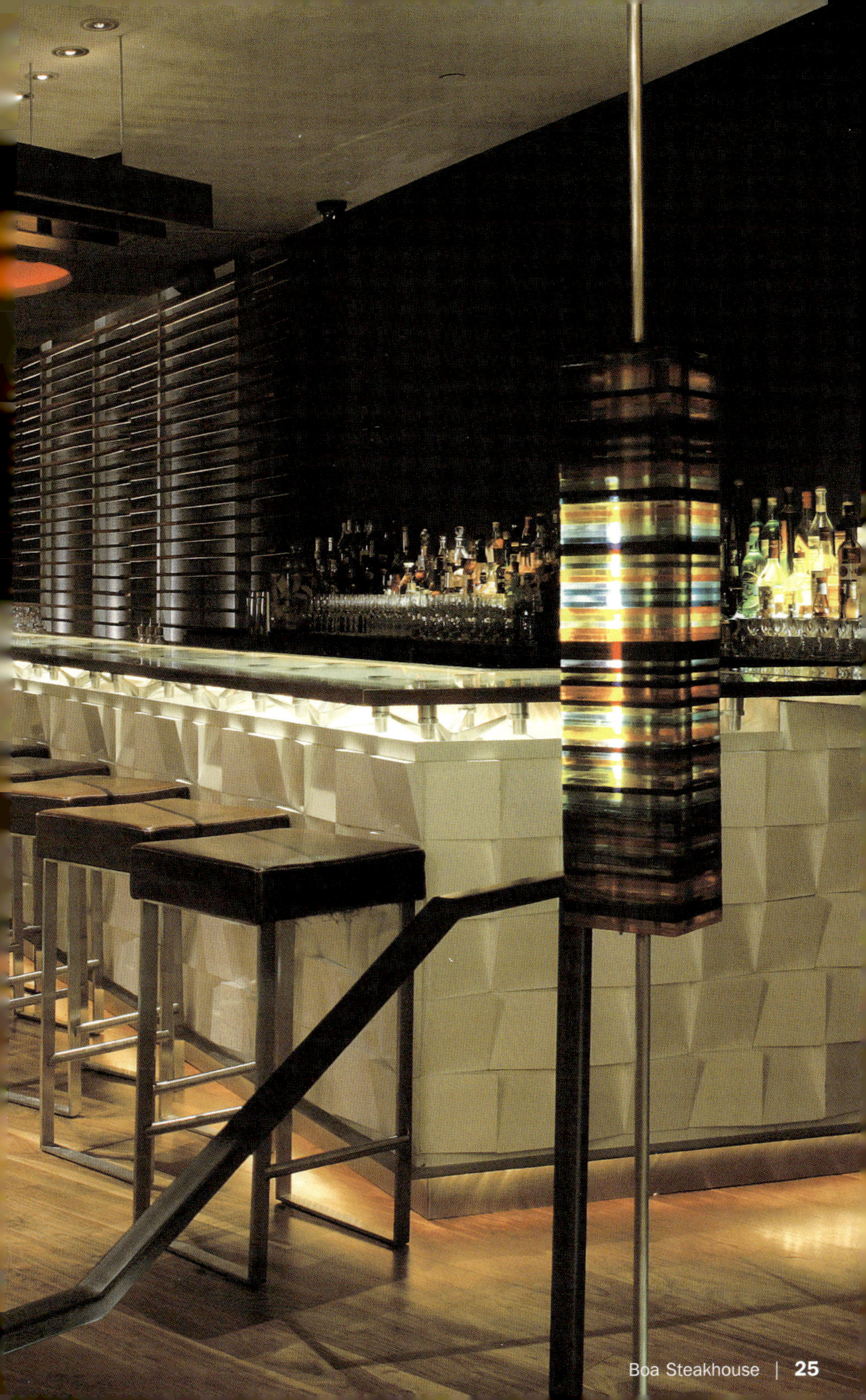

Surf & Turf

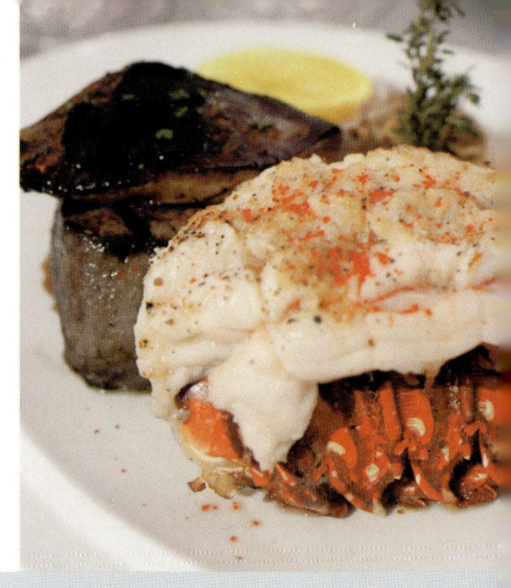

4 pieces beef fillet, 8 oz each
4 lobster tails
4 pieces foie gras, 3 oz each
Salt, pepper
8 tbsp "Huckleberry sauce"
Thyme twigs, lemons, pepper and paprika powder
for decoration

"Huckleberry sauce":
1 shallot, chopped
1 tbsp olive oil
100 ml Cassis liquor
100 ml port wine
100 ml red wine
200 ml veal fond
50 ml balsamic vinegar
2 twigs fresh thyme

1 bay leave
1 tsp pepper corns

Sautée shallot in oil, add all liquid ingredients and spices and reduce until it resembles a thick sauce.

Season beef fillets, lobster tails and foie gras and sear on both sides for 3 minutes. Turn the lobster meat inside out, arrange on plates and drizzle the foie gras with 2 tbsp sauce. Decorate with thyme twigs, lemons and sprinkle the lobster tails with pepper and red paprika powder.

4 Rinderfilets, je 225 g
4 Hummerschwänze
4 Stück Gänsestopfleber, je 85 g
Salz, Pfeffer
8 EL „Huckleberry Sauce"
Thymianzweige, Zitronen, Pfeffer und Paprikapulver
zur Dekoration

Für die „Huckleberry Sauce":
1 gehackte Schalotte
1 EL Olivenöl
100 ml Cassislikör
100 ml Portwein
100 ml Rotwein
200 ml Kalbsfond
50 ml Balsamico-Essig
2 Zweige frischer Thymian

1 Lorbeerblatt
1 TL Pfefferkörner

Die Schalotte in Öl kurz anbraten, die flüssigen Zutaten und die Gewürze hinzugeben und alles einreduzieren, bis eine dickflüssige Soße entstanden ist.

Rinderfilets, Hummerschwänze und Gänsestopfleber würzen und 3 Minuten auf beiden Seiten scharf anbraten. Das Hummerfleisch herauslösen, auf Tellern anrichten und die Gänsestopfleber mit 2 EL Soße beträufeln. Mit Thymianzweigen und Zitronenscheiben dekorieren und die Hummerschwänze mit Pfeffer und rotem Paprikapulver bestreuen.

4 filets de bœuf de 225 g
4 queues de homard
4 morceaux de foie gras d'oie de 85 g
Sel, poivre
8 c. à soupe de « sauce Huckleberry »
Branches de thym, citrons, poivre et poudre de paprika pour la garniture

Pour la « sauce Huckleberry » :
1 échalote hachée
1 c. à soupe d'huile d'olive
100 ml de liqueur de cassis
100 ml de porto
100 ml de vin rouge
200 ml de bouillon de veau
50 ml de vinaigre balsamique
2 branches de thym frais

1 feuille de laurier
1 c. à café de grains de poivre

Faire revenir brièvement l'échalote dans l'huile, ajouter les ingrédients liquides et les épices, puis laisser réduire afin d'obtenir une sauce épaisse.

Assaisonner les filets de bœuf, les queues de homard et les morceaux de foie gras et bien les saisir 3 minutes de chaque côté. Décortiquer le homard et disposer la chair sur les assiettes, puis verser 2 c. à soupe de sauce sur les morceaux de foie gras. Garnir de branches de thym et de rondelles de citron. Poivrer les queues de homard et les saupoudrer de paprika.

4 filetes de ternera de 225 g cada uno
4 colas de langosta
4 escalopes de foie gras, de 85 g cada uno
Sal, pimienta
8 cucharadas de "Huckleberry sauce"
Ramita de tomillo, limones, pimientas y pimentón para decorar

Para la "Huckleberry sauce":
1 chalote picado
1 cucharada de aceite de oliva
100 ml de licor de cassis
100 ml de oporto
100 ml de vino tinto
200 ml de fondo de cordero
50 ml de vinagre balsámico
2 ramitas de tomillo fresco

1 hoja de laurel
1 cucharadita de granos de pimienta

Rehogue brevemente el chalote en aceite, añada los líquidos y las especias y deje que reduzca hasta obtener una salsa espesa.

Condimente los filetes de ternera, las colas de langosta y los escalopes de foie gras y sofríalos a fuego fuerte por ambos lados durante 3 minutos. Saque la carne de la langosta, coloque los ingredientes en los platos y vierta por encima del hígado 2 cucharadas de salsa. Decore con ramitas de tomillo y rodajas de limón y espolvoree las colas de langosta con pimienta y pimentón rojo.

4 filetti di manzo di 225 g ciascuno
4 code di astice
4 pezzi di foie gras di 85 g ciascuno
Sale, pepe
8 cucchiai di "Huckleberry sauce"
Per la guarnizione: ramoscelli di timo, limone, pepe e paprika

Per la "Huckleberry sauce":
1 scalogno tritato
1 cucchiaio di olio di oliva
100 ml di liquore di Cassis
100 ml di vino Porto
100 ml di vino rosso
200 ml di fondo di vitello
50 ml di aceto balsamico
2 ramoscelli di timo fresco

1 foglia di alloro
1 cucchiaino di grani di pepe

Rosolare brevemente lo scalogno nell'olio, unire i liquidi e gli aromi e lasciar restringere fino ad ottenere una salsa densa.

Condire i filetti di manzo, le code di astice ed il foie gras e rosolarli a fuoco vivo per 3 minuti da entrambi i lati. Estrarre la polpa di astice, disporla sui piatti e pillottare il foie gras con 2 cucchiai di salsa. Guarnire con ramoscelli di timo e fettine di limone e spruzzare le code di astice con pepe e paprika.

Bradley Ogden

Design: Engstrom Design Group | Chef & Owner: Bradley Ogden

3570 Las Vegas Boulevard S | Las Vegas, NV 89109 | Caesars Palace
Phone: +1 702 731 7731
www.caesars.com
Opening hours: Daily 5 pm to 11 pm, bar nightly from 4:30 pm to 11 pm
Average price: $ 40
Cuisine: American
Special features: Accentuated with the inviting elements of water

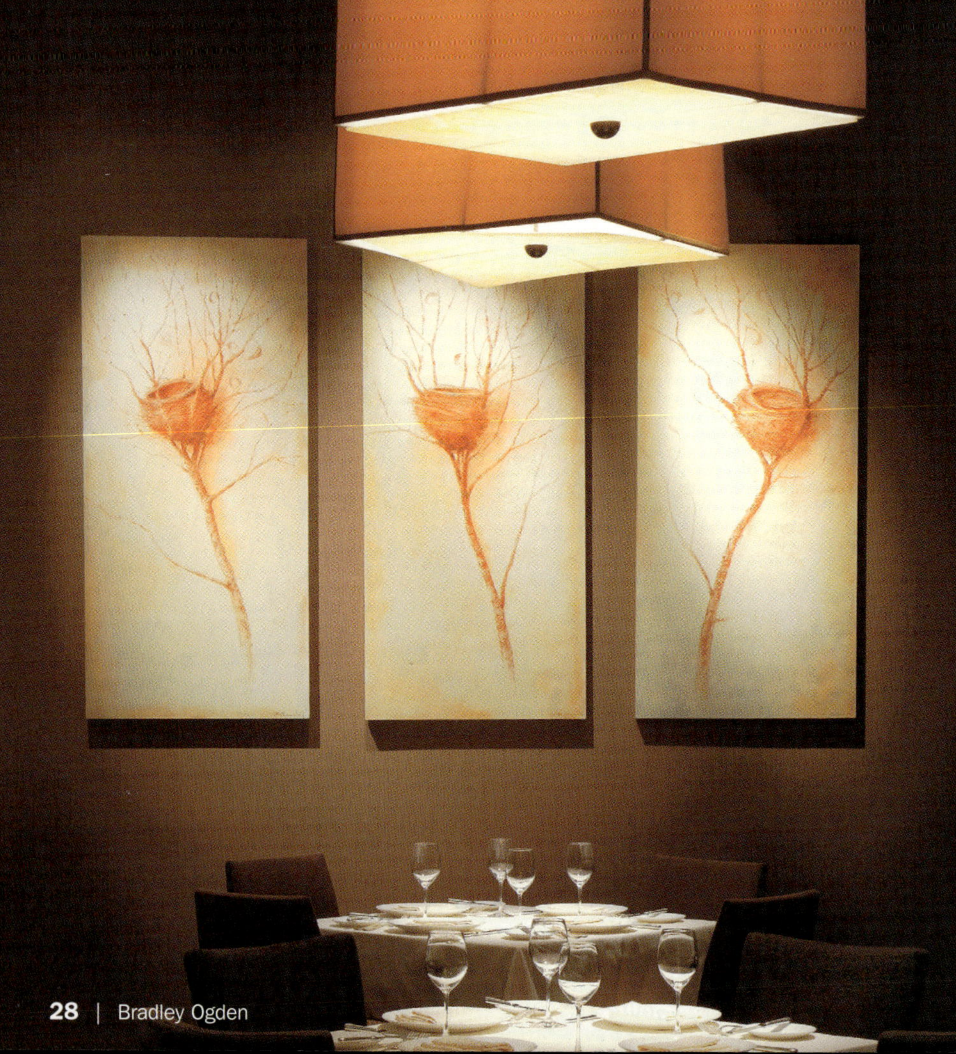

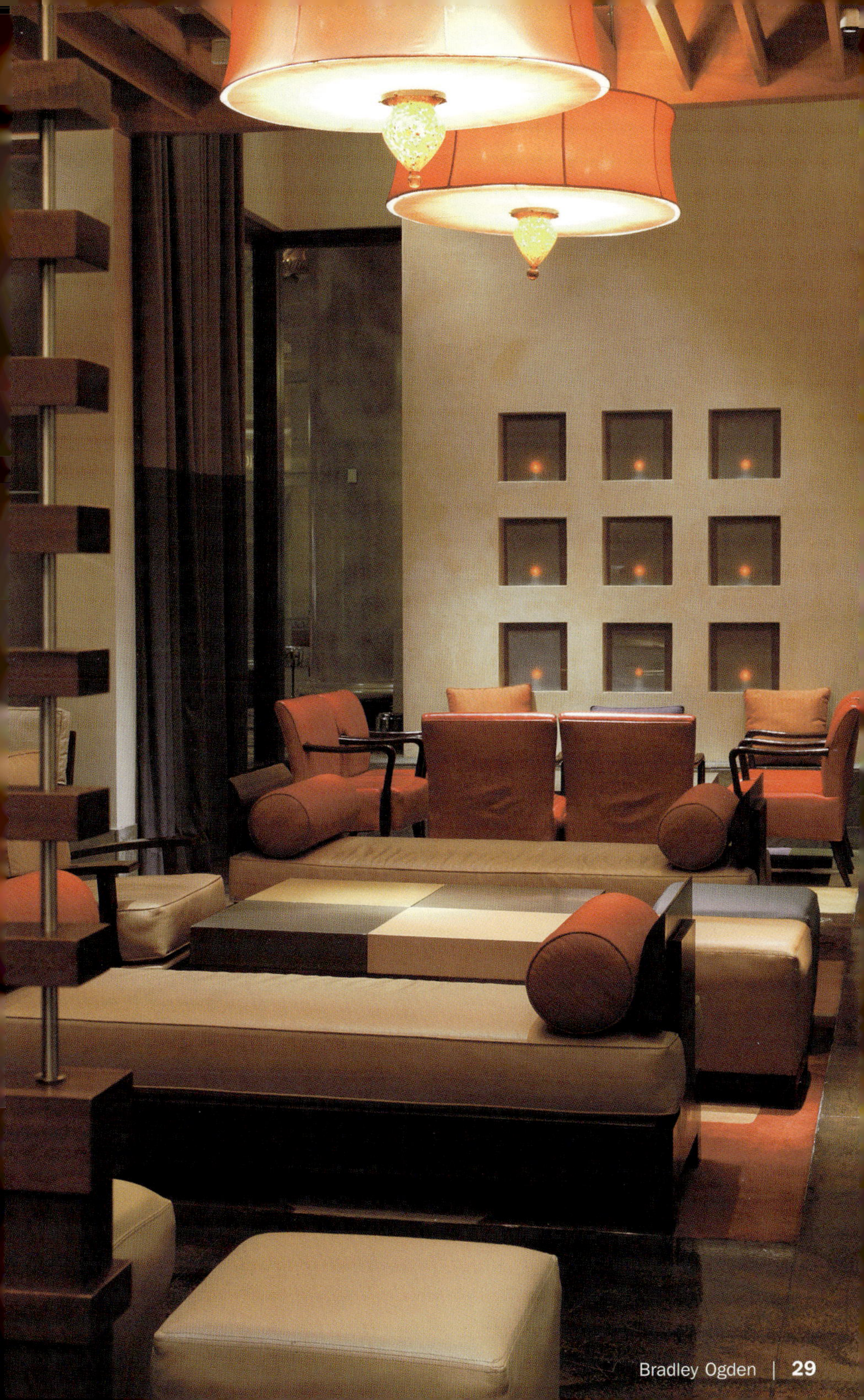

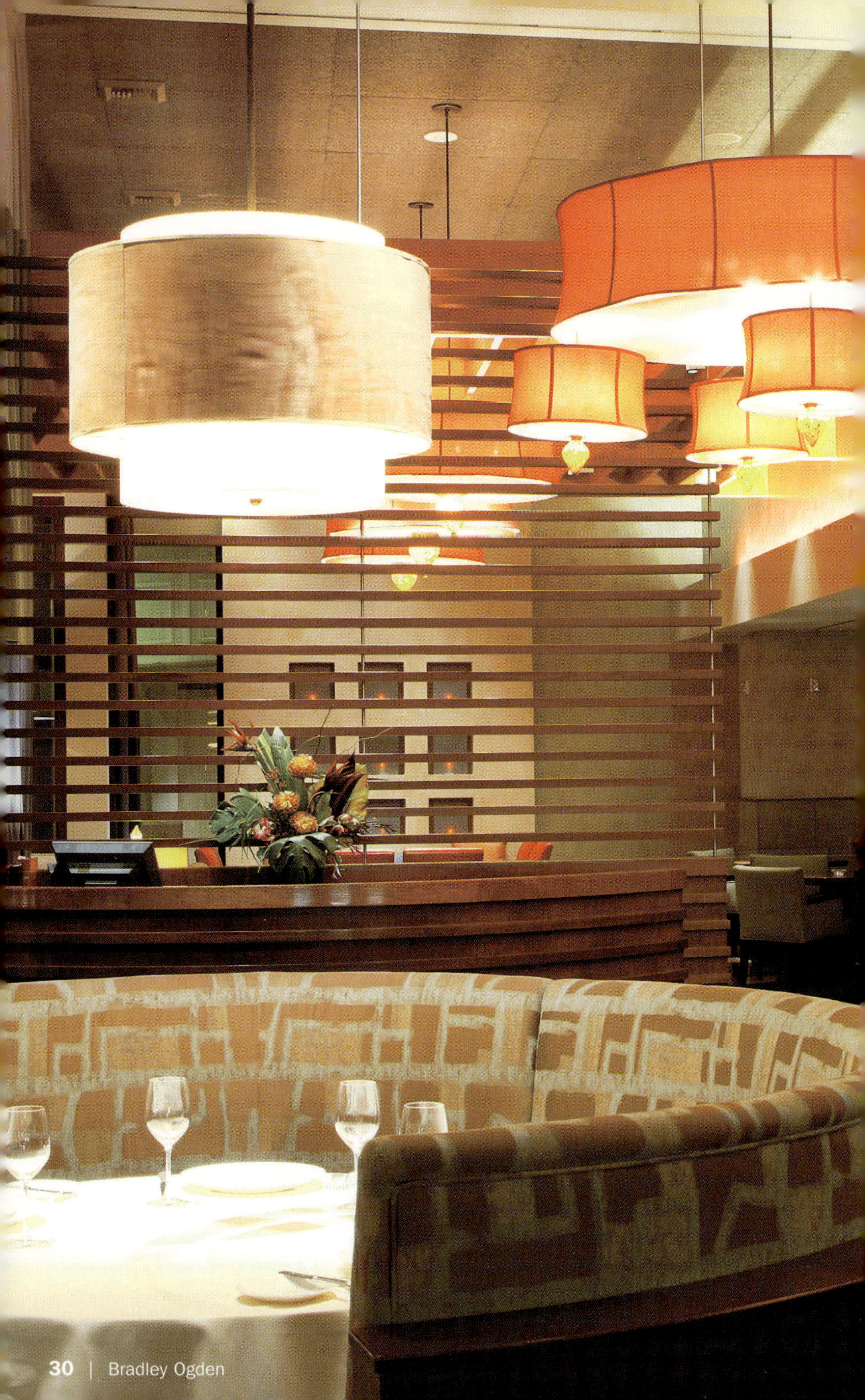

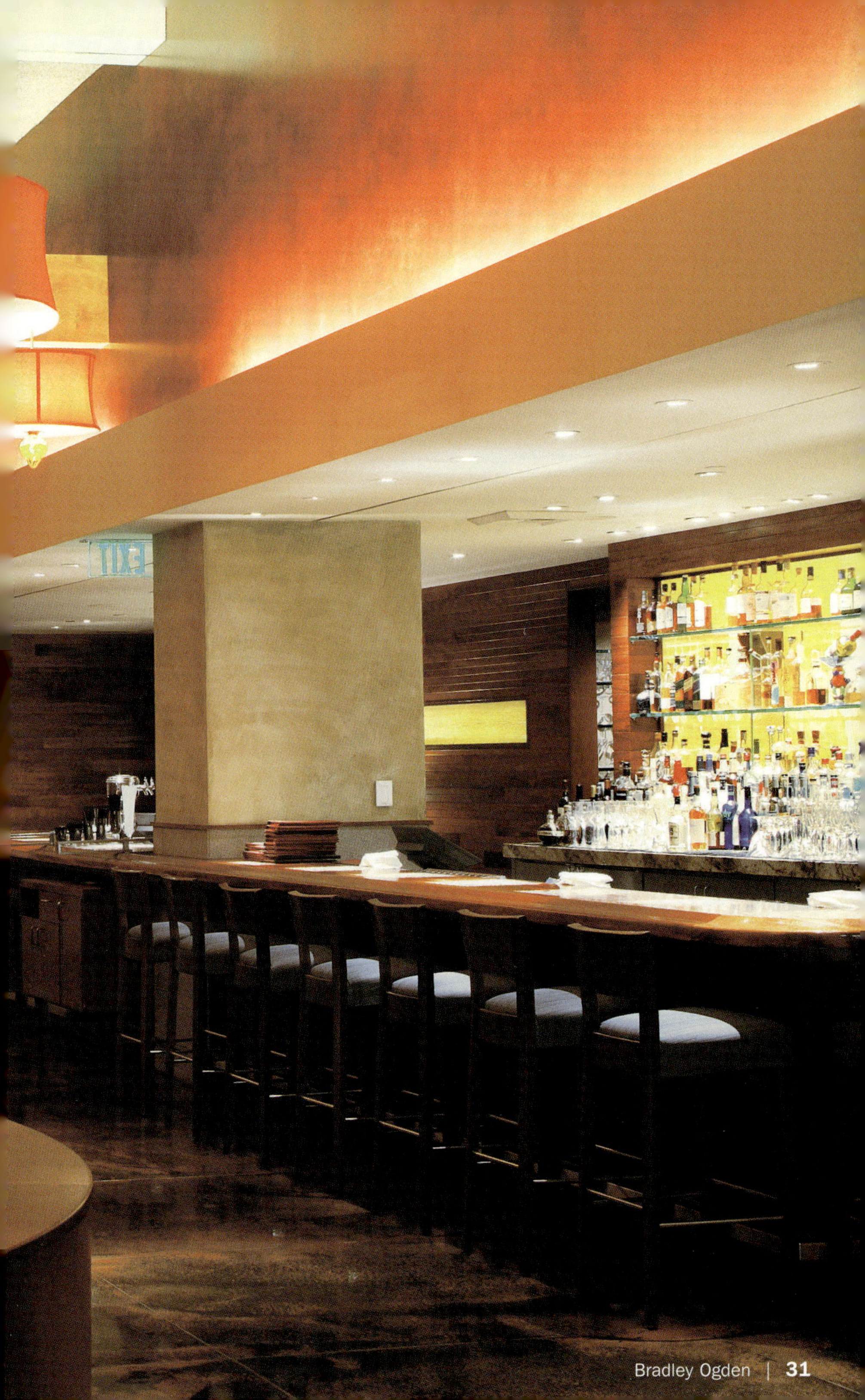

Chinois

Design: Todd-Avery Lenehan, Barbara Lazaroff, Steve Jones
Chef: Terence Fong, David Robins | Owner: Wolfgang Puck

3500 Las Vegas Boulevard S | Las Vegas, NV 89109 | The Forum Shops of Caesars
Phone: +1 702 737 9700
www.wolfgangpuck.com
Opening hours: Sat–Sun 11:30 am to 10 pm, Mon–Fri 5 pm to 10 pm
Average price: $ 17
Cuisine: Fusion, sushi

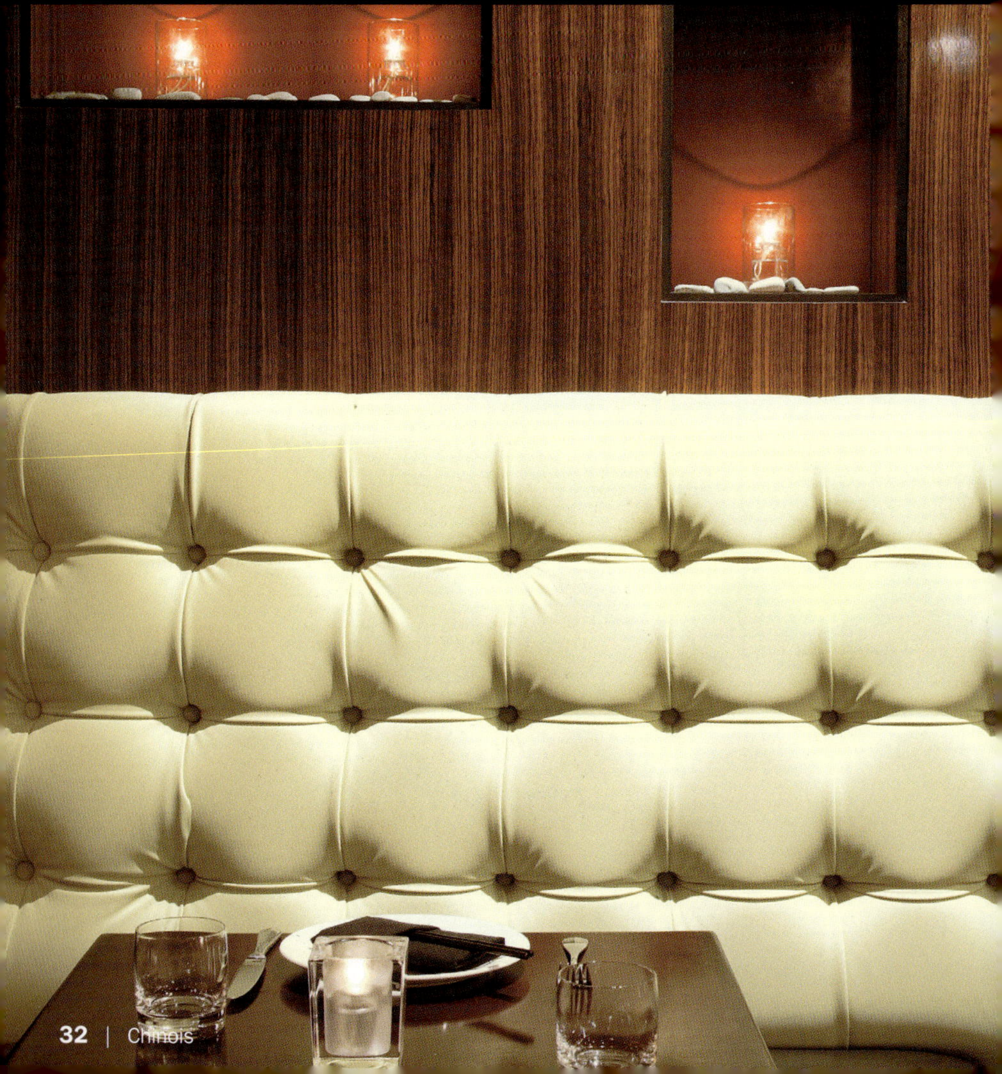

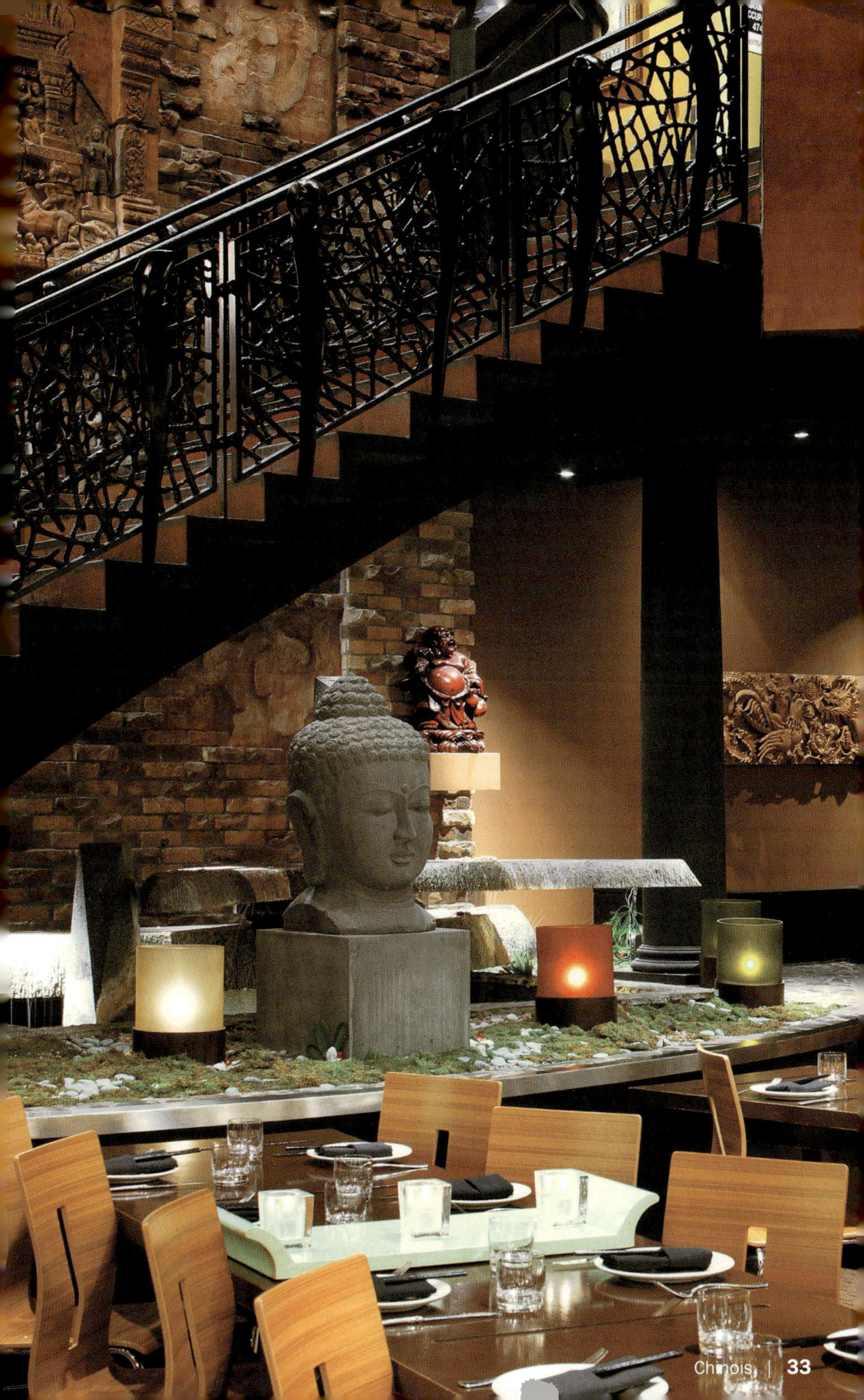

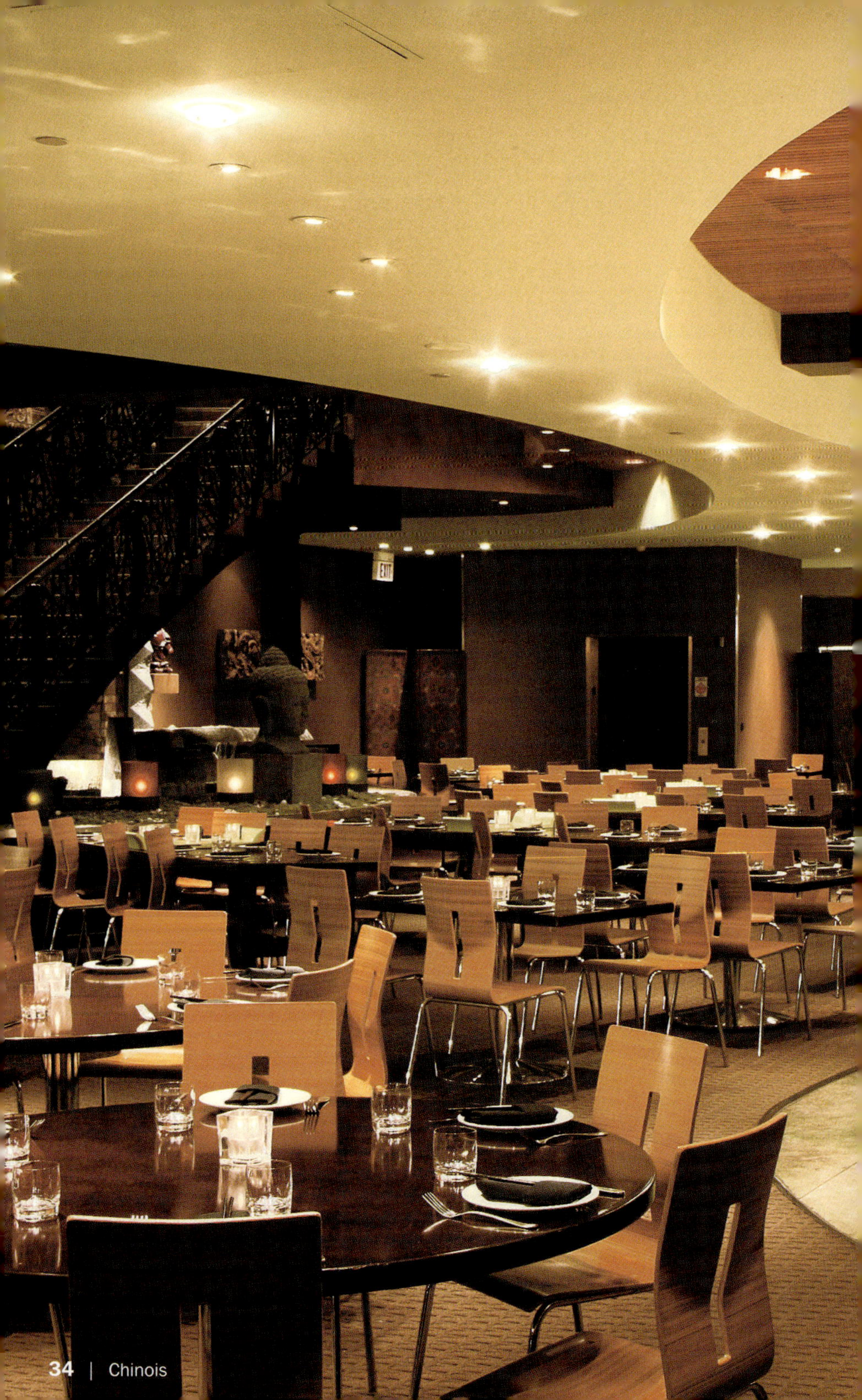

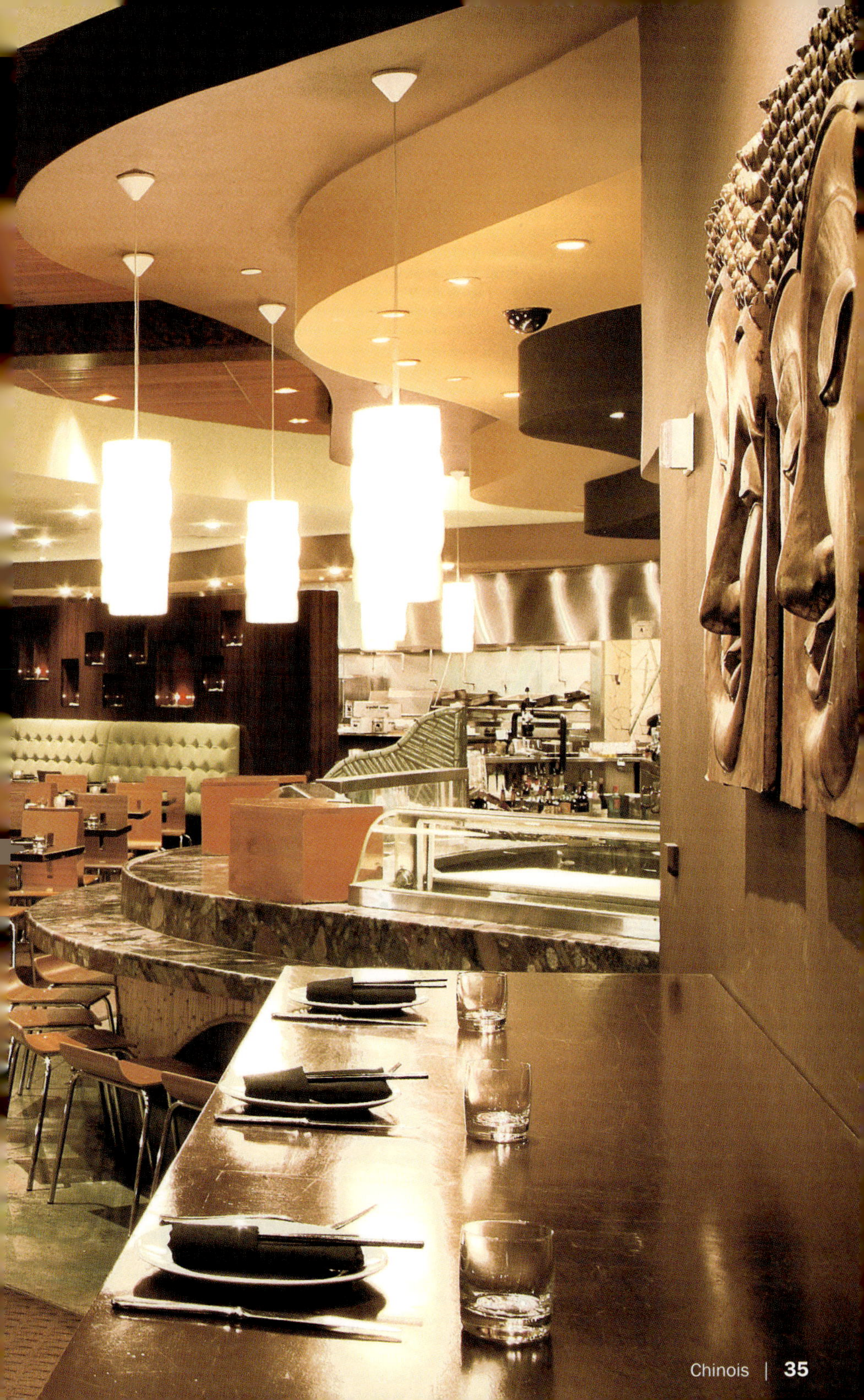

Chicken Spring Rolls

Frühlingsrollen mit Hühnchen

Rouleaux de printemps au poulet

Rollos de primavera con pollo

Involtini primavera con pollo

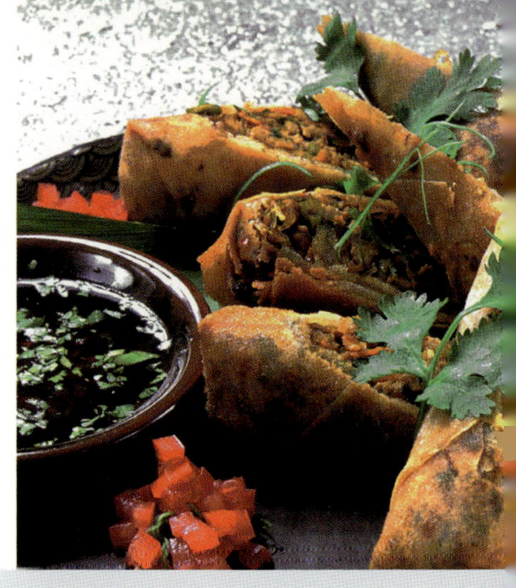

3 lb 4 oz ground chicken
200 ml soybean oil
2 onions, diced
2 cloves of garlic, chopped
2 oz ginger, chopped
2 spring onions, julienne
½ Napa cabbage, julienne
2 carrots, julienne
10 oz shiitake mushrooms, chopped
3 tbsp peanuts, chopped
3 oz bean sprouts
2 oz curry powder
4 oz tamarind, wet paste
120 ml soy sauce
4 oz brown sugar
120 ml red wine vinegar
3 oz chili, chopped
Salt, pepper

Heat half the soybean oil in a wok. Stir-fry chicken until it turns a dark brown color. Remove from the wok and strain. Clean wok, heat up the second half of the soybean oil and stir-fry all vegetables until tender. Add the other ingredients and season. Mix with the ground chicken and season again, if necessary.

2 packages of spring roll skins (approx. 20 skins each)
Flour-water mixture
Oil for deep-frying
Soy sauce for dipping
Spread the spring roll skins and divide the mixture onto them. Brush the edges with the flour-water mixture and shape into spring rolls. Deep-fry in 320 °F hot oil until the skins turn a golden color.

1.500 g gehacktes Hühnerfleisch
200 ml Sojabohnenöl
2 gewürfelte Zwiebeln
2 gehackte Knoblauchzehen
55 g gehackter Ingwer
2 in feine Streifen geschnittene Frühlings-zwiebeln
½ in feine Streifen geschnittener Pak Choy
2 in feine Streifen geschnittene Karotten
285 g gehackte Shiitakepilze
3 EL gehackte Erdnüsse
85 g Bohnensprossen
55 g Currypulver
115 g Tamarindenpaste
120 ml Sojasoße
115 g brauner Zucker
120 ml Rotweinessig
85 g gehackte Chili
Salz, Pfeffer

Die Hälfte des Sojabohnenöls in einem Wok erhitzen. Das Hühnchen unter Rühren anbraten, bis es eine dunkelbraune Färbung angenommen hat. Aus dem Wok nehmen und abtropfen lassen. Den Wok reinigen, das restliche Sojabohnenöl erhitzen und das Gemüse unter Rühren anbraten, bis es weich ist. Die anderen Zutaten hinzufügen und würzen. Mit dem Hühnerfleisch vermischen und bei Bedarf nochmals abschmecken.

2 Packungen Teigblätter für Frühlingsrollen (je ca. 20 Blätter)
Mischung aus Mehl und Wasser
Öl zum Frittieren
Sojasoße zum Dippen
Die Teigblätter für Frühlingsrollen auslegen und die Mischung darauf verteilen. Die Ränder mit der Mehl-Wasser-Mischung bestreichen und Frühlingsrollen formen. In 160 °C heißem Öl frittieren, bis sie goldbraun sind.

1.500 g de blanc de poulet haché
200 ml d'huile de soja
2 oignons coupés en dés
2 gousses d'ail hachées
55 g de gingembre haché
2 oignons de printemps émincés
½ chou pak-choi coupé en julienne
2 carottes coupées en julienne
285 g de champignons shiitake hachés
3 c. à soupe de cacahuètes hachées
85 g de pousses de soja
55 g de poudre de curry
115 g de pâte de tamarin
120 ml de sauce de soja
115 g de sucre brun
120 ml de vinaigre de vin rouge
85 g de piment haché
Sel, poivre

Faire chauffer la moitié de l'huile de soja dans un wok. Saisir le poulet en remuant jusqu'à ce qu'il brunisse bien. Ôter du feu et égoutter. Nettoyer le wok, faire chauffer le reste d'huile de soja et saisir les légumes en remuant jusqu'à ce qu'ils ramollissent. Ajouter les autres ingrédients et épicer. Incorporer le poulet et relever l'assaisonnement si nécessaire.

2 paquets de feuilles de riz (20 feuilles dans chaque)
Mélange de farine et d'eau
Huile pour la friture
Sauce de soja pour tremper les rouleaux
Étaler les feuilles de riz et répartir le mélange dessus. Enduire les bords du mélange farine-eau et préparer les rouleaux. Les faire frire dans l'huile à une température de 160 °C jusqu'à ce qu'ils soient bien dorés.

1.500 g de carne de pollo picada
200 ml de aceite de soja
2 cebollas en dados
2 dientes de ajo picados
55 g de jengibre picado
2 cebolletas en juliana
½ de pak choy en juliana
2 zanahorias en juliana
285 g de setas shiitake en juliana
3 cucharadas de cacahuetes picados
85 g brotes de judías
55 g de curry molido
115 g de pasta de tamarindo
120 ml de salsa de soja
115 g de azúcar moreno
120 ml de vinagre de vino tinto
85 g de guindilla picada
Sal, pimienta

Caliente la mitad del aceite de soja en un wok. Sofría el pollo removiendo hasta que tenga un color marrón oscuro. Saque el pollo del wok y deje que escurra. Limpie el wok, caliente el resto del aceite y rehogue la verdura sin dejar de remover hasta que esté tierna. Incorpore los demás ingredientes y condimente. Mézclelos con la carne de pollo y vuelva a sazonar si fuera necesario.

2 paquetes de láminas para rollos de primavera (aprox. 20 láminas cada uno)
Mezcla de harina y agua
Aceite para freír
Salsa de soja para mojar
Extienda las láminas y reparta por encima la mezcla. Pinte los bordes con la mezcla de agua y harina y forme los rollos. Fríalos en aceite caliente a 160 °C hasta que estén dorados.

1.500 g di carne di pollo tritata
200 ml di olio di semi di soia
2 cipolle tagliate a dadini
2 spicchi d'aglio tritati
55 g di zenzero tritato
2 cipollotti tagliati a julienne
½ pak-choy (cavolo cinese) tagliato a julienne
3 carote tagliate a julienne
285 g di funghi shitake tritati
2 cucchiai di arachidi tritate
85 g di germogli di fagioli
55 g di polvere di curry
115 g pasta di tamarindo
120 ml di salsa di soia
115 g di zucchero bruno
120 ml di aceto di vino rosso
85 g di peperoncino tritato
Sale, pepe

Scaldare in un wok la metà dell'olio di semi di soia. Rosolare il pollo rigirandolo, finché non sarà dorato. Estrarlo dal wok e sgocciolarlo. Pulire il wok, scaldare il rimanente olio di semi di soia e rosolare le verdure rimestandole, finché non saranno tenere. Aggiungere gli altri ingredienti e condire. Unire la carne di pollo, assaggiare e, se necessario, regolare il condimento.

2 confezioni di fogli di pasta di riso per involtini primavera di circa 20 fogli ciascuna
Composto di acqua e farina
Olio per friggere
Salsa di soia per intingere
Stendere i fogli e ripartirvi dentro il composto. Spennellare i bordi con acqua e farina e formare gli involtini. Friggerli in olio caldo a 160 °C finché non siano dorati.

Craftsteak

Design: Bentel&Bentel | Chef: Christopher Albrecht
Owners: Tom Colicchio, MGM Grand Hotel & Casino

3799 Las Vegas Boulevard S | Las Vegas, NV 89109 | MGM Grand Hotel & Casino
Phone: +1 702 891 7318
www.mgmgrand.com
Opening hours: Daily 5:30 pm to 10:30 pm
Average price: $ 52
Cuisine: Steakhouse
Special features: Extensive whiskey selection

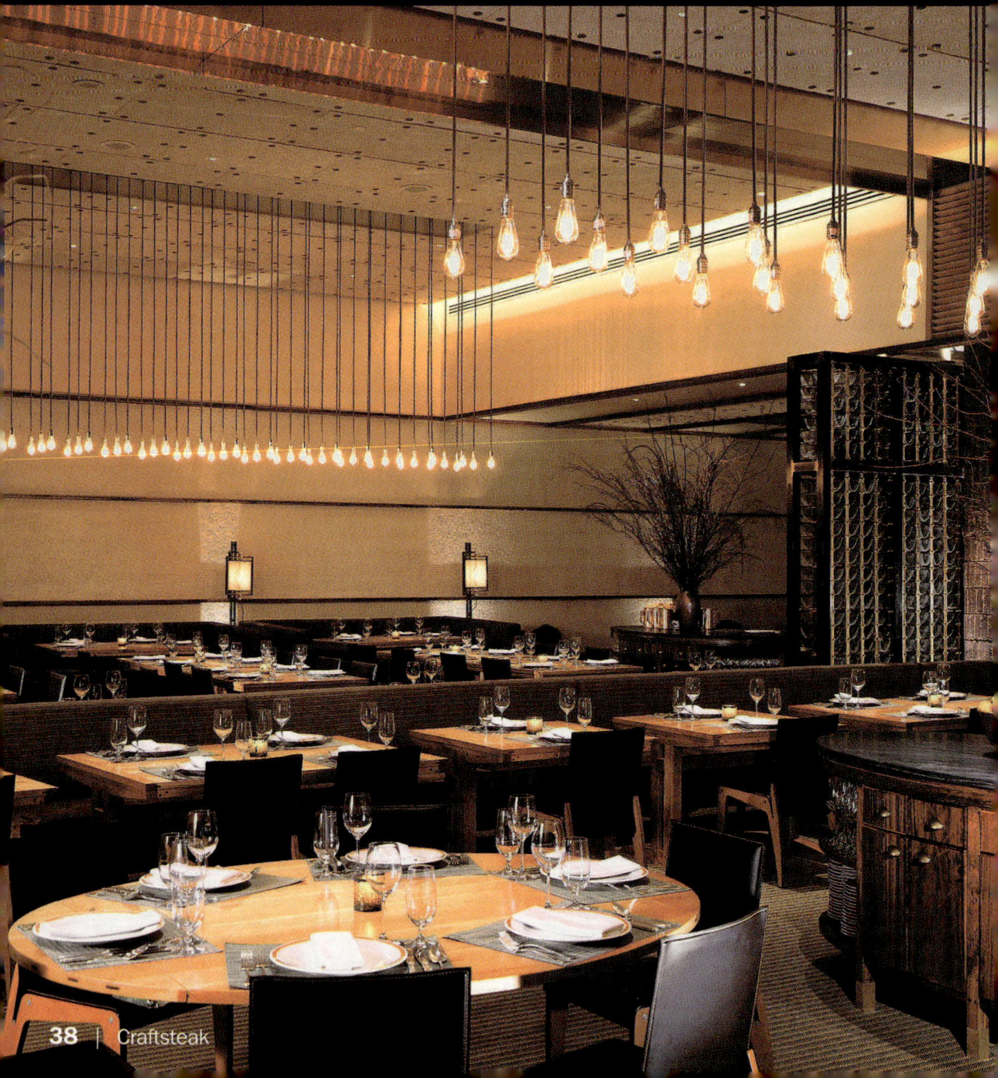

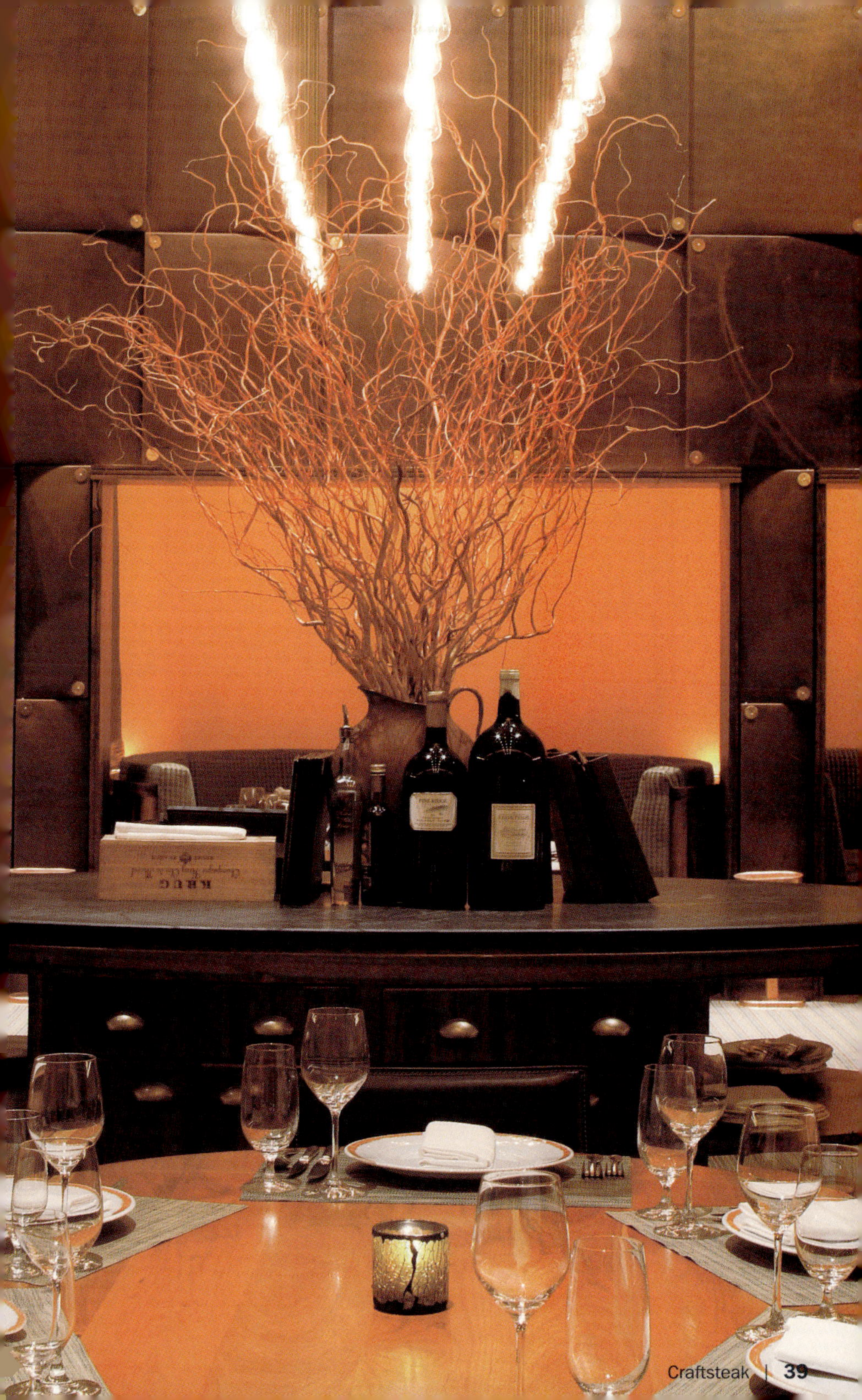

Roasted Rib Steak for Two

Gebratenes Rippensteak für Zwei

Entrecôte pour deux

Entrecot para dos

Costolette arrosto per due

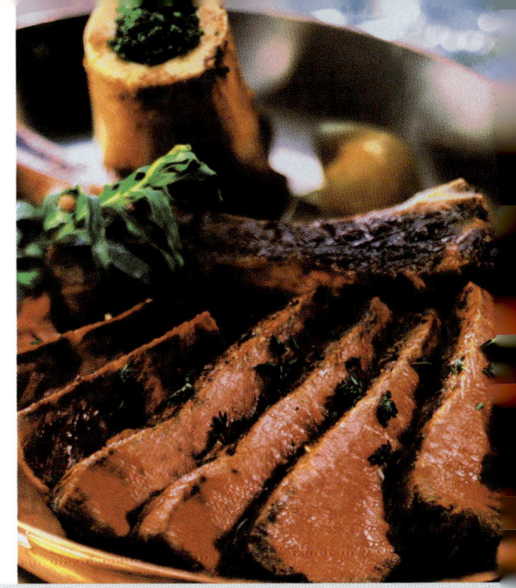

2 beef rib steaks, 32 oz each
Salt, pepper
3 tbsp peanut oil
8 shallots, peeled
4 marrowbones
4 twigs of tarragon

Fresh thyme and chives for decoration

Season the steaks and sear in hot oil from both sides for 2 minutes, add the marrowbones and the shallots and roast at 325 °F for 10–15 minutes. During the roasting process the meat and bone will produce juices. Baste the steaks with those meat juices occasionally. After 10 minutes add the tarragon twigs and baste one more time. Cut the steaks in slices and arrange with the bones and the shallots on four plates. Decorate with thyme and chives.

2 Rippensteaks vom Rind, je 900 g
Salz, Pfeffer
3 EL Erdnussöl
8 geschälte Schalotten
4 Markknochen
4 Estragonzweige

Frischer Thymian und Schnittlauch zur Dekoration

Steaks würzen und in heißem Öl von beiden Seiten 2 Minuten scharf anbraten. Dann die Markknochen und die Schalotten hinzugeben und 10–15 Minuten bei 160 °C schmoren. Bei diesem Vorgang tritt Saft aus dem Fleisch und den Knochen aus. Die Steaks gelegentlich mit diesem Fleischsaft begießen. Nach 10 Minuten die Estragonzweige hinzugeben und noch einmal begießen. Die Steaks in Scheiben schneiden und mit den Knochen und den Schalotten auf vier Tellern anrichten. Mit Thymian und Schnittlauch dekorieren.

2 entrecôtes de bœuf de 900 g
Sel, poivre
3 c. à soupe d'huile d'arachide
8 échalotes épluchées
4 os à moelle
4 branches d'estragon

Thym et ciboulette frais pour la garniture

Assaisonner les entrecôtes et les saisir dans l'huile chaude 2 minutes de chaque côté. Ajouter les os à moelle et les échalotes et laisser braiser 10–15 minutes à 160 °C. Pendant ce temps, la viande et les os émettent du jus. Arroser de temps à autre les entrecôtes de ce jus. Au bout de 10 minutes, ajouter les branches d'estragon et arroser une nouvelle fois. Couper les entrecôtes en tranches et les dresser sur quatre assiettes avec les os et les échalotes. Garnir de thym et de ciboulette.

2 entrecotes de ternera de 900 g cada uno
Sal, pimienta
3 cucharadas de aceite de cacahuete
8 chalotes pelados
4 huesos con tuétano
4 ramitas de estragón

Tomillo fresco y cebollino para decorar

Sazone los entrecotes y fríalos por ambos lados durante 2 minutos en aceite caliente. Añada después los huesos y los chalotes y rehogue entre 10 y 15 minutos a 160 °C. Durante este proceso la carne y los huesos producen un jugo. Vierta de vez en cuando este caldo por encima de la carne. Después de 10 minutos incorpore el estragón y vuelva a verter el jugo por encima. Corte después los entrecotes en lonchas y póngalos en cuatro platos junto con los huesos y los chalotes. Decore con el tomillo y el cebollino.

2 costolette di manzo di 900 g ciascuna
Sale, pepe
3 cucchiai di olio di arachidi
8 scalogni sbucciati
4 ossi con midollo
4 rametti di dragoncello

Per la guarnizione: timo ed erba cipollina freschi

Condire le bistecche e rosolarle a fuoco vivo in olio caldo da entrambi i lati per circa 2 minuti. Unire gli ossi e gli scalogni e lasciar cuocere a 160 °C per 10–15 minuti. Bagnare ogni tanto le bistecche con il loro succo. Dopo 10 minuti, aggiungere i rametti di dragoncello e bagnare ancora una volta. Affettare la carne e disporla su quattro piatti con gli ossi e gli scalogni. Guarnire con il timo e l'erba cipollina.

Daniel Boulud Brasserie

Design: Jeffrey Beers | Chef: Daniel Boulud
Owner: Wynn Las Vegas

3131 Las Vegas Boulevard S | Las Vegas, NV 89109 | Wynn Las Vegas
www.wynnlasvegas.com
Opening hours: Daily 5:30 pm to 10:30 pm
Average price: $ 40
Cuisine: French
Special features: Patio seating

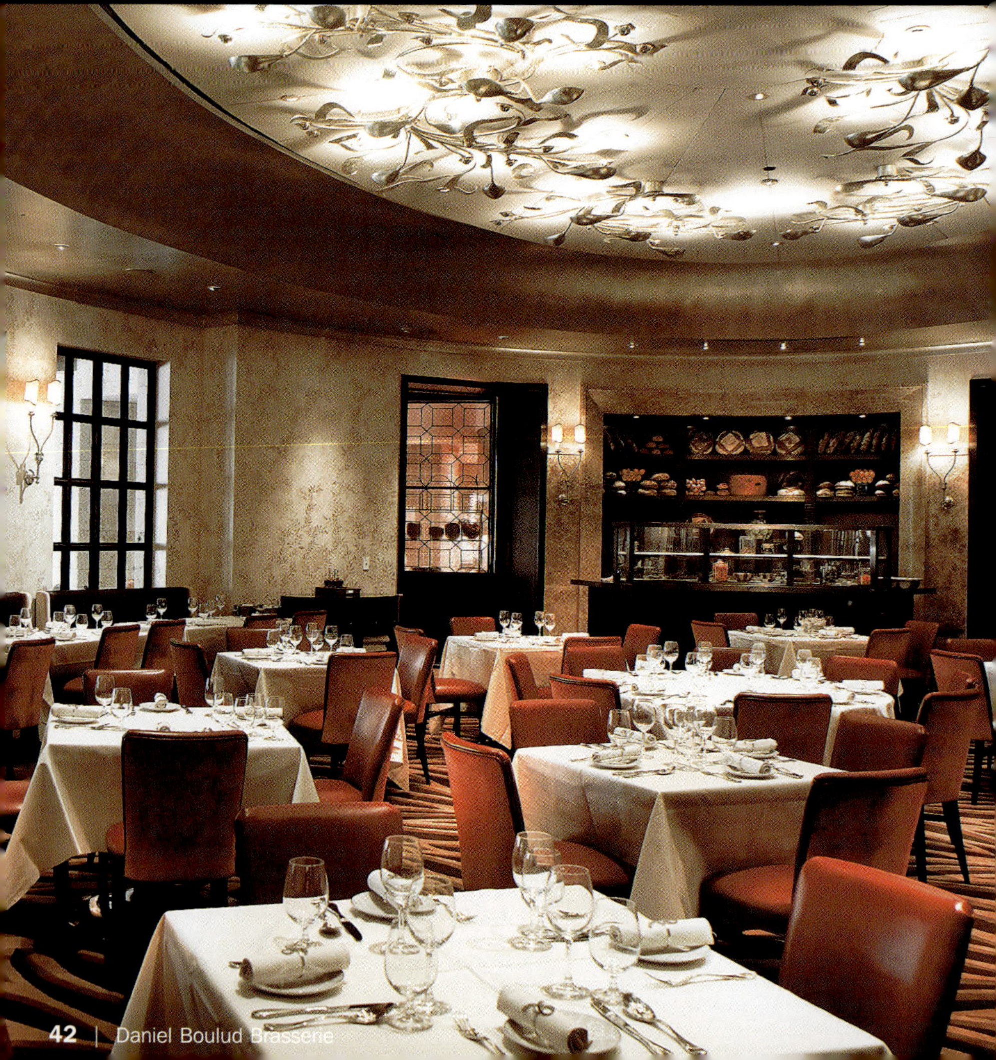

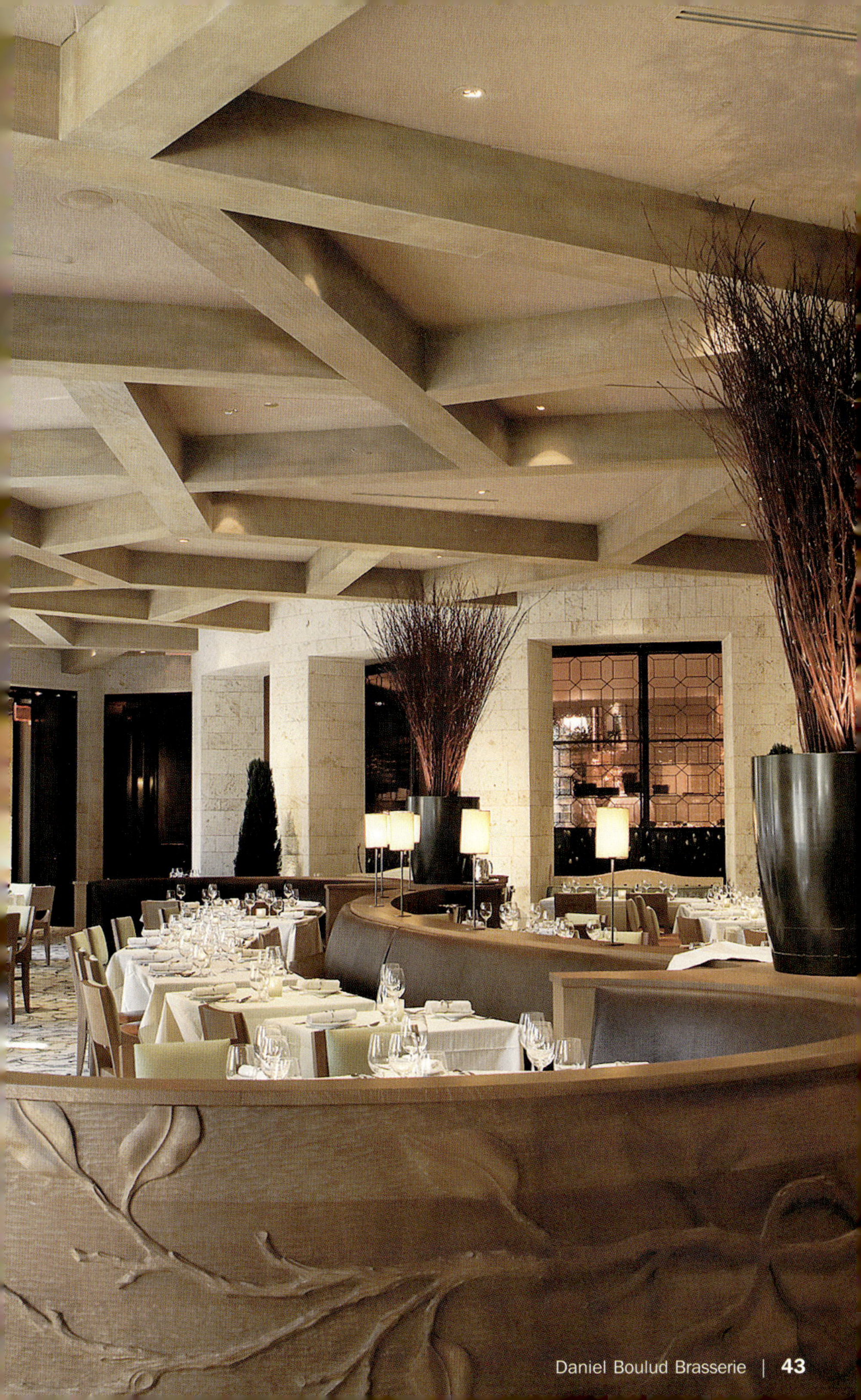

Eiffel Tower **Restaurant**

Design: Bill Johnson | Chef: Jean Joho
Owner: Lettuce Entertain You

3655 Las Vegas Boulevard S | Las Vegas, NV 89109 | Paris Las Vegas
Phone: +1 702 948 6937
www.chefjoho.com
Opening hours: Daily 11 am to 3 pm, Sun–Thu 5 pm to 10:15 pm, Fri–Sat 5 pm to 10:45 pm
Average price: $ 41
Cuisine: French
Special features: Panoramic view of the Las Vegas strip and water show

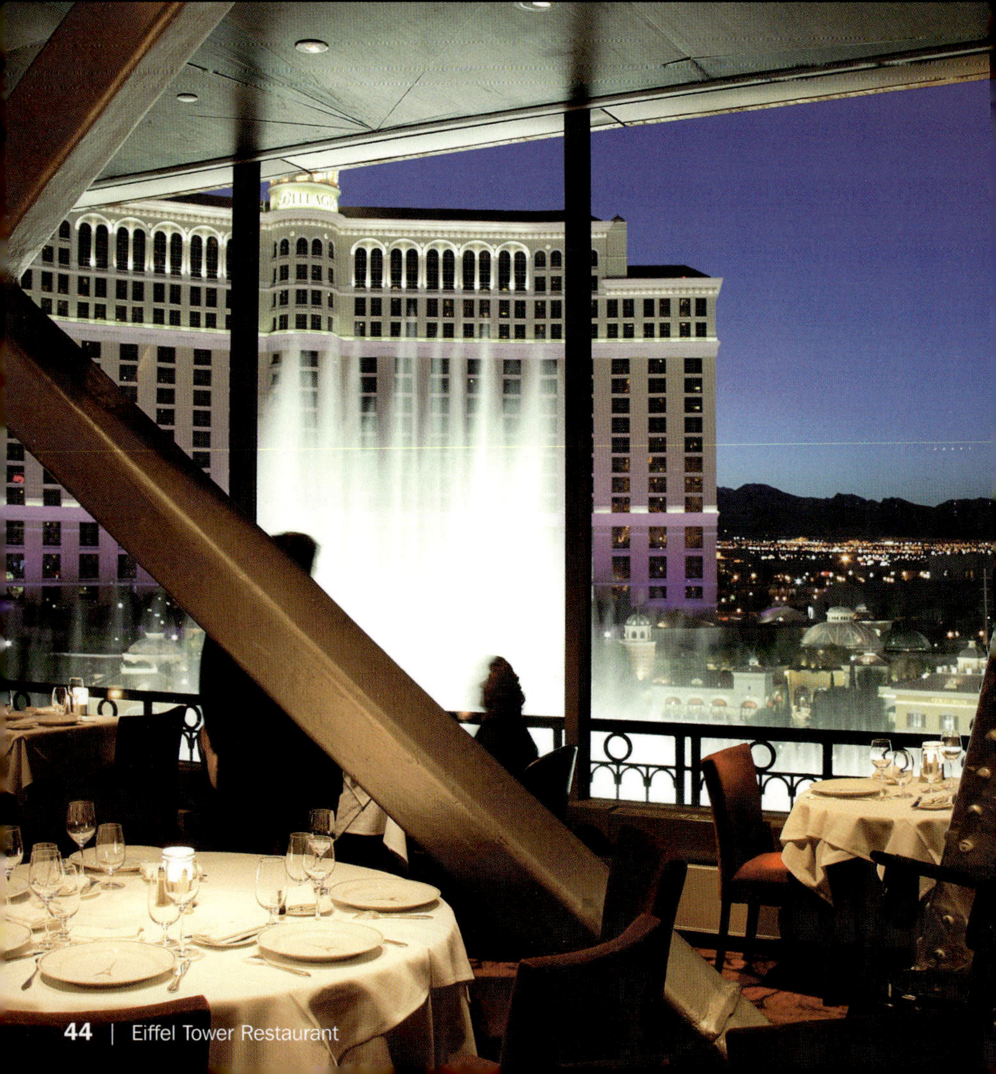

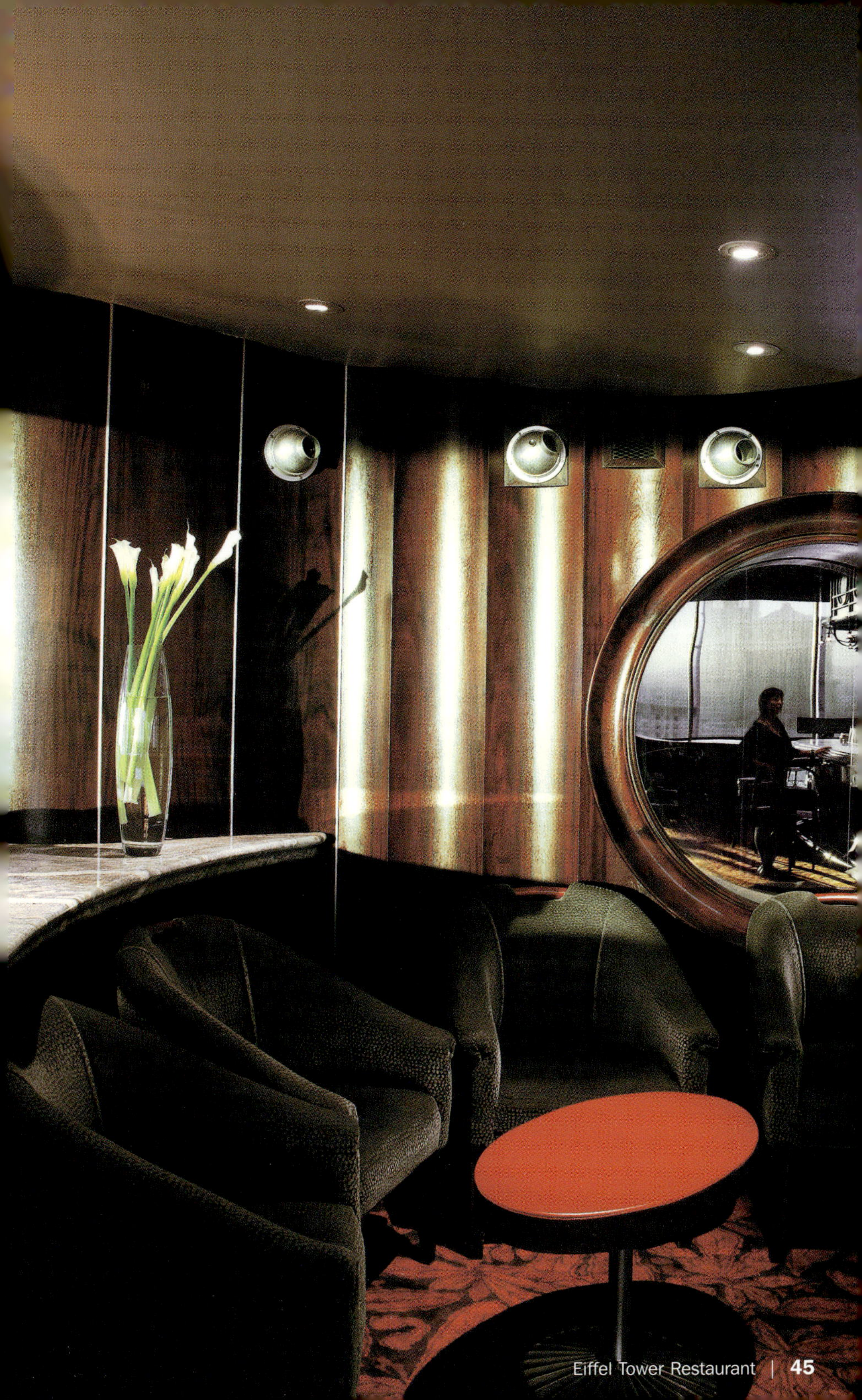

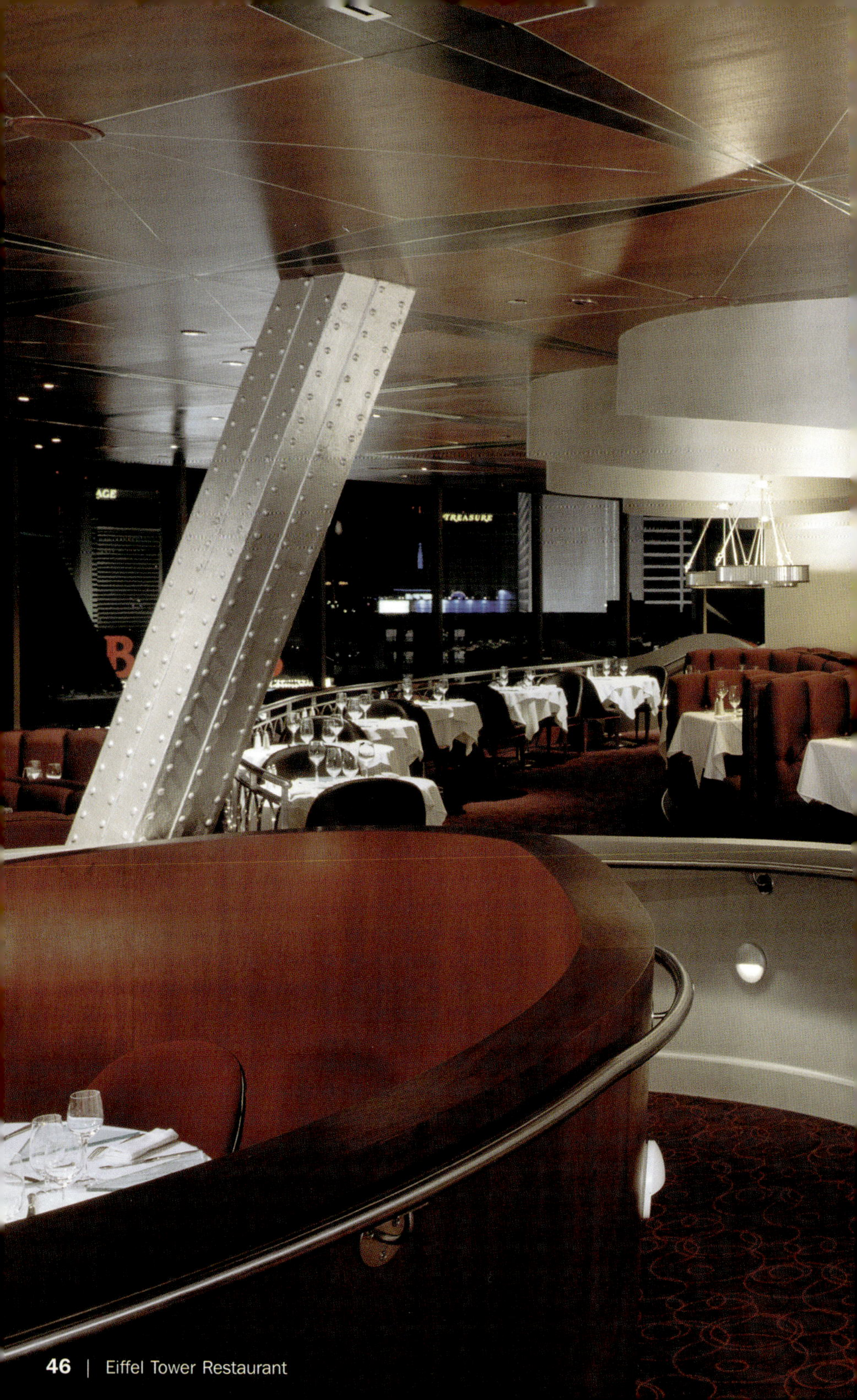

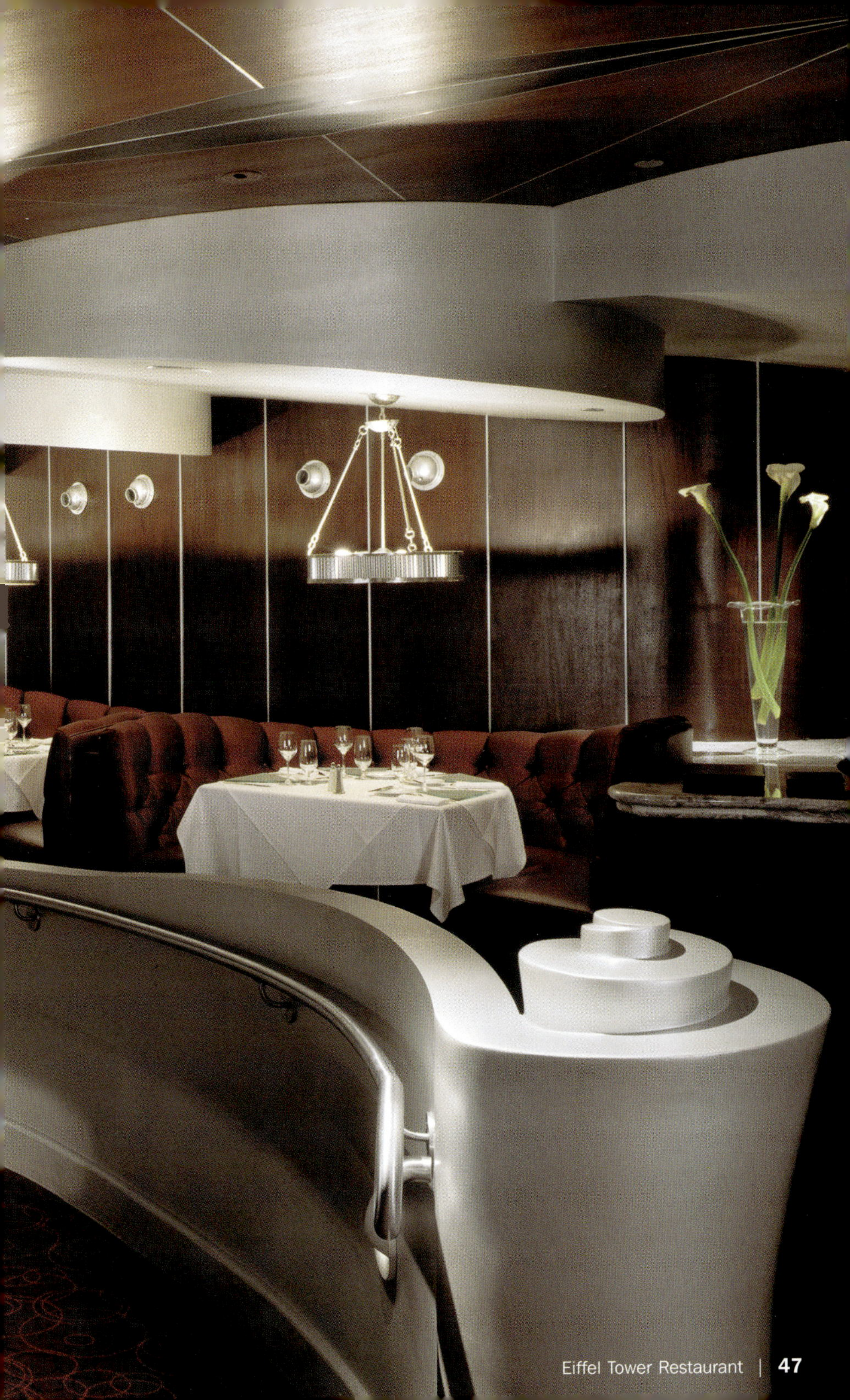

Fiamma

Design: Yabu Pushelberg | Chef: Michael White
Owners: Stephen Hanson, MGM Grand Hotel & Casino

3799 Las Vegas Boulevard S | Las Vegas, NV 89109 | MGM Grand Hotel & Casino
Phone: +1 702 891 7600
www.mgmgrand.com
Opening hours: 5:30 pm to 10:30 pm
Average price: $ 33
Cuisine: Italian
Special features: Private screening room

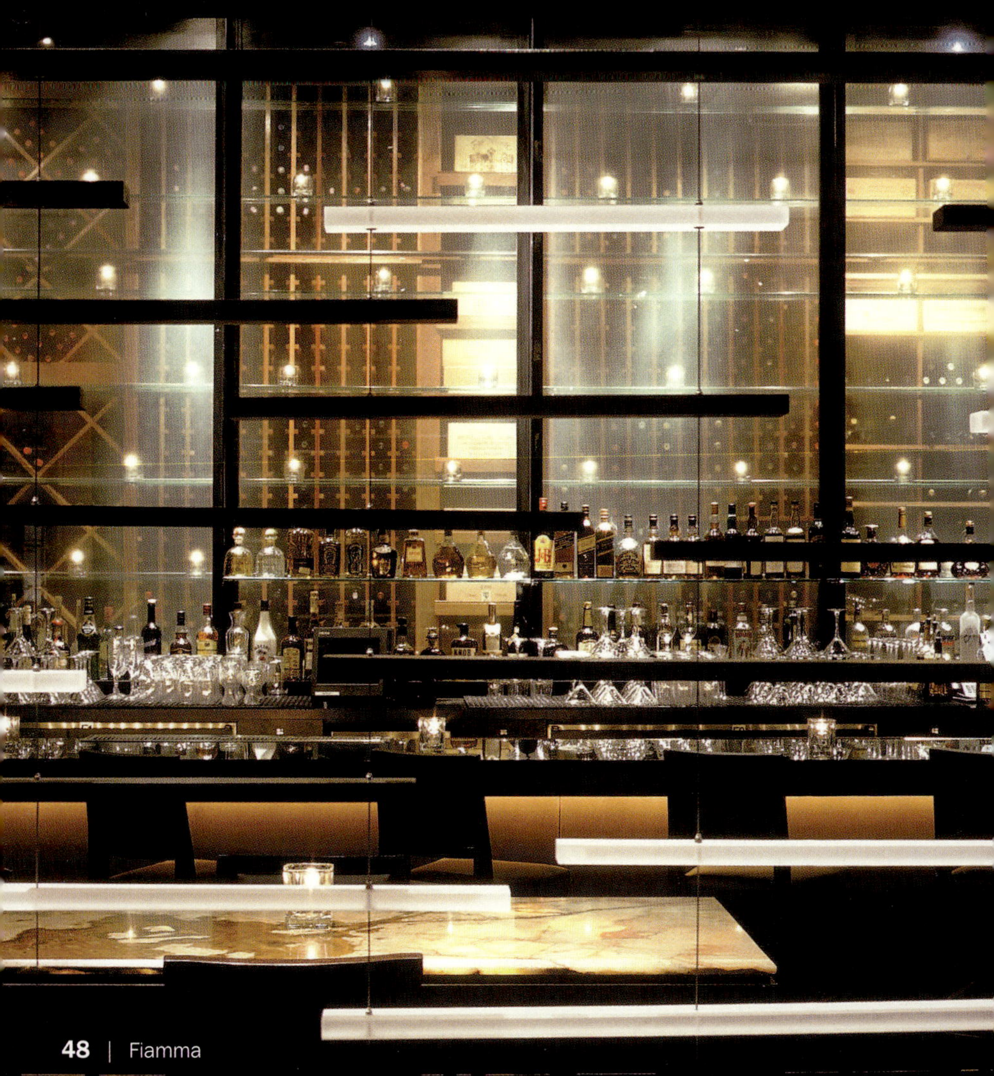

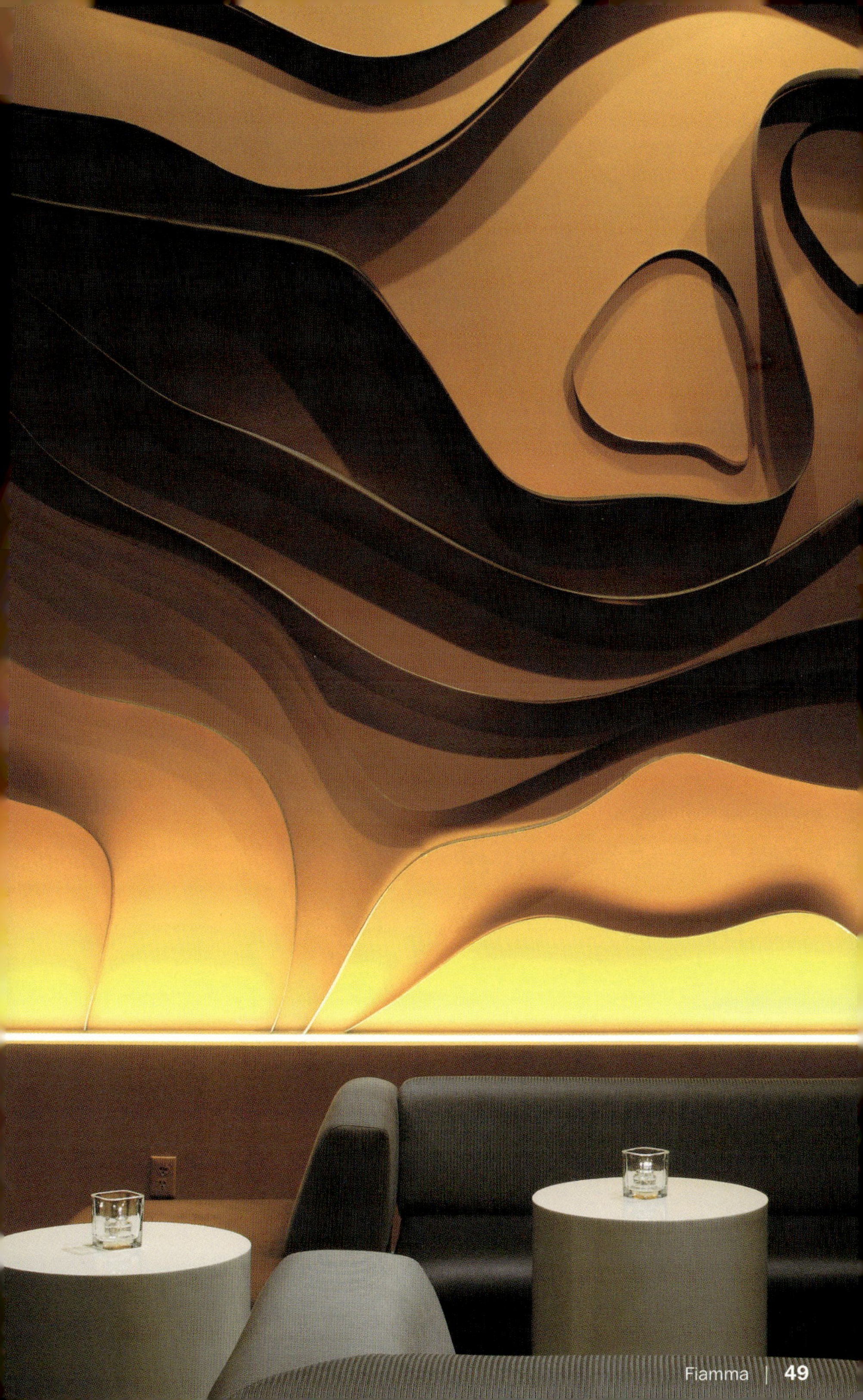

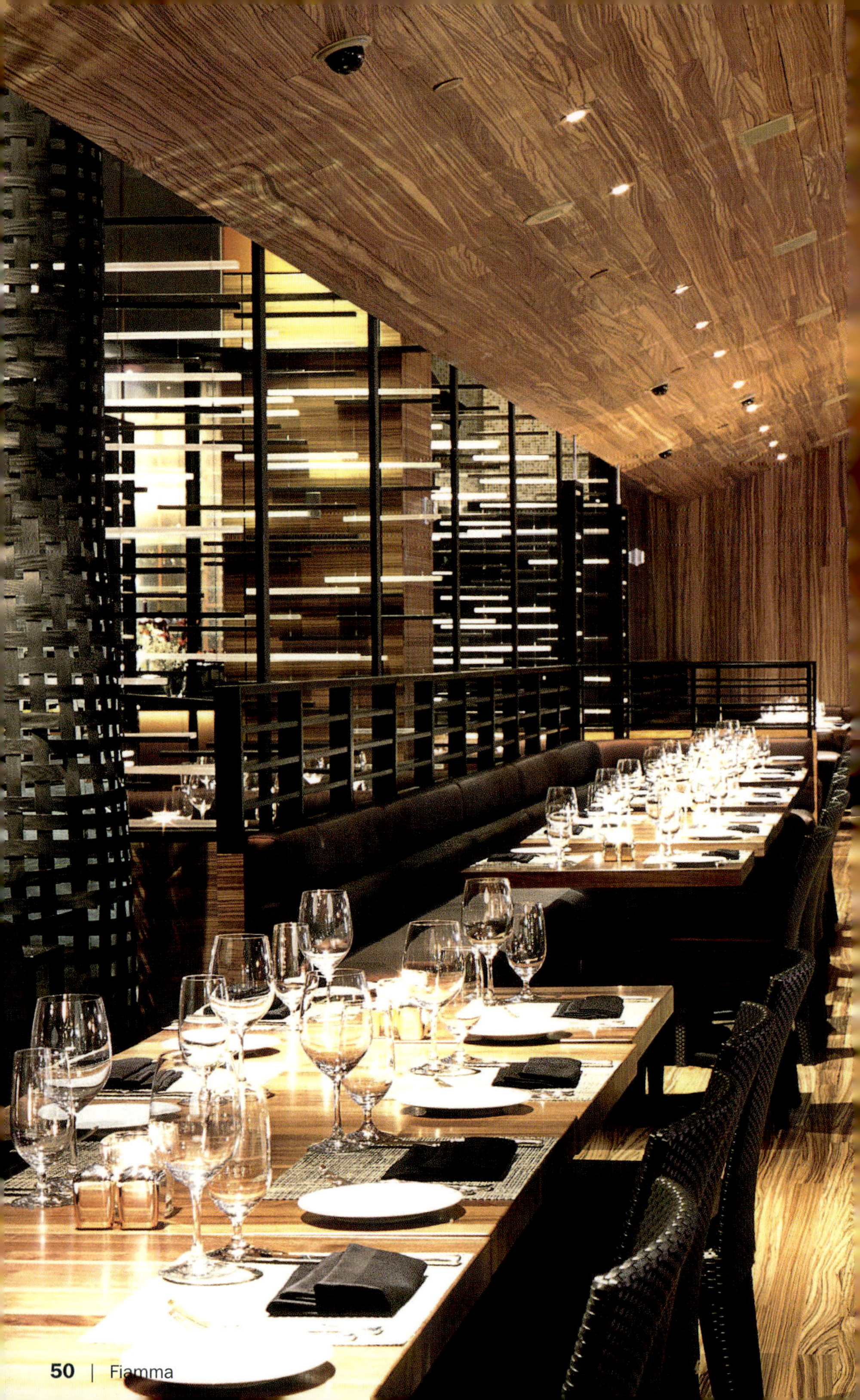

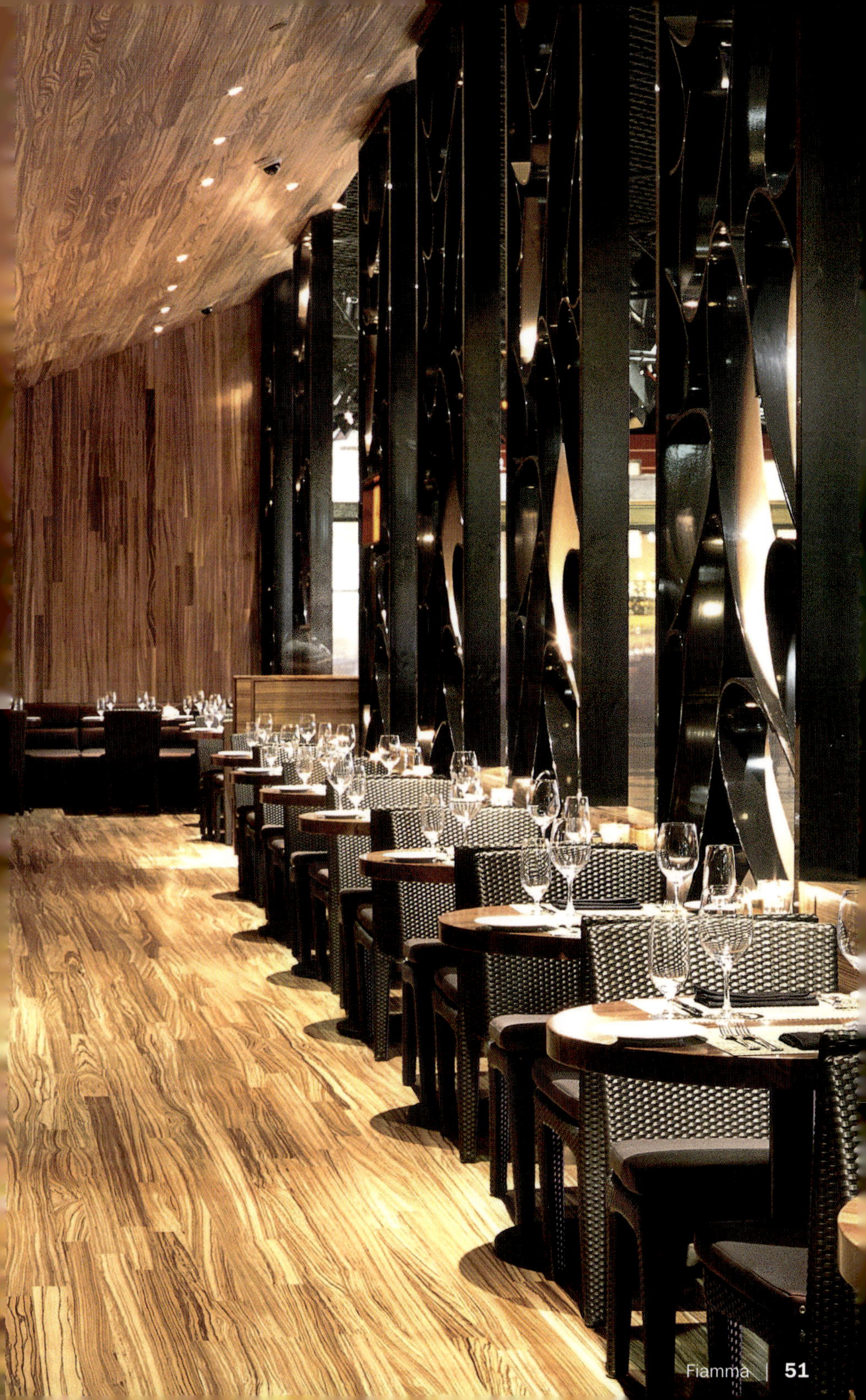

Ricotta Tortellini

Ricotta Tortellini
Tortellini à la ricotta
Ricotta Tortellini
Tortellini alla ricotta

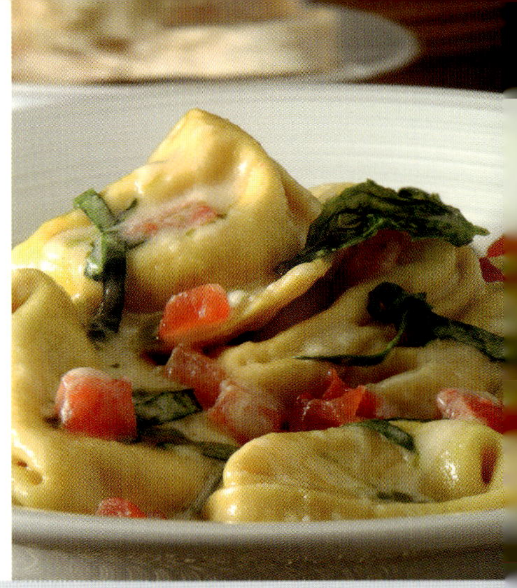

Dough:
15 oz flour
3 large eggs
6 egg yolks
Salt
Combine all ingredients and work into a soft dough. Chill for at least 1 hour, but remember to remove dough from the refrigerator 1 hour prior to use.

Filling:
9 oz ricotta cheese
4 tbsp parmesan, grated
1 egg
Salt, pepper, nutmeg
Place all ingredients in a bowl, season, whisk and chill.

Roll out the dough to about 0,1 in. thickness, then cut out squares (2 x 2 in.). Place 1 tsp of the ricotta mixture in the middle of each square, brush the edges with water, fold the square into a triangle and shape into a tortellini. Makes about 32 tortellini. Boil the tortellini in salted water for 2 minutes.

2 tbsp butter
4 tomatoes, skinned, seeded and diced
8 slices smoked bacon, diced
2 tbsp basil leaves, torn
4 tbsp parmesan, grated
Salt, pepper
In the meantime, heat the butter in a pan, add the tomatoes and bacon and season. Add the strained tortellini to the pan, stir in basil leaves and parmesan. Season again, if necessary.

Für den Teig:
425 g Mehl
3 große Eier
6 Eigelbe
Salz
Alle Zutaten miteinander vermengen und zu einem weichen Teig verarbeiten. Mindestens 1 Stunde kühl stellen, den Teig jedoch 1 Stunde vor der Weiterverarbeitung wieder aus dem Kühlschrank holen.

Für die Füllung:
250 g Ricottakäse
4 EL geriebener Parmesan
1 Ei
Salz, Pfeffer, Muskat
Alle Zutaten in eine Schüssel geben, würzen, mit dem Schneebesen schlagen und kühl stellen.

Den Teig ungefähr 3 mm dünn ausrollen und in Quadrate von ca. 5 x 5 cm schneiden. 1 TL der Ricottamischung in die Mitte jedes Quadrates geben, die Ränder mit Wasser bestreichen, zu einem Dreieck falten und daraus Tortellinis formen. Ergibt ca. 32 Tortellini. Tortellini 2 Minuten in Salzwasser garen lassen.

2 EL Butter
4 gehäutete, entkernte und in Würfel geschnittene Tomaten
8 Scheiben gewürfelter, geräucherter Speck
2 EL zerrissene Basilikumblätter
4 EL geriebener Parmesan
Salz, Pfeffer
In der Zwischenzeit die Butter in einer Pfanne erhitzen, Tomaten und Speck hinzufügen und würzen. Tortellini abgießen und dazugeben und Basilikumblätter und Parmesan unterrühren. Falls nötig, nochmals abschmecken.

Pour la pâte :
425 g de farine
3 gros œufs
6 jaunes d'œuf
Sel
Mélanger tous les ingrédients et préparer la pâte. La réserver au frais au moins 1 heure, puis la sortir du réfrigérateur 1 heure avant de la travailler.

Pour la farce :
250 g de ricotta
4 c. à soupe de parmesan râpé
1 œuf
Sel, poivre, muscade
Verser tous les ingrédients dans un plat creux, les assaisonner, les battre au fouet et les garder au frais.

Préparer une pâte de 3 mm d'épaisseur et la découper en carrés de 5 x 5 cm. Verser 1 c. à café de mélange à la ricotta au milieu de chaque carré, badigeonner d'eau les bords, plier les pâtes en triangles et préparer 32 tortellini. Les cuire 2 minutes dans l'eau salée.

2 c. à soupe de beurre
4 tomates pelées, épépinées et coupées en dés
8 tranches de lard fumé coupées en dés
2 c. à soupe de feuilles de basilic découpées
4 c. à soupe de parmesan râpé
Sel, poivre
Entre-temps, chauffer le beurre dans une poêle, ajouter les tomates et le lard, puis assaisonner. Jeter l'eau des tortellini, les verser dans la poêle, puis incorporer le basilic et le parmesan. Relever l'assaisonnement si nécessaire.

Para la pasta:
425 g de harina
3 huevos grandes
6 yemas
Sal
Mezcle todos los ingredientes y amase hasta conseguir una pasta suave. Déjela enfriar por lo menos 1 hora y sáquela del frigorífico 1 hora antes de seguir trabajando con ella.

Para el relleno:
250 g de queso ricotta
4 cucharadas de queso parmesano rallado
1 huevo
Sal, pimienta, nuez moscada
Ponga todos los ingredientes en un cuenco, sazone, remueva con unas varillas y ponga la mezcla en el frigorífico.
Extienda con el rodillo la pasta hasta conseguir un grosor de unos 3 mm y corte cuadrados de

aprox. 5 x 5 cm. Ponga en el centro de cada cuadrado 1 cucharadita de la mezcla de ricotta, pinte los bordes con agua, doble los cuadrados en un triángulo y deles después la forma de tortellini. Obtendrá unos 32 tortellini. Deje que se cuezan en su punto durante 2 minutos en agua con sal.

2 cucharadas de mantequilla
4 tomates pelados, despepitados y cortados en dados
8 lonchas de beicon ahumado en dados
2 cucharadas de hojas de albahacas deshechas
4 cucharadas de queso parmesano rallado
Sal, pimienta
Mientras se hacen los tortellini caliente la mantequilla en una sartén, añada los tomates y el beicon y sazone. Escurra los tortellini y añádalos a la sartén junto con la albahaca y el queso parmesano y remueva. Condimente nuevamente si fuera necesario.

Per la pasta sfoglia:
425 g di farina
3 uova grosse
6 tuorli d'uovo
Sale
Mescolare tutti gli ingredienti e lavorarli fino ad ottenere una pasta morbida. Lasciare in frigo per almeno 1 ora. Estrarre tuttavia la pasta dal frigorifero almeno 1 ora prima della successiva lavorazione.

Per il ripieno:
250 g di ricotta
4 cucchiai di parmigiano grattugiato
1 uovo
Sale, pepe, noce moscata
Mettere tutti gli ingredienti in una ciotola, condirli, mescolarli con la frusta e mettere in frigo il composto.

Stendere una sfoglia dello spessore di circa 3 mm e ricavarne dei quadrati di circa 5 x 5 cm. Mettere 1 cucchiaino di ripieno al centro di ogni quadrato, spennellarne i bordi con acqua, piegarli a triangolo e formare i tortellini. Le quantità sono sufficienti per circa 32 tortellini. Cuocerli per 2 minuti in acqua salata.

2 cucchiai di burro
4 pomodori spellati, privati dei semi e tagliati a dadini
8 fette di speck affumicato tagliato a dadini
2 cucchiai di foglie di basilico sminuzzato
4 cucchiai di parmigiano grattugiato
Sale, pepe
Nel frattempo, scaldare il burro in una padella, unire i pomodori e lo speck e condire. Scolare i tortellini e versarli nella salsa, aggiungendo le foglie di basilico ed il parmigiano. Assaggiare ed eventualmente regolare il condimento.

Fix

Design: Graft architects | Chef: Brian Massi
Owner: LightGroup

3600 Las Vegas Boulevard S | Las Vegas, NV 89109 | Bellagio Las Vegas
Phone: +1 877 234 6358
www.bellagio.com
Opening hours: Sun–Thu 5 pm to midnight, Fri and Sat 5 pm to 2 am
Average price: $ 60
Cuisine: Contemporary American

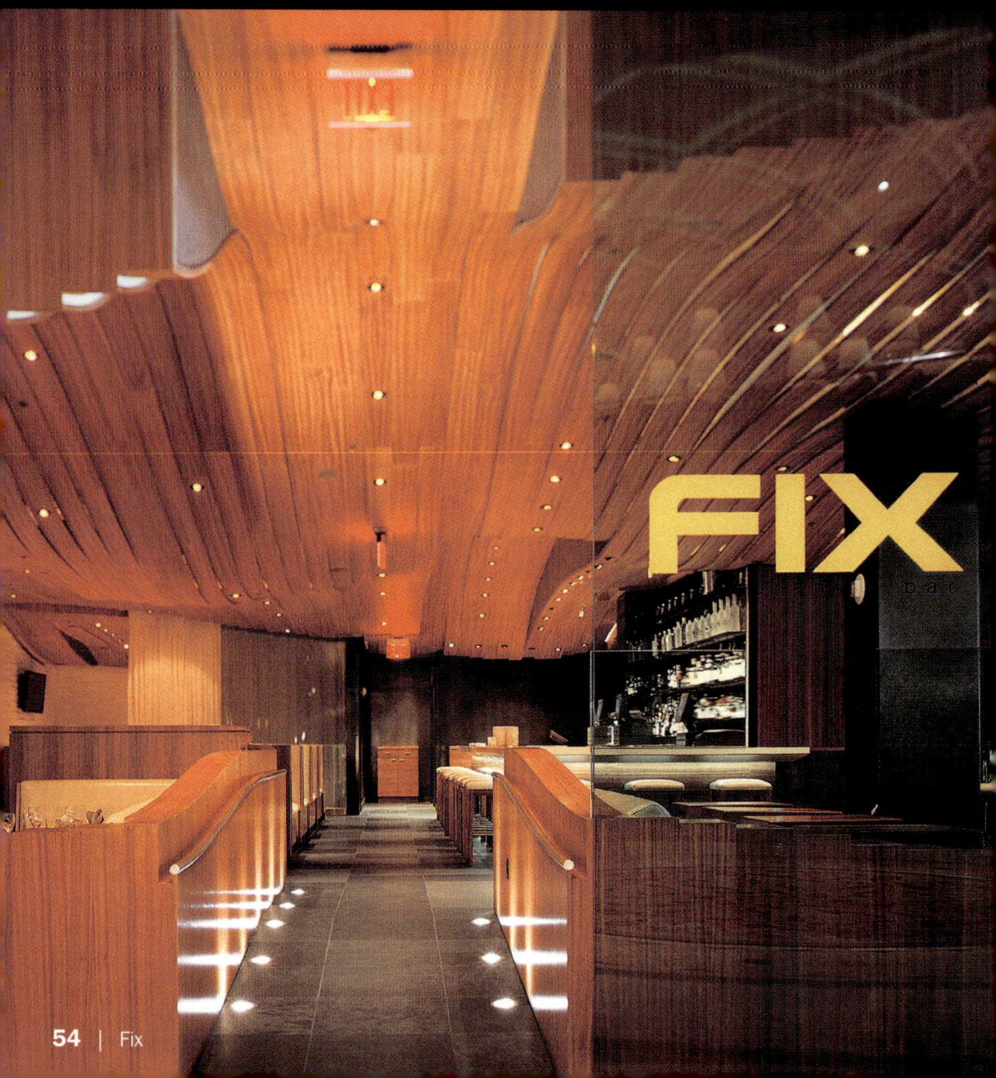

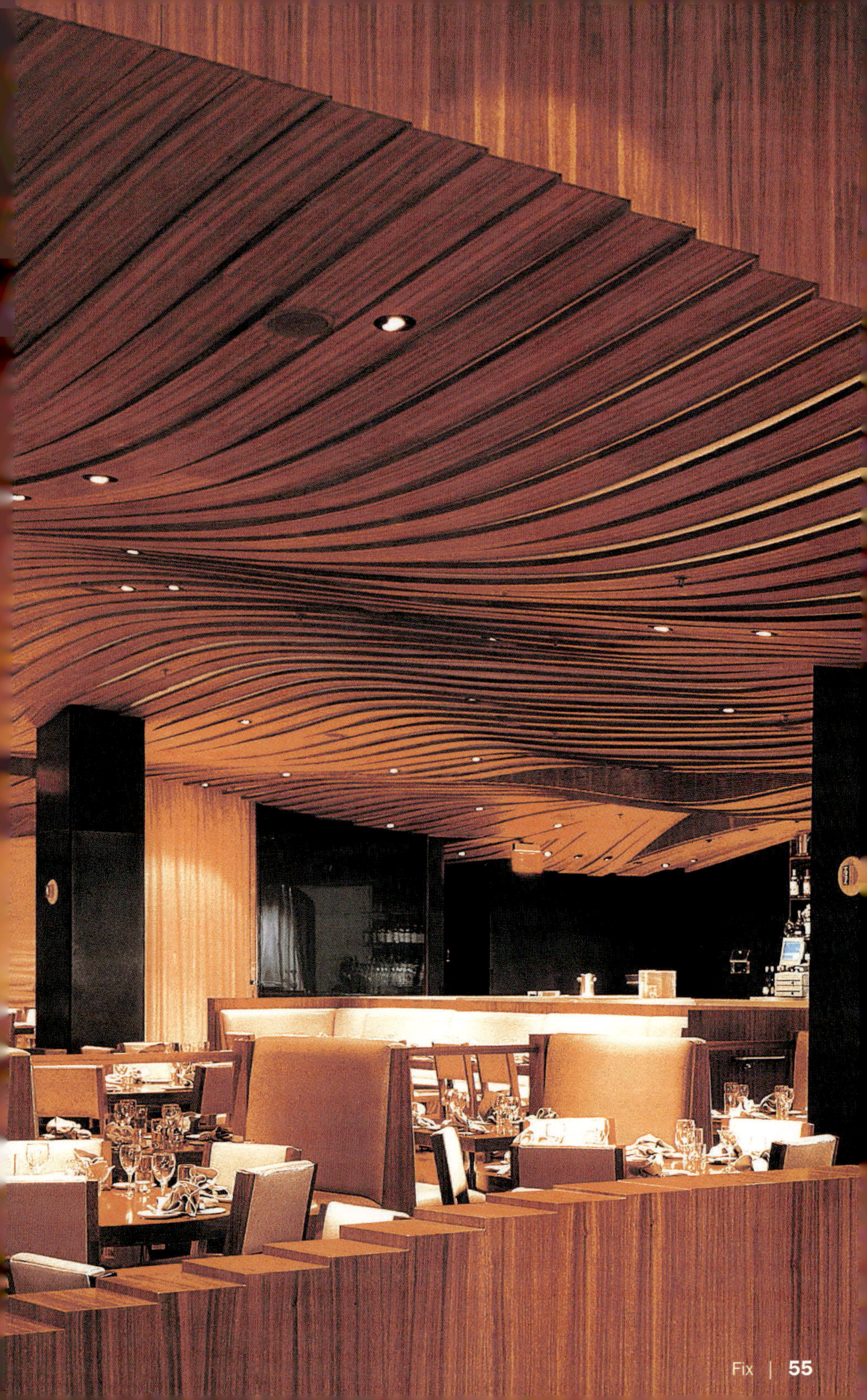

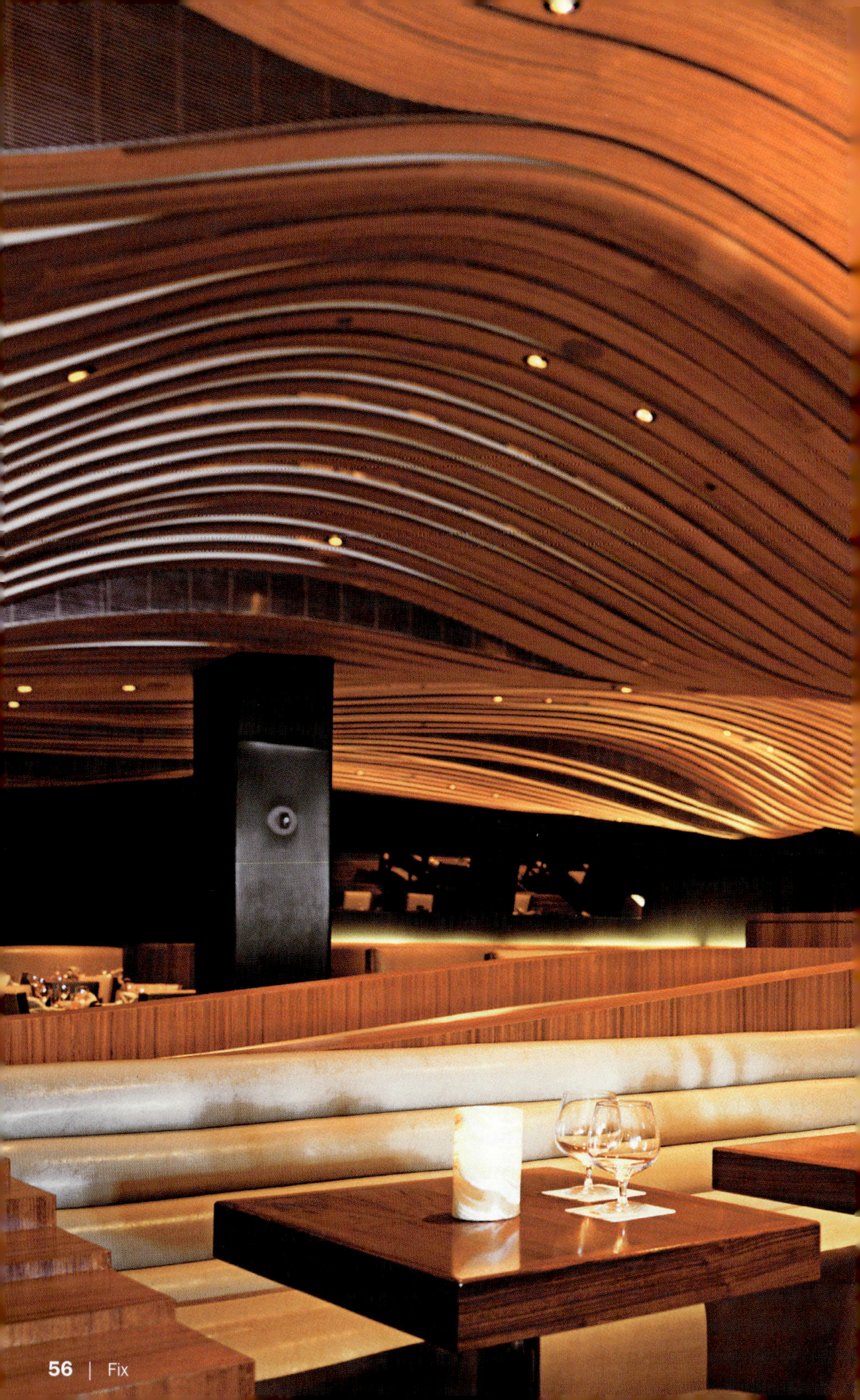

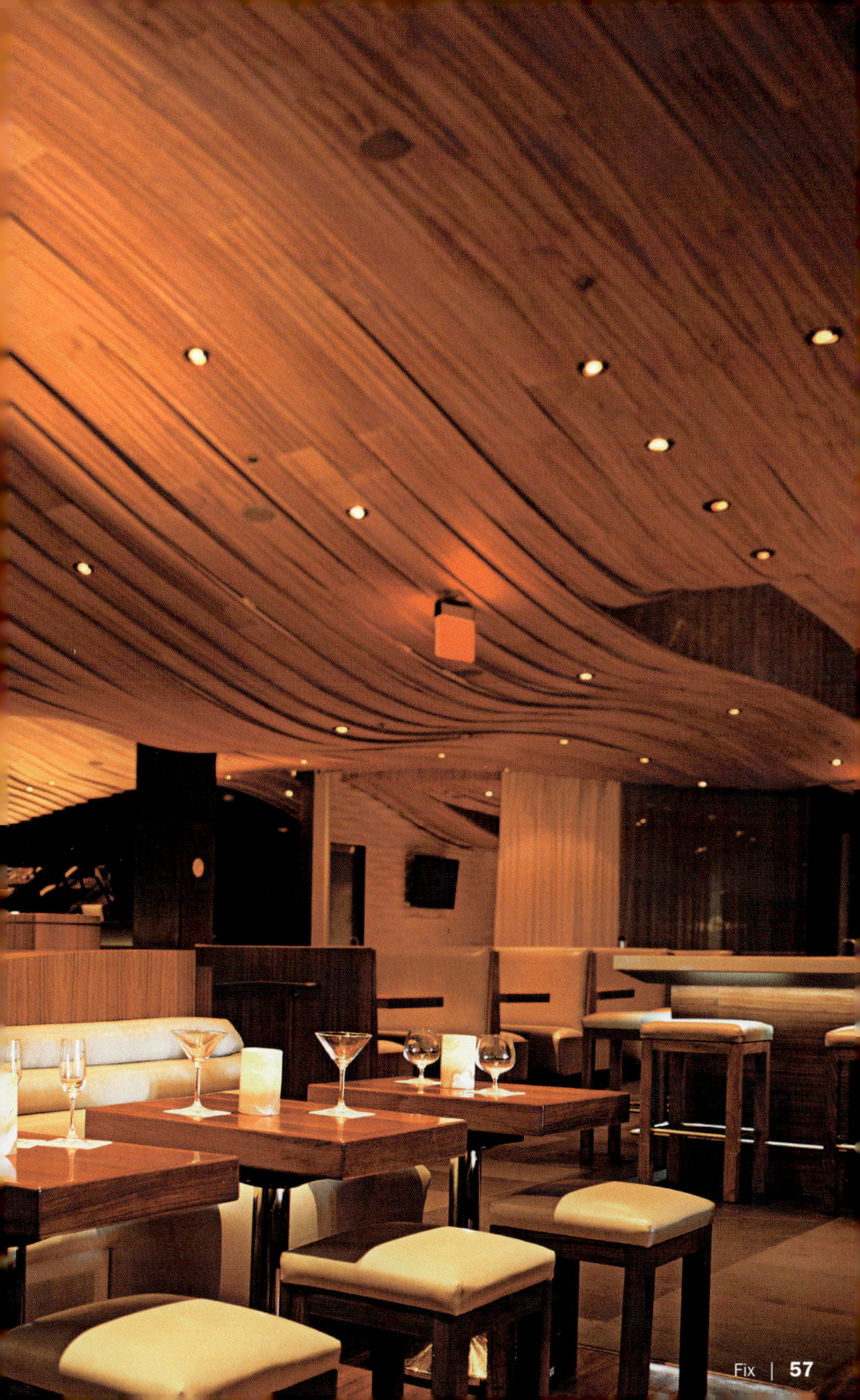

Fleur de Lys

Design: Stanlee Gatti | Chef: Hubert Keller
Owners: Hubert Keller, Mandalay Bay Resort & Casino

3950 Las Vegas Boulevard | Las Vegas, NV 89119 | Mandalay Bay Resort & Casino
Phone: +1 702 632 9400
www.mandalaybay.com
Opening hours: Daily 5:30 pm to 10:30 pm, lounge daily, 5 pm to 2 am
Average price: $ 82
Cuisine: French
Special features: Live floral sculpture of 3,000 roses

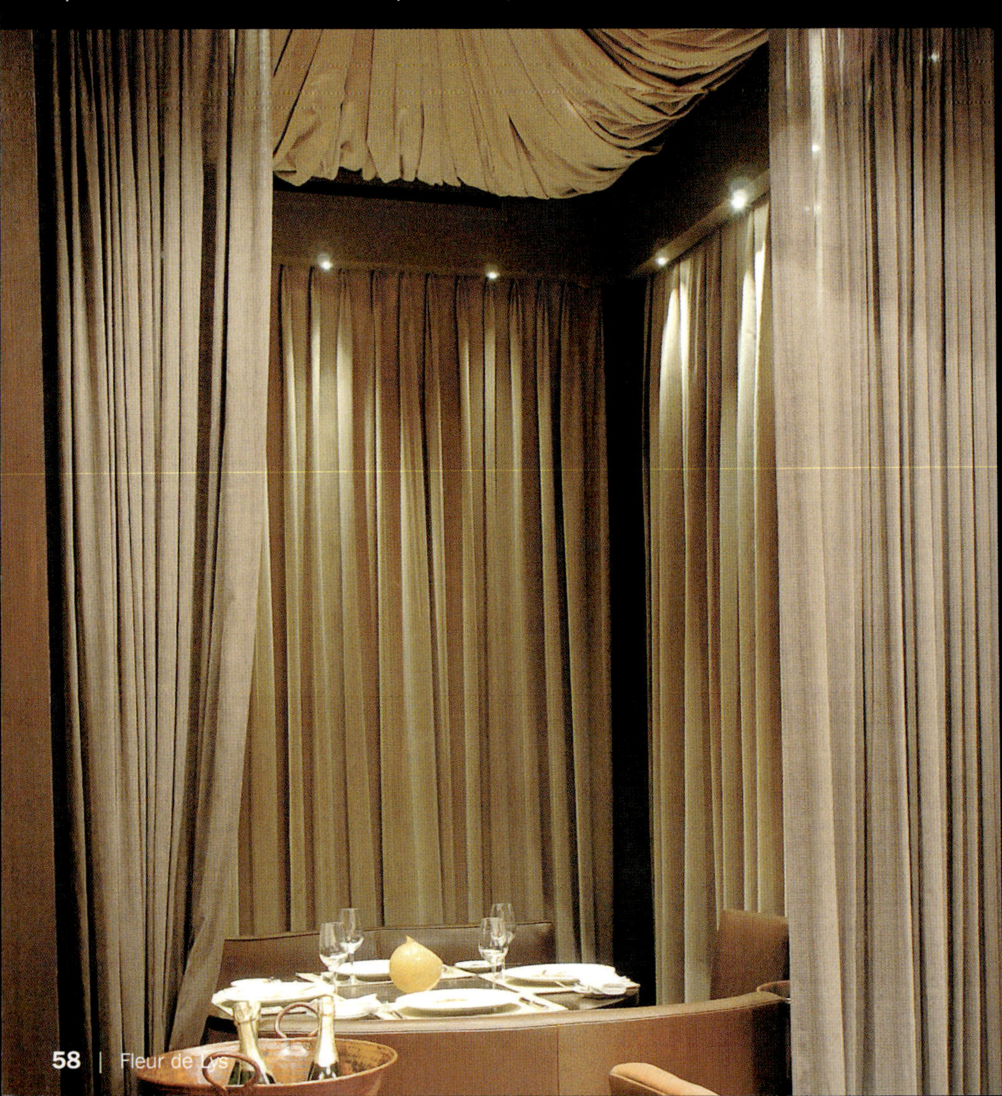

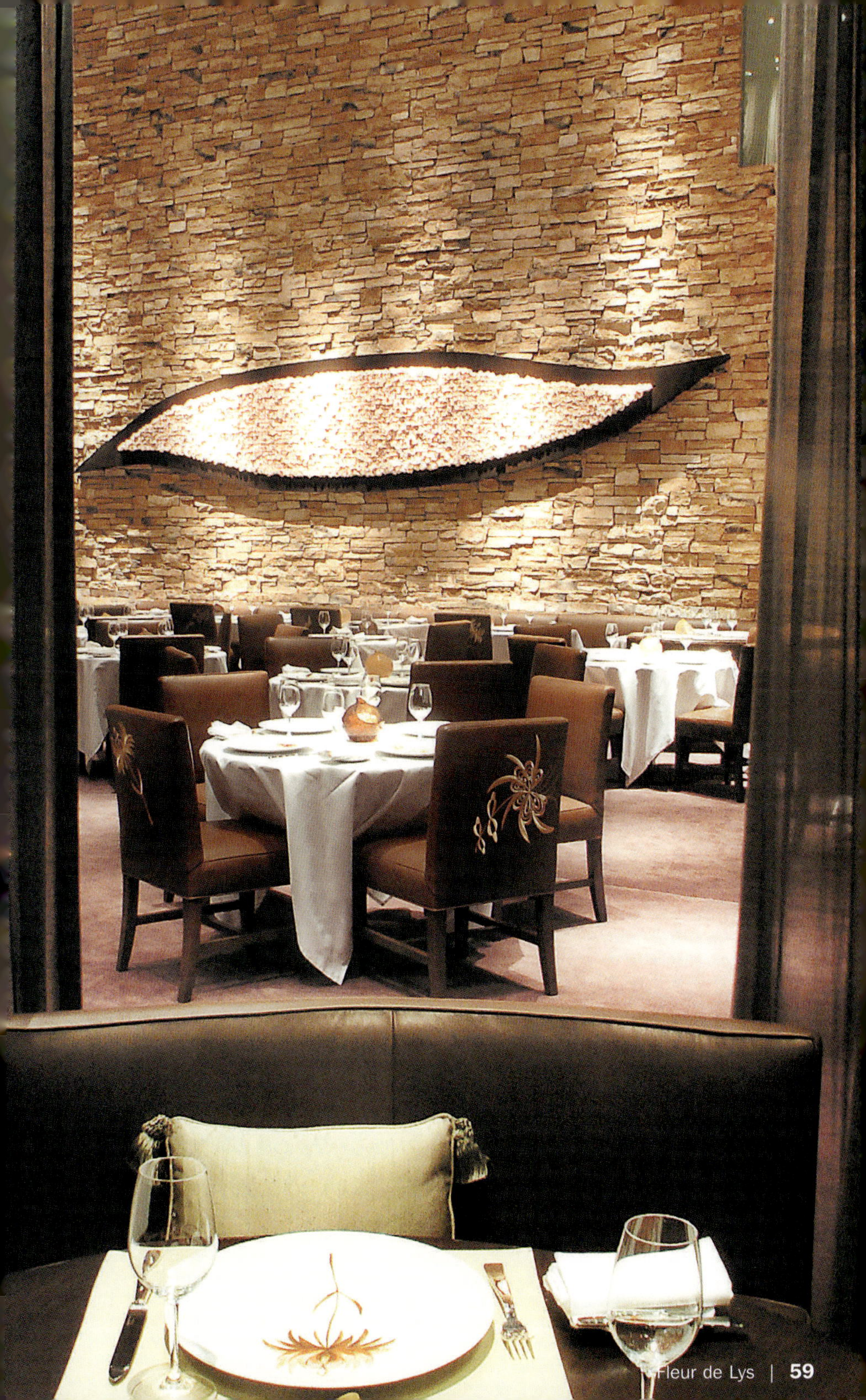

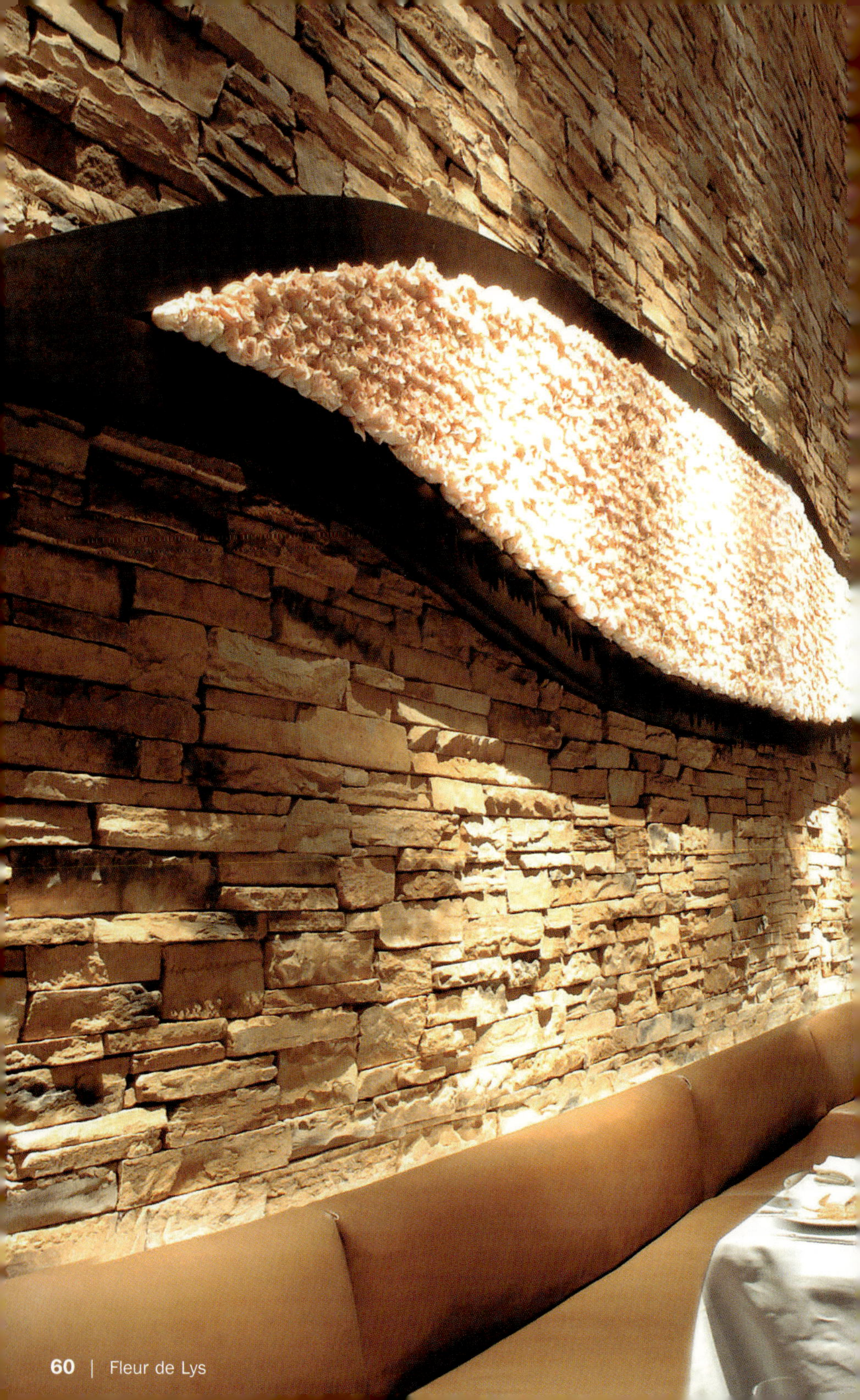

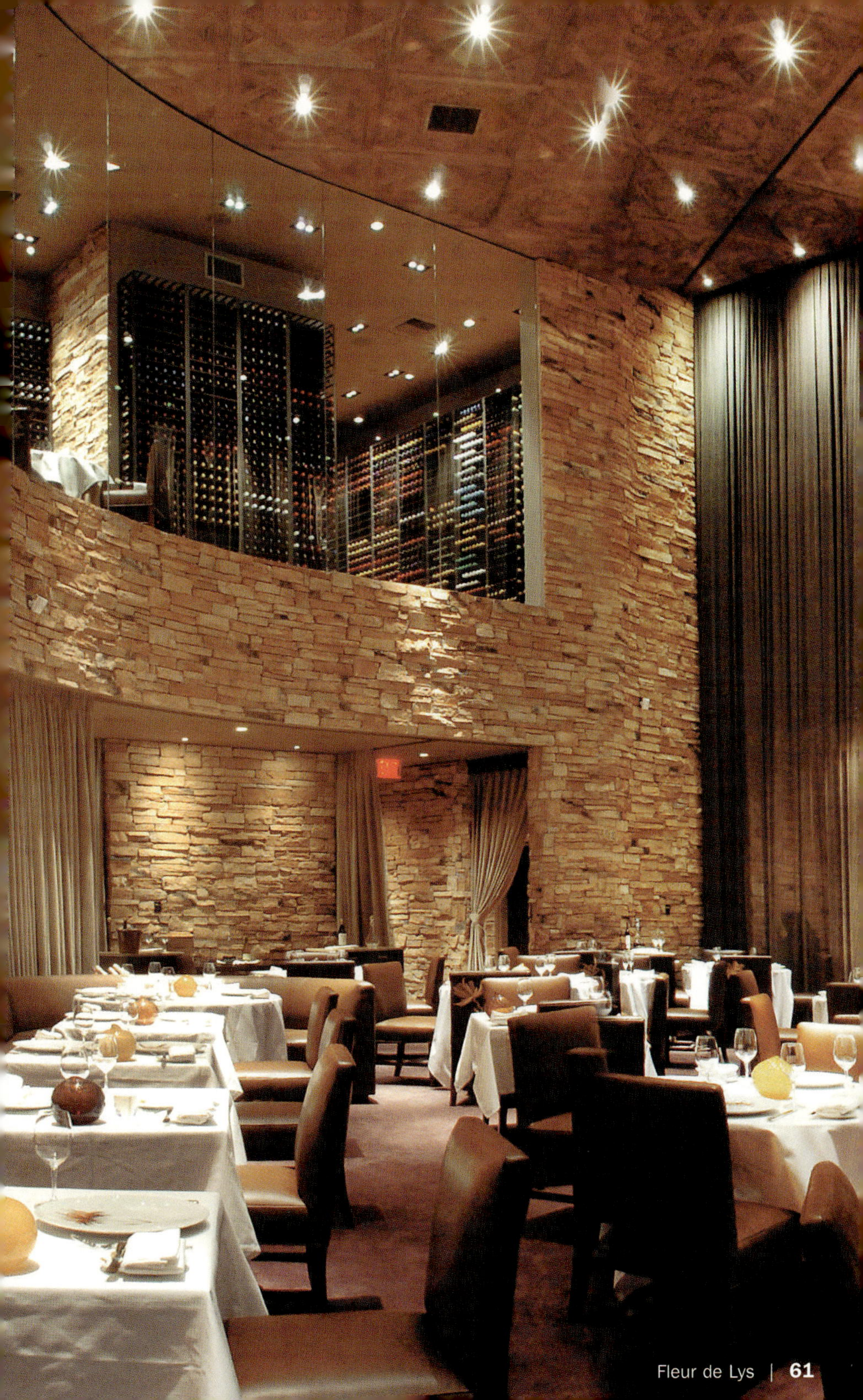

Seared Ah Tuna

Gebratener Tunfisch

Thon poêlé

Atún asado

Tonno arrosto

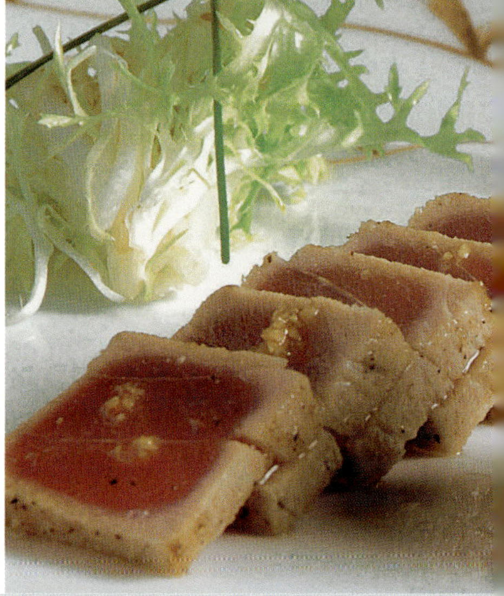

4 pieces of tuna (2 x 2 x 4 in.)
Salt, pepper
2 tbsp soy oil
Curry powder for decoration
Season tuna and sear in hot oil from all sides for 1 minute. Cut in thin slices and sprinkle with curry.

8 chanterelles, cleaned and halved
1 shallot, diced
1 tbsp butter
2 tbsp soy sauce
Salt, pepper
Parsley for decoration
Sautée chanterelles with shallots in hot butter, deglaze with soy sauce and season with salt and pepper. Garnish with parsley.

6 oz tuna, ground
1 tsp lemon juice

1 tsp shallots, finely chopped
1 tsp olive oil
Salt, pepper
4 slices daikon (radish), blanched
8 cherry tomatoes, quartered
8 sticks of chive
Combine all ingredients, season and fill into four metal rings. Remove the rings and wrap one slice of daikon around each tuna tartar. Decorate with tomato quarters and chives.
60 ml soy sauce
60 ml rice vinegar
120 ml olive oil
2 tsp ginger, grated
Mix all ingredients and fill the dip into four small serving dishes.
Garnish with plate with frisee lettuce and chives, if desired.

4 Tunfischstücke (5 x 5 x 10 cm)
Salz, Pfeffer
2 EL Sojaöl
Currypulver zur Dekoration
Tunfisch würzen und in heißem Öl von allen Seiten 1 Minute lang scharf anbraten. In dünne Scheiben schneiden und mit Curry bestreuen.

8 geputzte und halbierte Pfifferlinge
1 gewürfelte Schalotte
1 EL Butter
2 EL Sojasoße
Salz, Pfeffer
Petersilie zur Dekoration
Die Pfifferlinge mit der Schalotte in heißer Butter kurz anbraten, mit Sojasoße ablöschen und mit Salz und Pfeffer würzen. Mit Petersilie garnieren.

170 g gehackter Tunfisch
1 TL Zitronensaft

1 TL fein gehackte Schalotten
1 TL Olivenöl
Salz, Pfeffer
4 Scheiben blanchierter Daikon (japanischer weißer Rettich)
8 geviertelte Kirschtomaten
8 Halme Schnittlauch
Alle Zutaten zusammengeben, würzen und in vier Metallringe füllen. Die Ringe entfernen und je 1 Scheibe Daikon-Rettich um jede Portion Tunfischtartar wickeln. Mit Tomatenvierteln und Schnittlauch dekorieren.
60 ml Sojasoße
60 ml Reisessig
120 ml Olivenöl
2 TL Ingwer, gerieben
Alle Zutaten miteinander vermischen und den Dip in vier kleine Servierschalen geben.
Die Platte nach Wunsch mit Frisée-Salat und Schnittlauch garnieren.

4 morceaux de thon (5 x 5 x 10 cm)
Sel, poivre
2 c. à soupe d'huile de soja
Poudre de curry pour la garniture
Assaisonner le thon et bien le saisir dans l'huile chaude 1 minute sur toutes ses faces. Couper ensuite les morceaux de thon en fines tranches et les saupoudrer de curry.

8 girolles nettoyées et coupées en deux
1 échalote coupée en dés
1 c. à soupe de beurre
2 c. à soupe de sauce de soja
Sel, poivre
Persil pour la garniture
Faire brièvement revenir les girolles et l'échalote dans le beurre chaud, mouiller de sauce de soja, poivrer et saler. Garnir de persil.

170 g de thon haché
1 c. à café de jus de citron

1 c. à café d'échalote finement hachée
1 c. à café d'huile d'olive
Sel, poivre
4 tranches de daikon blanchies (radis blanc japonais)
8 tomates cerises coupées en quatre
8 tiges de ciboulette
Mélanger tous les ingrédients, les assaisonner et en remplir quatre anneaux en métal. Ôter les anneaux et envelopper chaque tartare de thon d'une tranche de daikon. Garnir de tomates cerises et de ciboulette.
60 ml de sauce de soja
60 ml de vinaigre de riz
120 ml d'huile d'olive
2 c. à café de gingembre râpé
Mélanger tous les ingrédients et servir le dip dans quatre petites coupes. Garnir librement les assiettes de salade frisée et de ciboulette.

4 trozos de atún (5 x 5 x 10 cm)
Sal, pimienta
2 cucharadas de aceite de soja
Curry molido para decorar
Sazone el atún y fríalo a fuego fuerte por todos los lados durante 1 minuto en aceite caliente. Córtelo en lonchas finas y esparza el curry.

8 rebozuelos limpios y cortados en mitades
1 chalote en dados
1 cucharada de mantequilla
2 cucharadas de salsa de soja
Sal, pimienta
Perejil para decorar
Rehogue brevemente los rebozuelos con el chalote en mantequilla caliente, vierta por encima la salsa de soja y salpimiente. Decore con perejil.

170 g de atún picado
1 cucharadita de zumo de limón

1 cucharadita de chalote finamente picado
1 cucharadita de aceite de oliva
Sal, pimienta
4 lonchas de daikon escaldado (rábano blanco japonés)
8 tomates cereza en cuartos
8 tallos de cebollino
Mezcle todos los ingredientes, condimente y rellene cuatro anillos metálicos. Retire los anillos y envuelva cada tartar de atún con una loncha de rábano daikon. Decore con cuartos de tomate y cebollino.
60 ml de salsa de soja
60 ml de vinagre de arroz
120 ml de aceite de oliva
2 cucharaditas de jengibre, rallado
Mezcle todos los ingredientes y reparta la salsa en cuatro cuencos pequeños. Si lo desea decore la bandeja con lechuga frisé y cebollino.

4 tranci di tonno (5 x 5 x 10 cm)
Sale, pepe
2 cucchiai di olio di soia
Per la guarnizione: polvere di curry
Condire il tonno e rosolarlo a fuoco vivo in olio caldo per 1 minuto da tutti i lati. Tagliarlo a fette sottili e cospargerlo di curry.

8 funghi galletti puliti e tagliati a metà
1 scalogno tagliato a dadini
1 cucchiaio di burro
2 cucchiai di salsa di soia
Sale, pepe
Per la guarnizione: prezzemolo
Rosolare brevemente i funghi e lo scalogno nel burro caldo, bagnare con la salsa di soia, salare e pepare. Guarnire con il prezzemolo.

170 g di tonno tritato
1 cucchiaino di succo di limone

1 cucchiaino di scalogno finemente tritato
1 cucchiaino di olio di oliva
Sale, pepe
4 fette di daikon (rafano bianco giapponese) scottato
8 pomodorini tagliati in quattro
8 steli di erba cipollina
Mescolare tutti gli ingredienti, condirli e farcire con il composto quattro anelli di metallo. Togliere gli anelli ed avvolgere una fetta di daikon attorno ad ogni porzione di tonno. Guarnire con i quarti di pomodoro e l'erba cipollina.
60 ml di salsa di soia
60 ml di aceto di riso
120 ml di olio di oliva
2 cucchiaini di zenzero grattugiato
Mescolare tutti gli ingredienti e ripartire l'intingolo in quattro ciotoline. Eventualmente, guarnire il piatto di portata con insalata riccia ed erba cipollina.

Little Buddha

Design: Rockwell Group | Chef: Gerald Canales, Masato
Nakabayashi | Owners: Raymond Visan, George Maloof

4321 Flamingo Road | Las Vegas, NV 89103 | The Palms Casino Las Vegas
Phone: +1 702 942 7778
www.littlebuddhalasvegas.com
Opening hours: Daily 5:30 pm to 11 pm
Average price: $ 22
Cuisine: Pacific Rim, French influences, sushi
Special features: Famous for its original music compilations

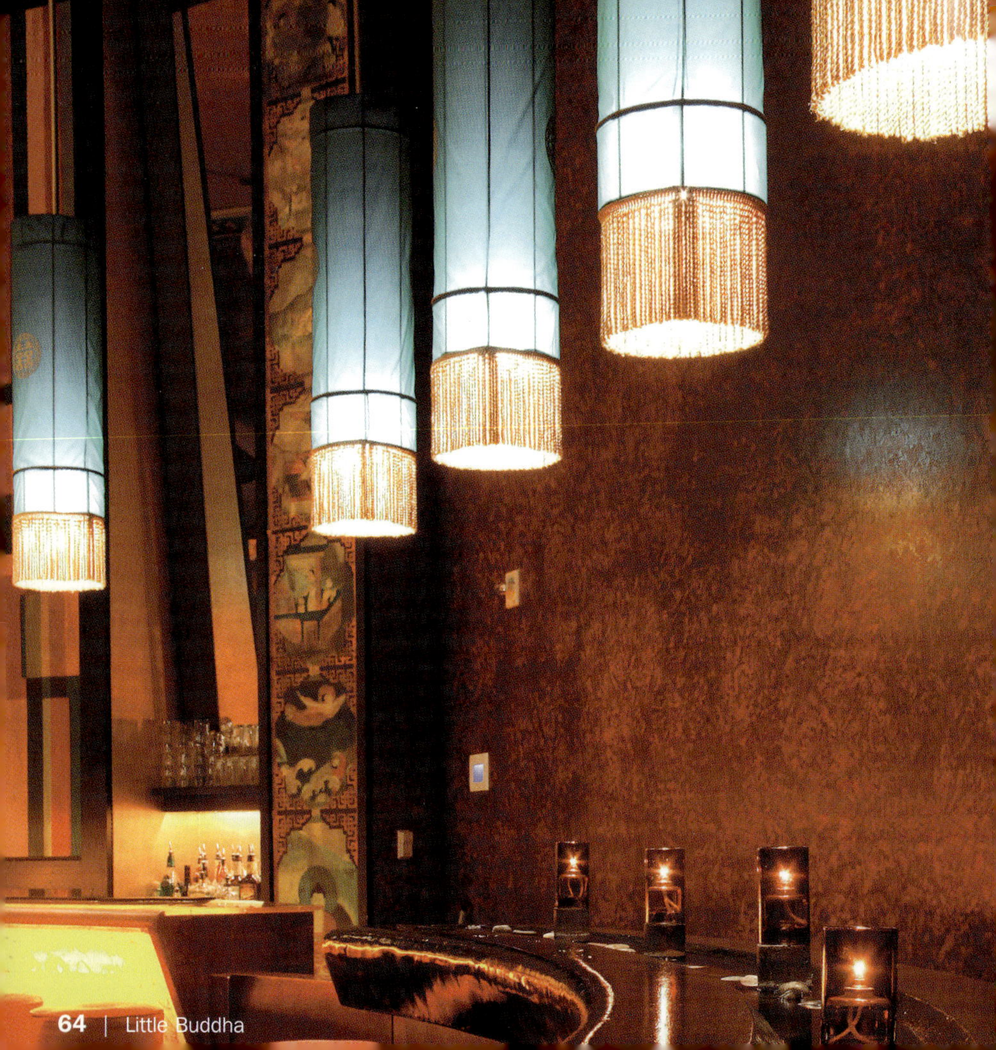

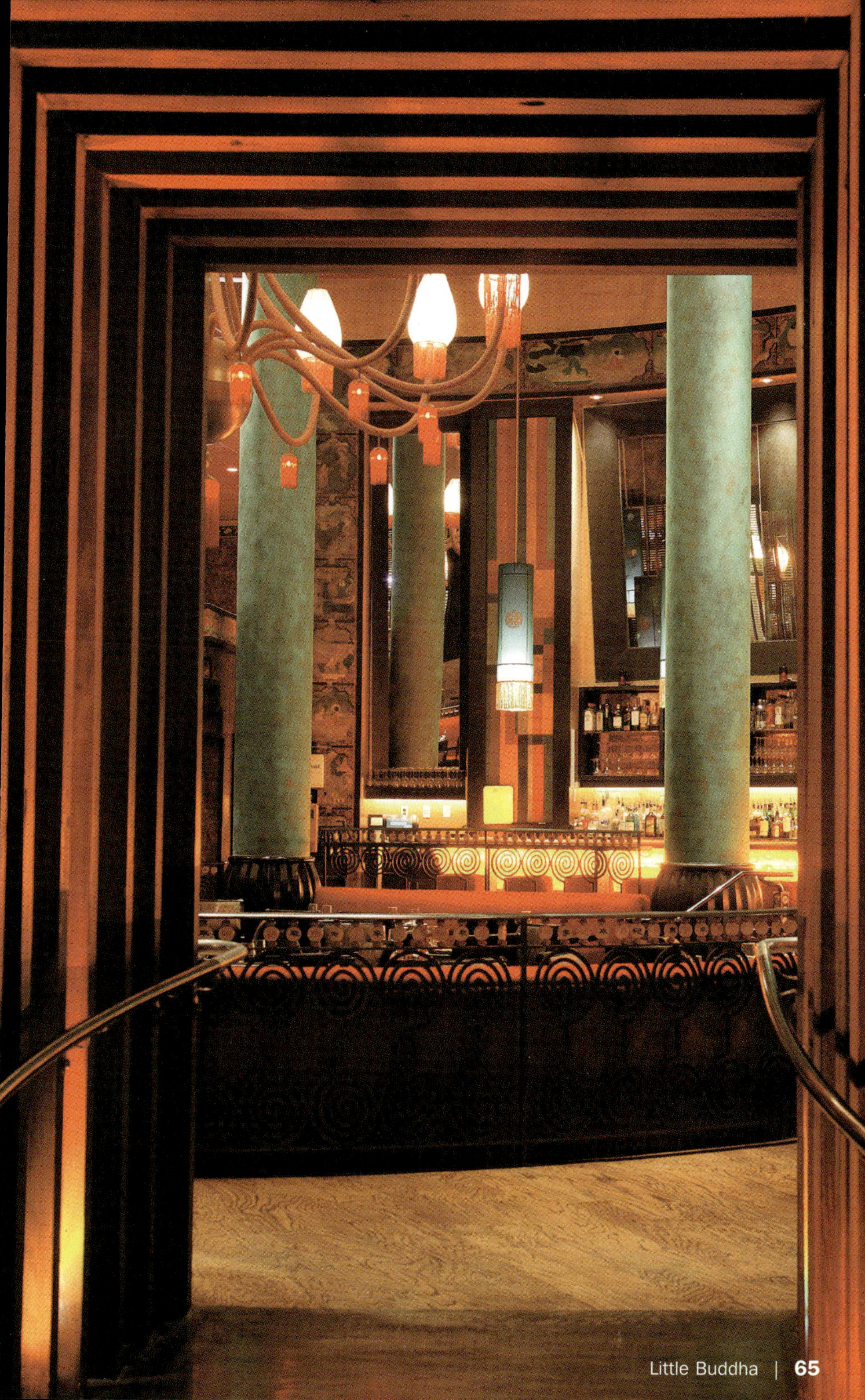

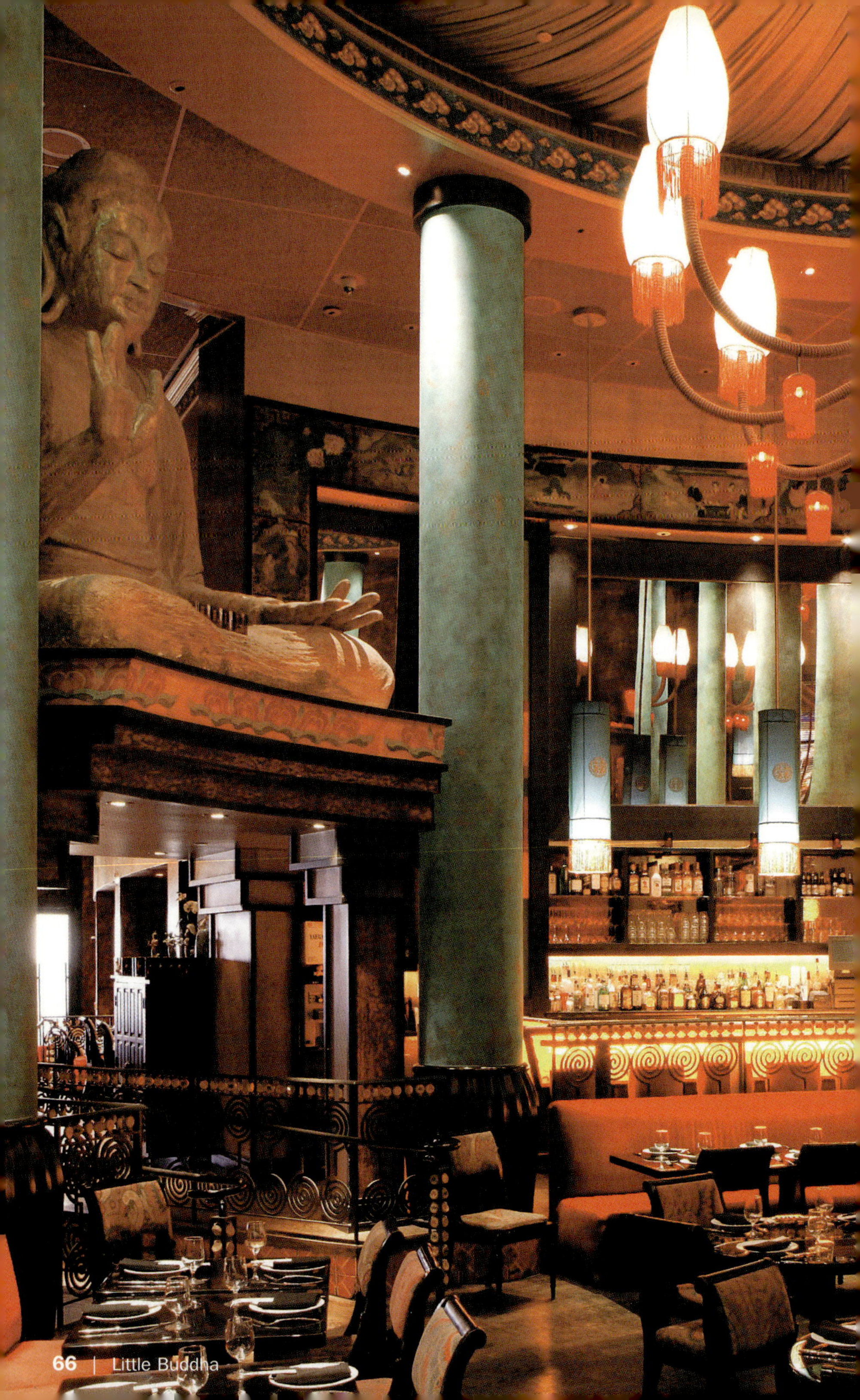

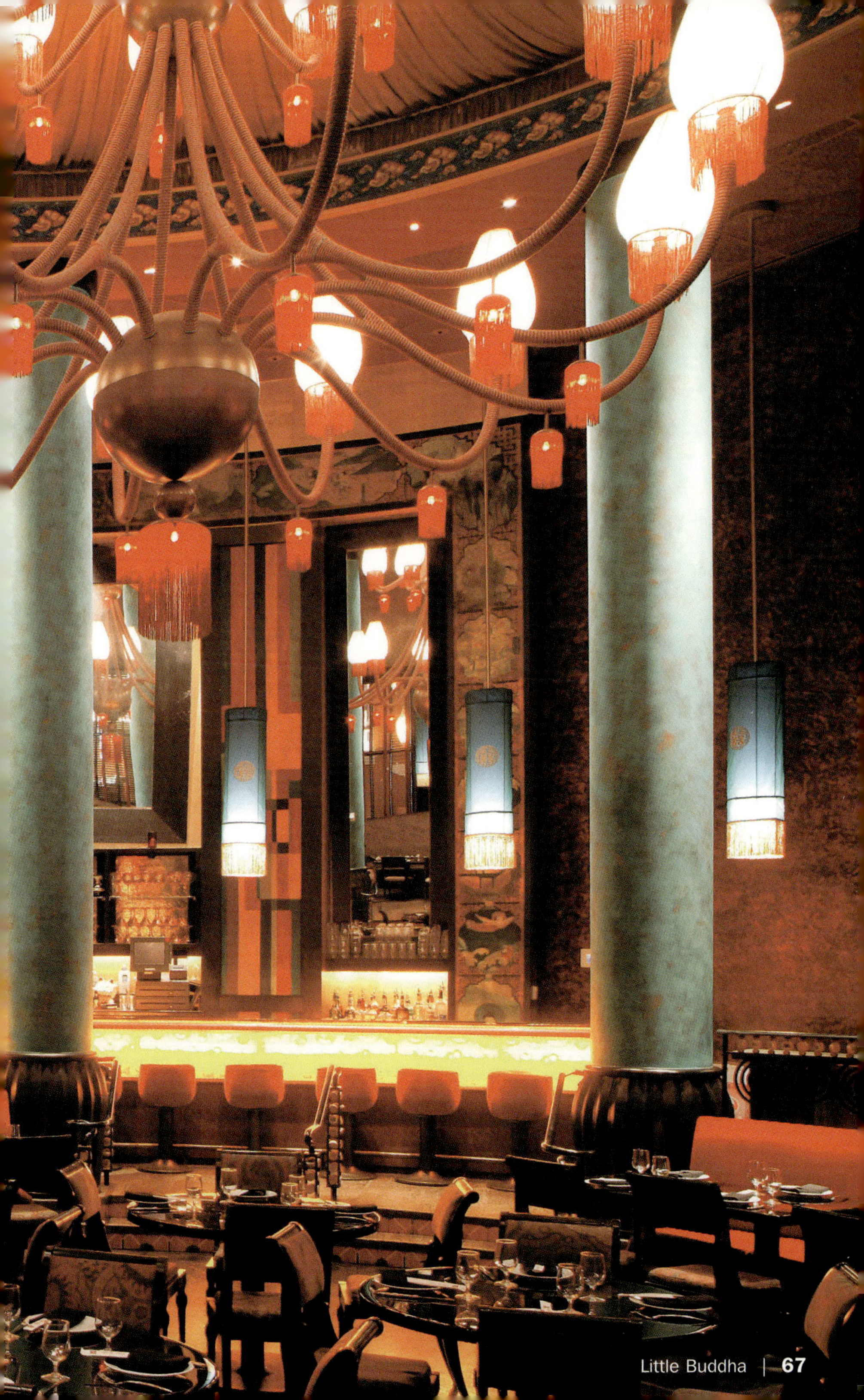

Mesa Grill

Design: Rockwell Group | Chef & Owner: Bobby Flay

3570 Las Vegas Boulevard S | Las Vegas, NV 89109 | Caesars Palace
Phone: +1 702 731 7731
www.caesars.com
Opening hours: Daily 5 pm to 11 pm, Mon–Fri 11 am to 2:30 pm, Sat–Sun 10:30 am to 3 pm
Average price: $ 35
Cuisine: Southwestern
Special features: 20-foot rotisserie with a giant grill and custom quesadilla oven

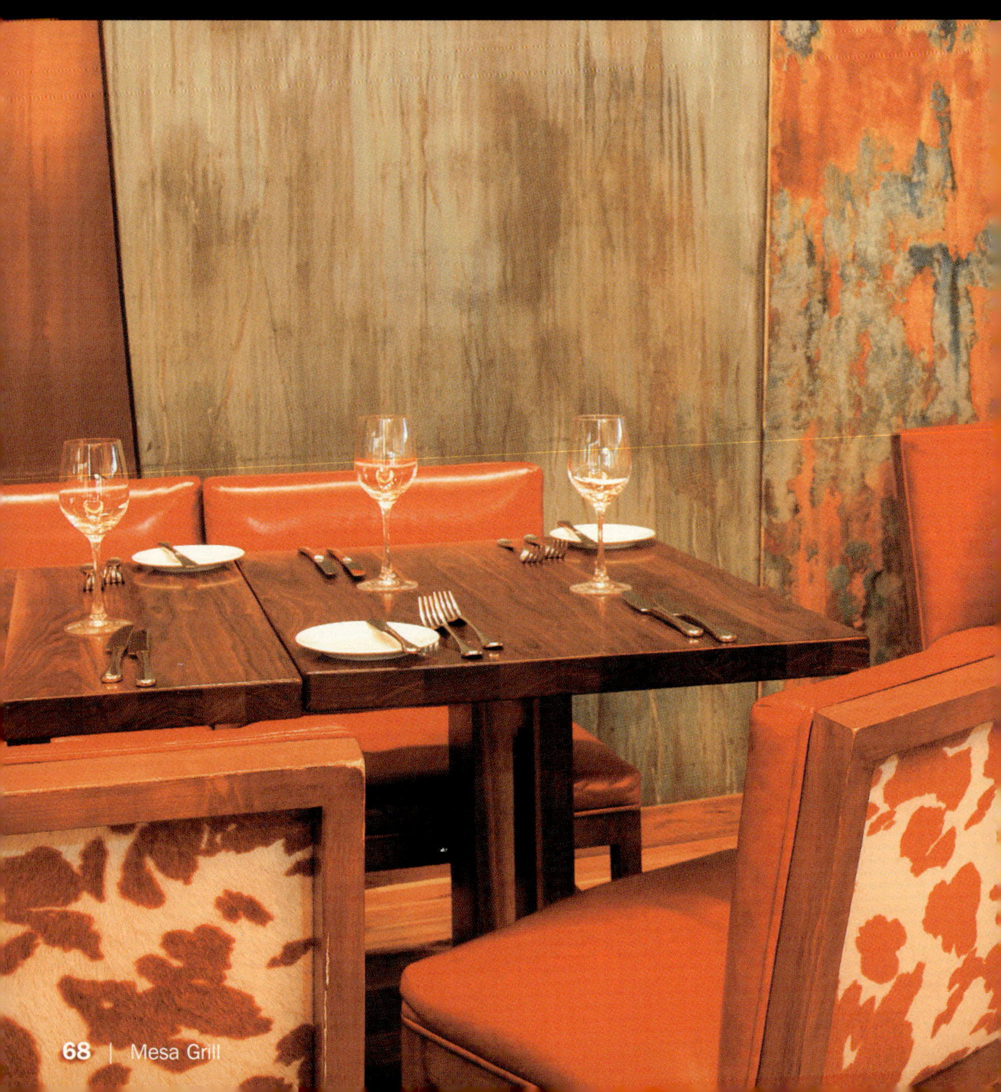

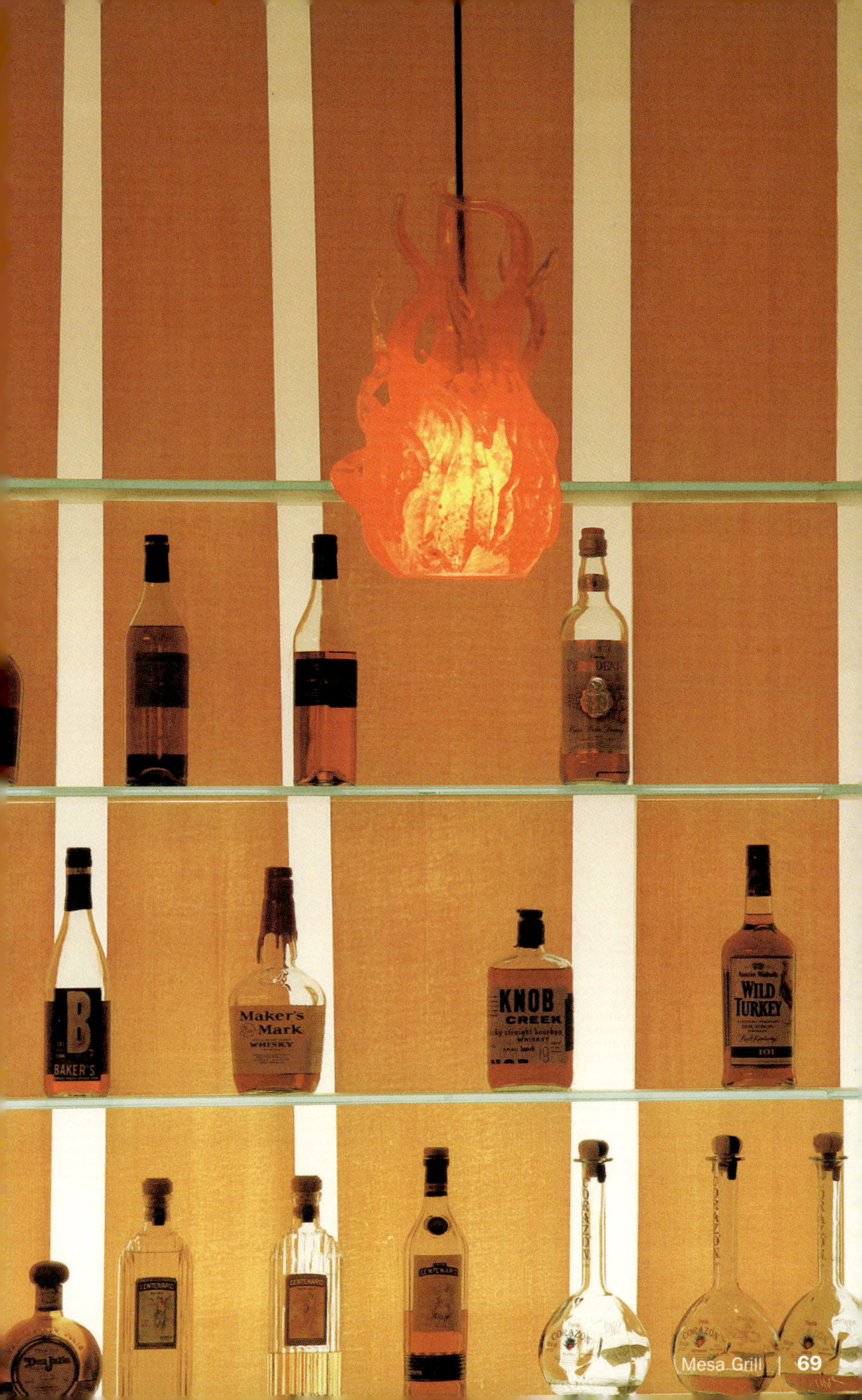
Mesa Grill | 69

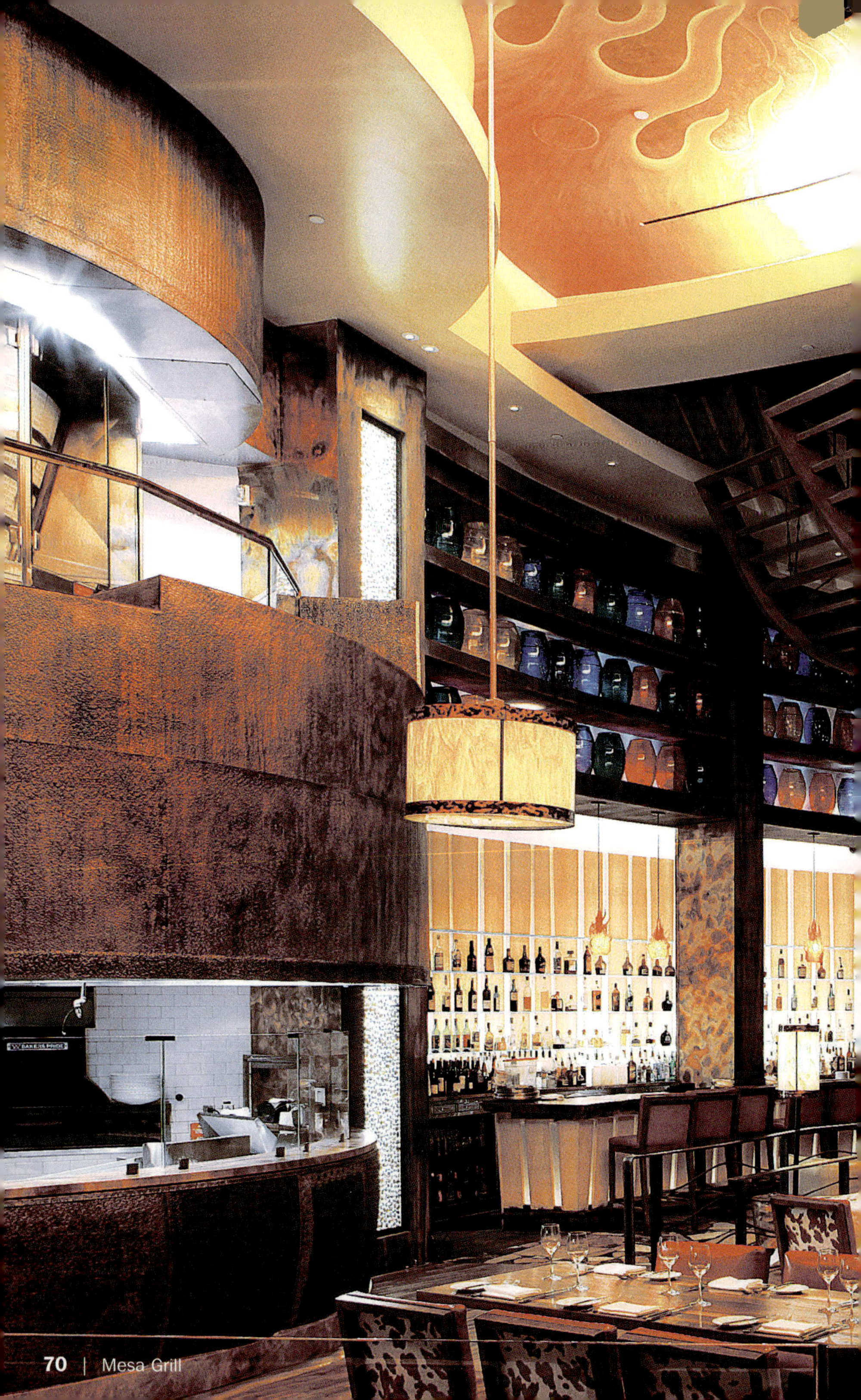

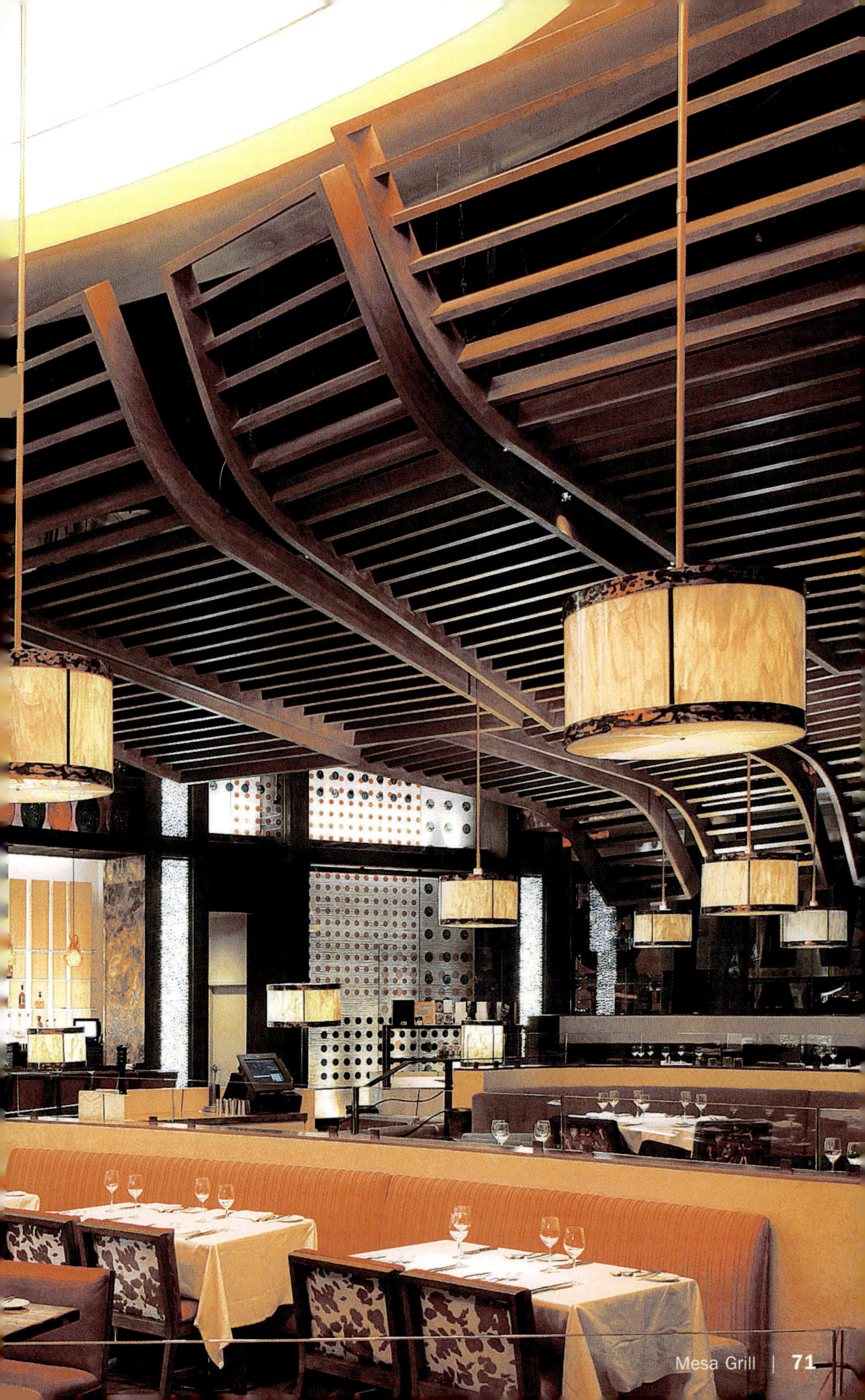

Michael Mina

Designer: Tony Chi | Chef & Owner: Michael Mina

3600 Las Vegas Boulevard S | Las Vegas, NV 89109 | Bellagio Hotel & Casino
Phone: +1 702 693 8199
www.michaelmina.net
Opening hours: Daily 5:30 pm to 10 pm
Average price: $ 85
Cuisine: Contemporary seafood, refined American cuisine
Special features: Semi-private dining room, pool view

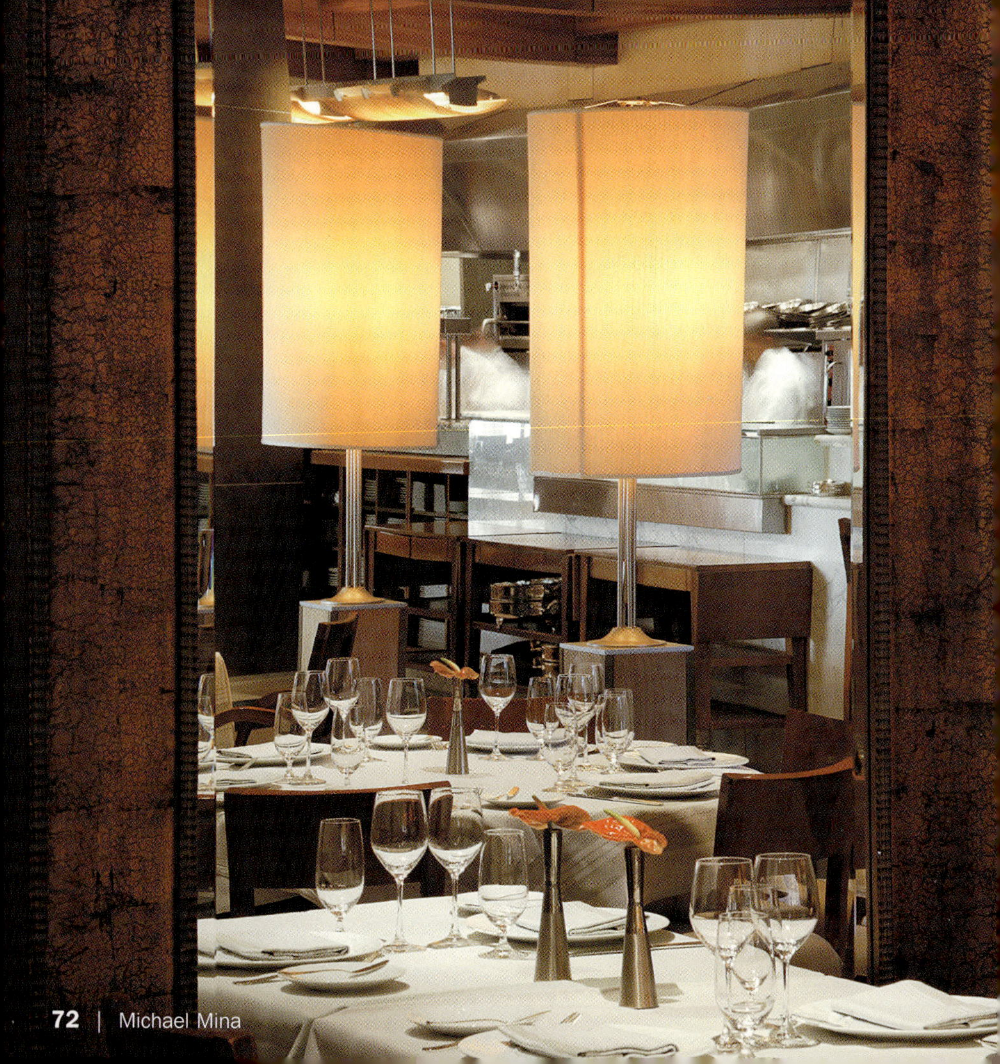

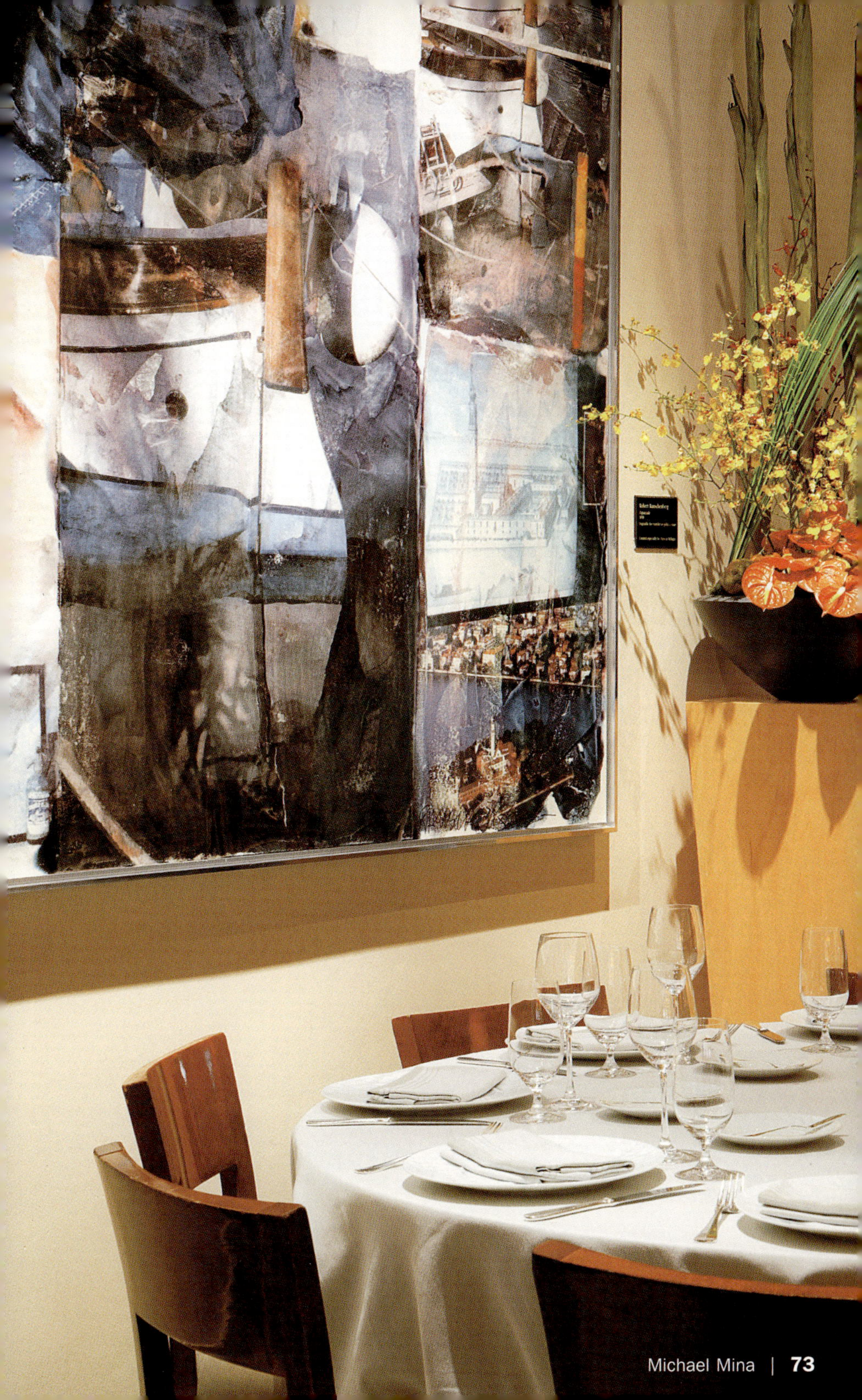

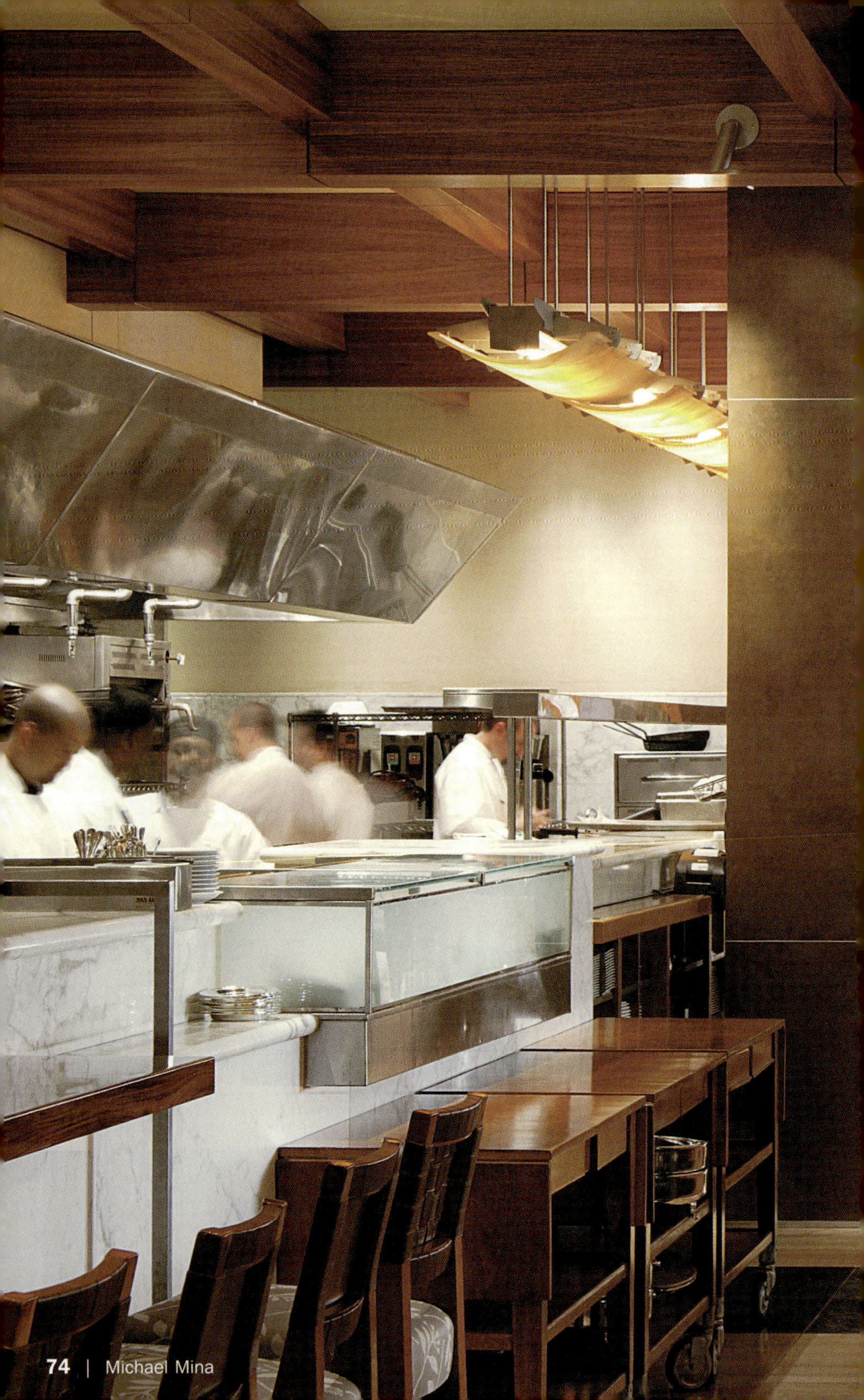

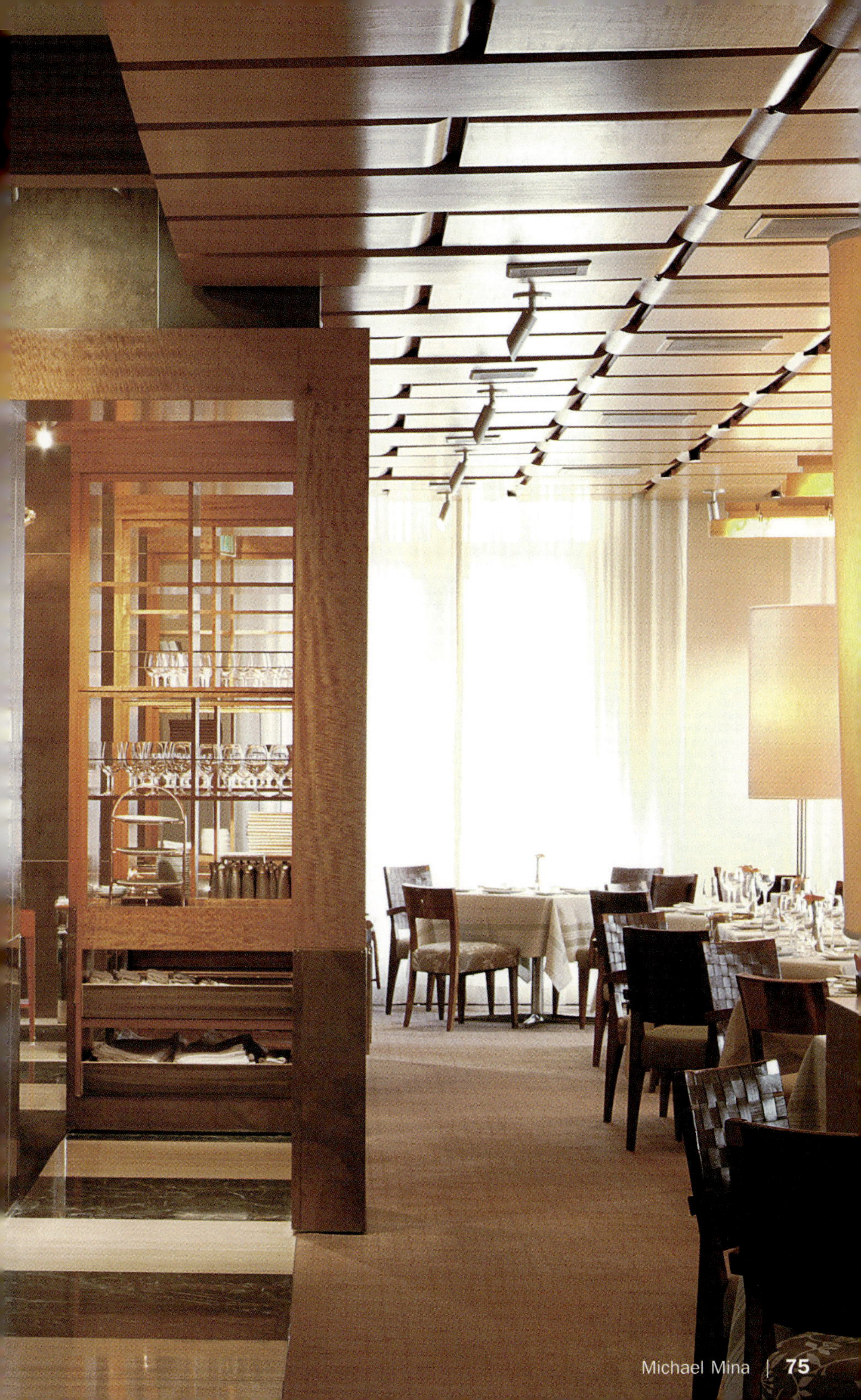

Mix

Design: Patrick Jouin | Chef: Alain Ducasse
Owners: Alain Ducasse, Mandalay Bay Resort & Casino

3950 Las Vegas Boulevard S | Las Vegas, NV 89119 | THEhotel at Mandalay Bay Resort & Casino
Phone: +1 702 632 9500
www.mandalaybay.com
Opening hours: Daily 5:30 pm to 10:30 pm
Average price: $ 42
Cuisine: American, French
Special features: View from the 64th floor, 24-ft glass chandelier

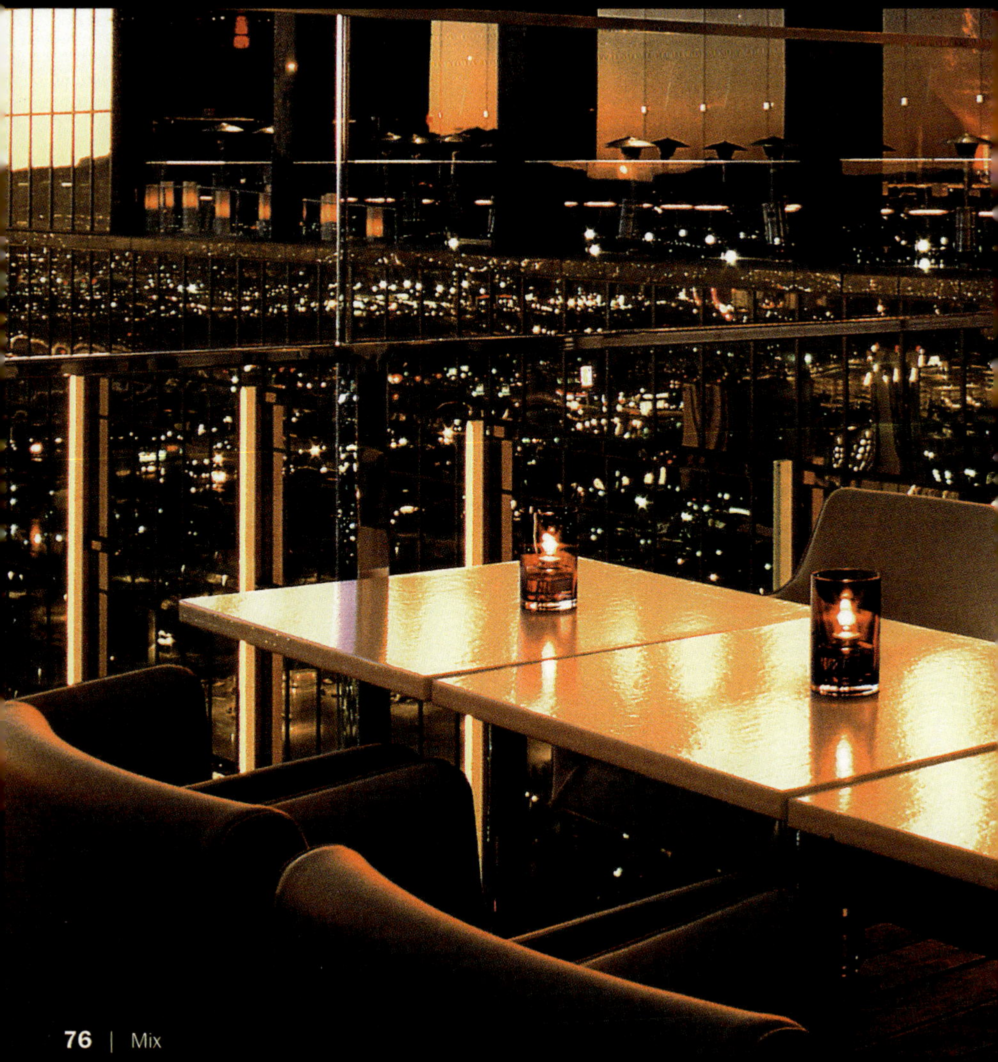

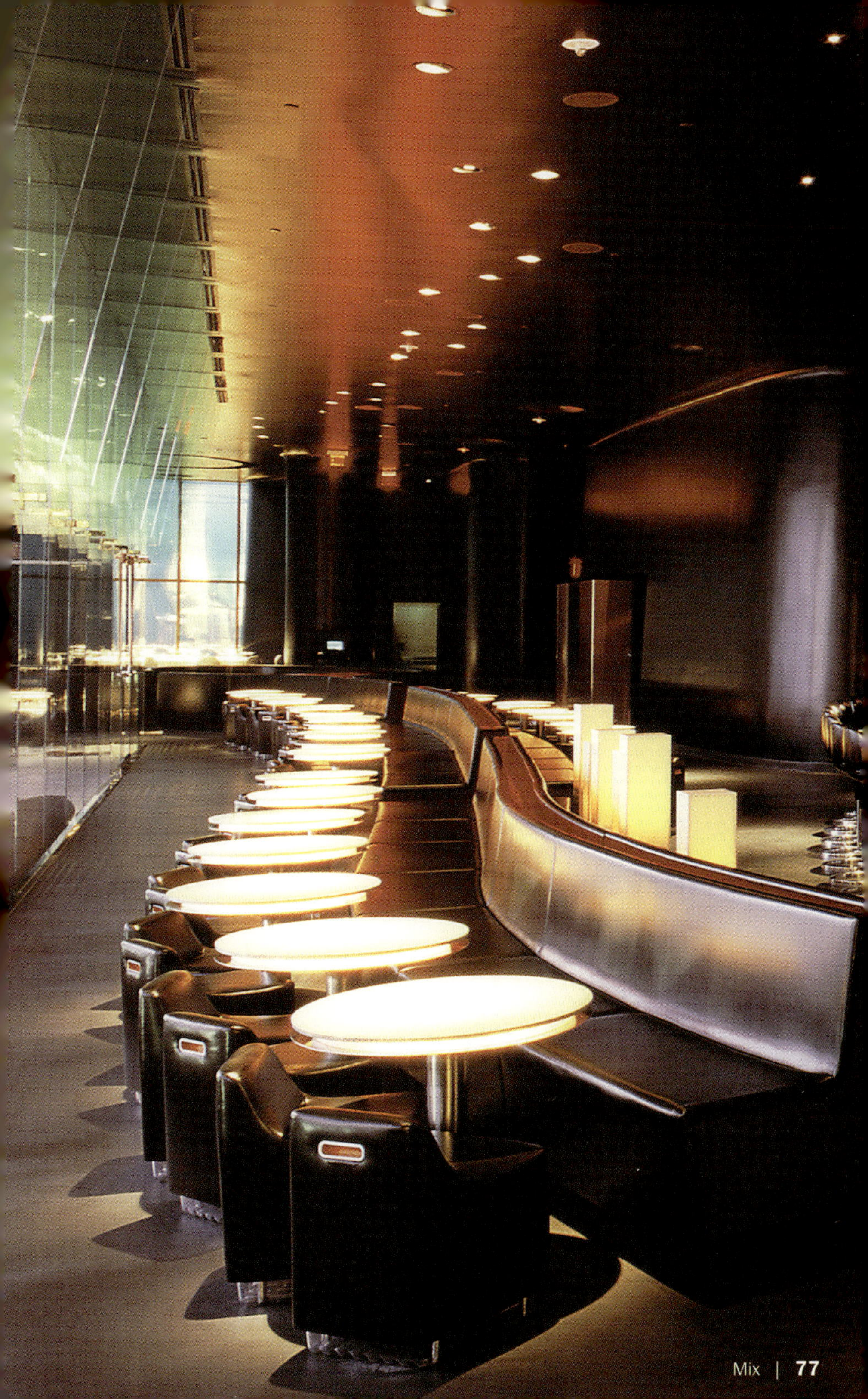

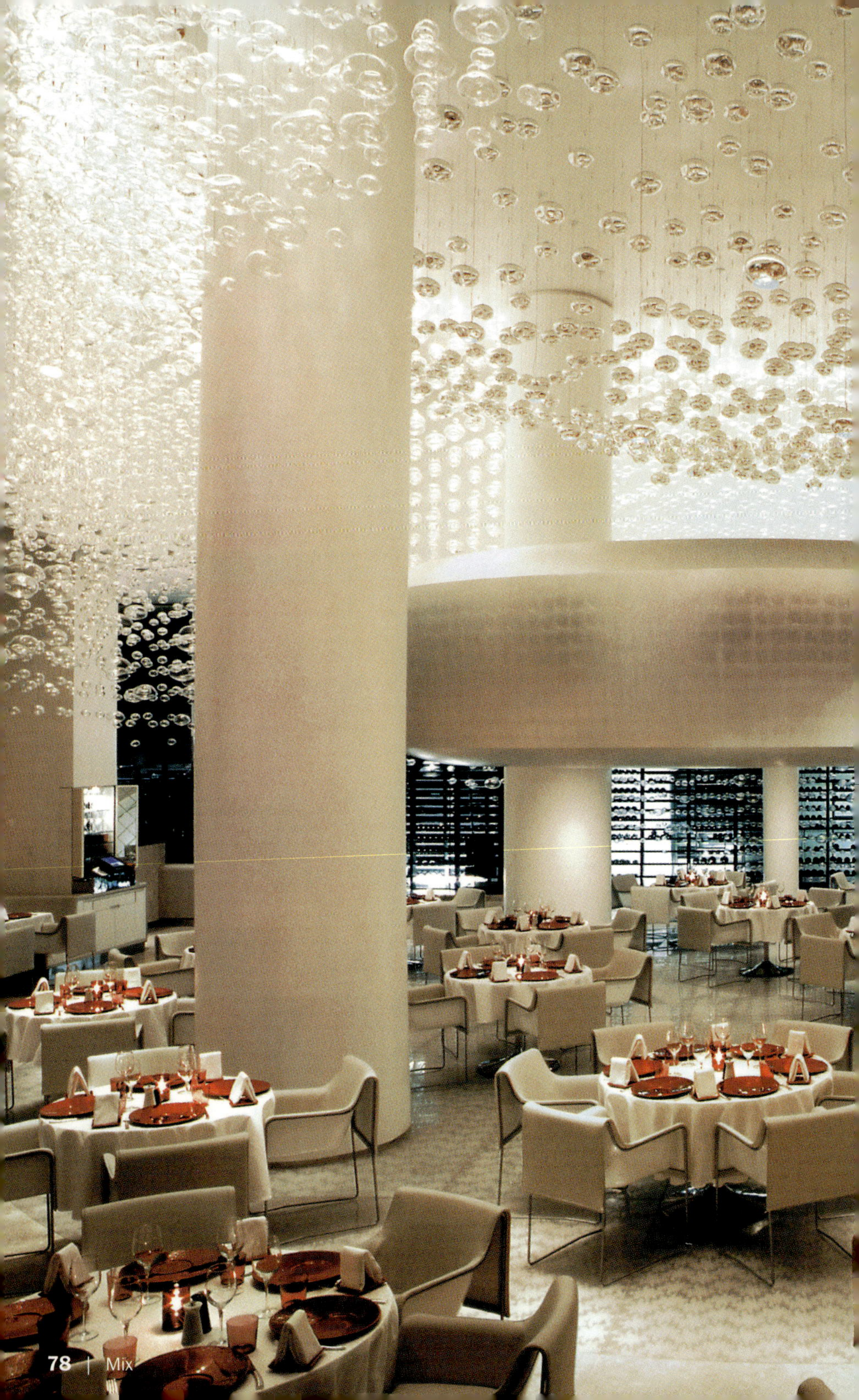

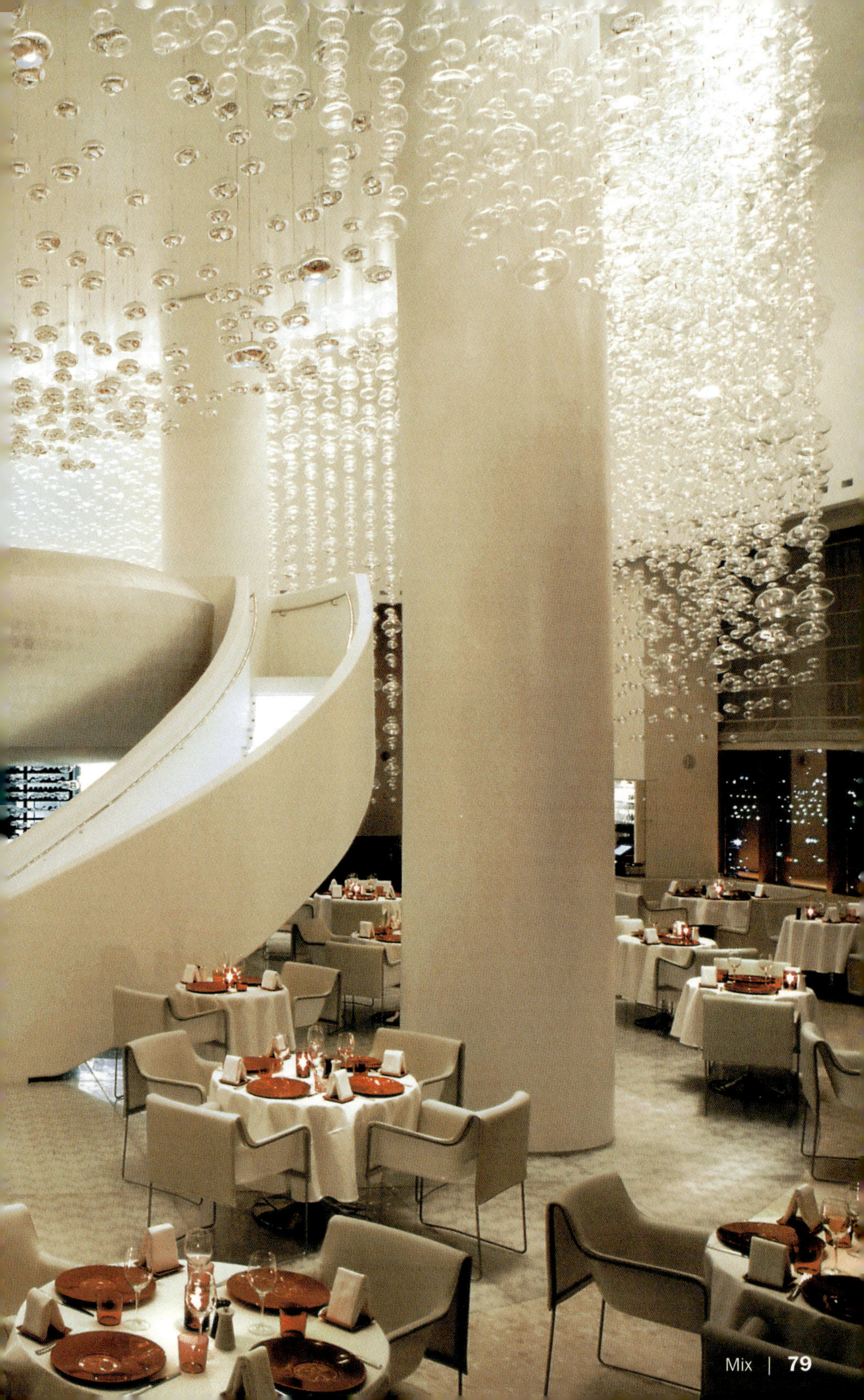

N9NE Steakhouse

Design & Owners: Michael Morton, Scott DeGraff
Chef: Barry S Dakake

4321 W Flamingo Road | Las Vegas, NV 89103 | The Palms Casino Las Vegas
Phone: +1 702 933 9900
www.n9negroup.com
Opening hours: Sun–Thu 5 pm to 11 pm, Fri–Sat 5 pm to 11:30 pm
Average price: $ 75
Cuisine: Seafood, steakhouse
Special features: Champagne caviar bar

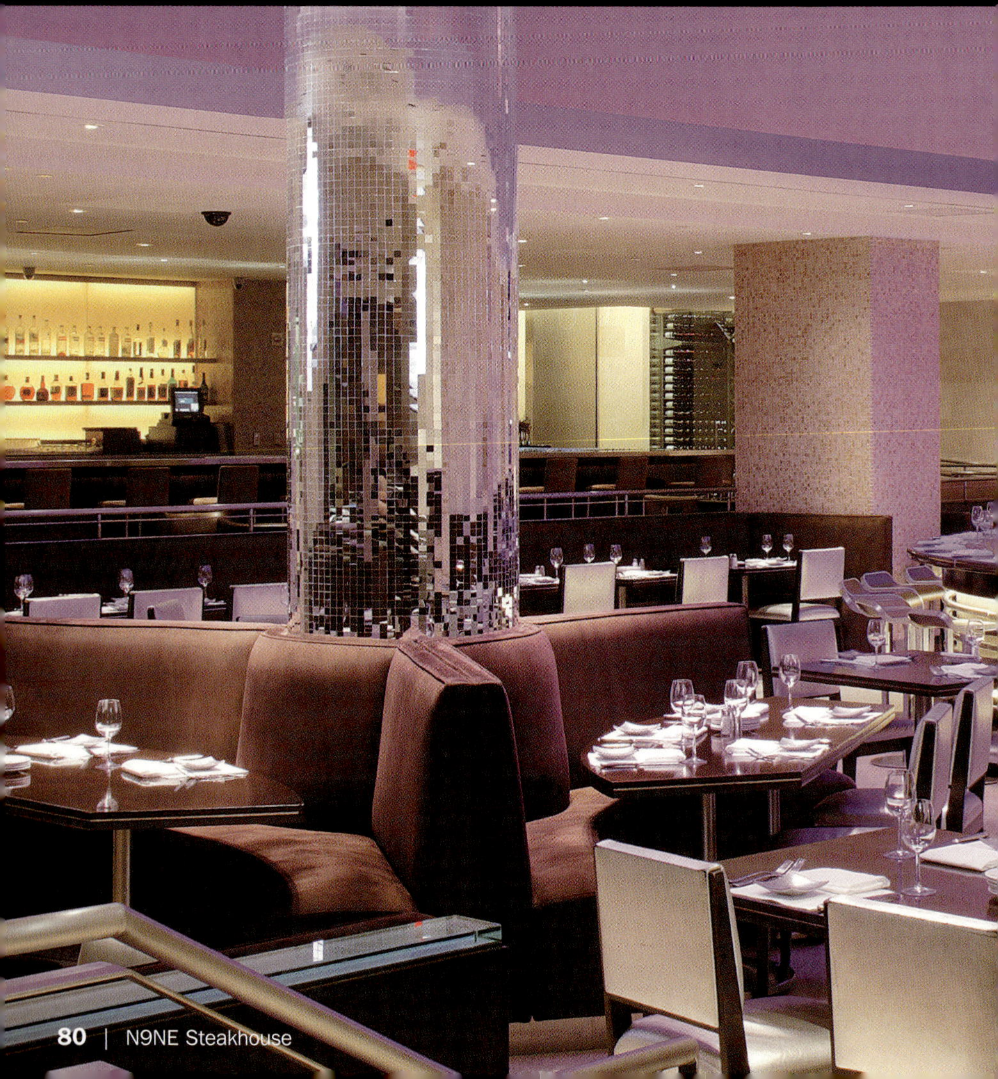

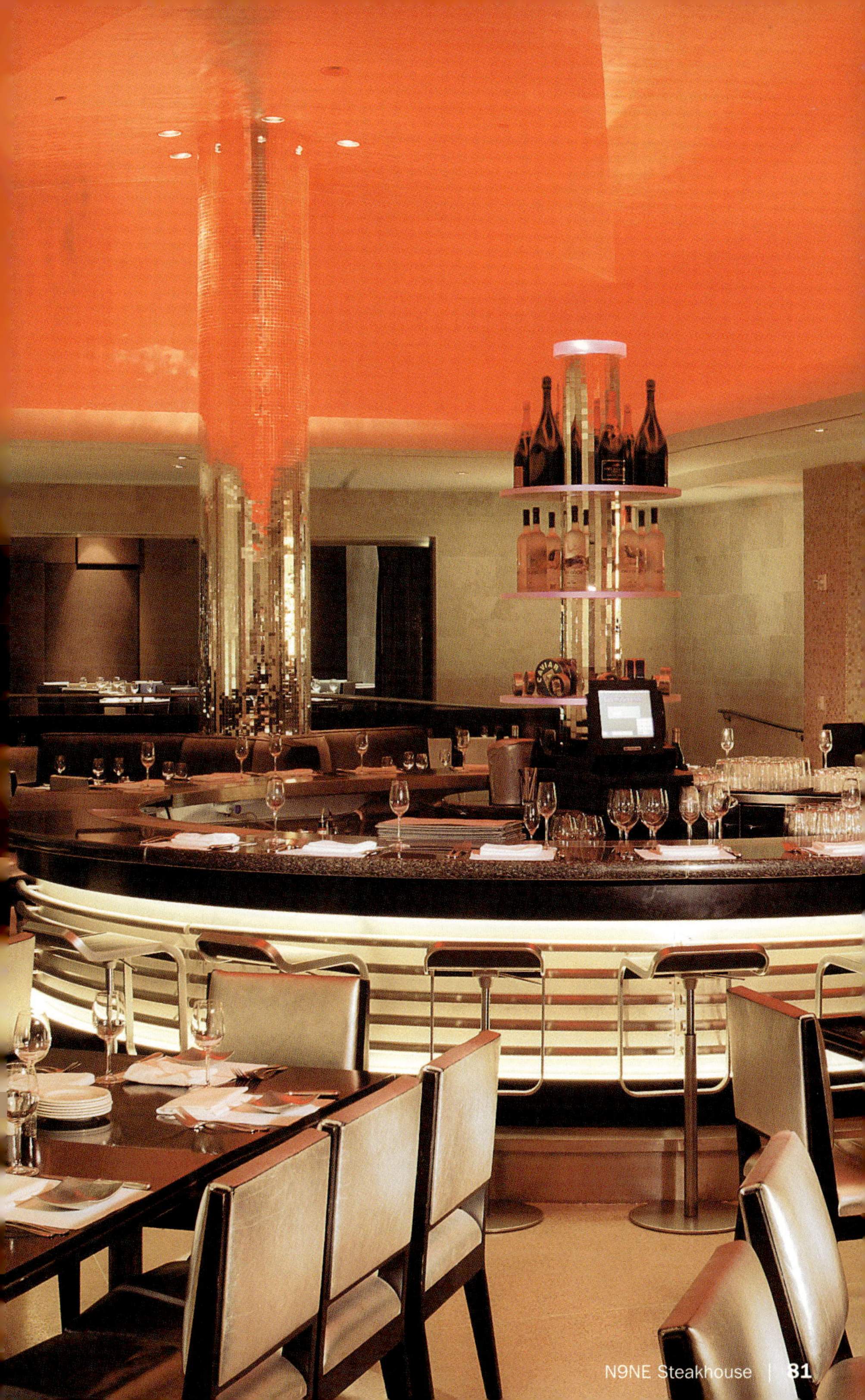

Two Cones

Waffelduo

Duo de cornets

Dúo de cucuruchos

Duo di waffel

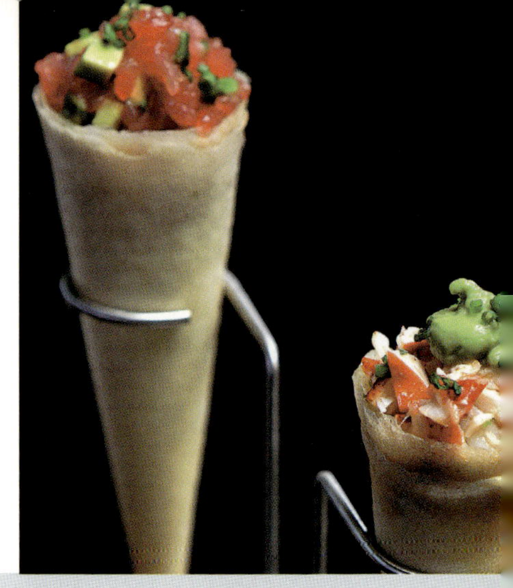

4 sheets of bric dough, cut in half diagonally
12 oz tuna, diced
2 avocados, peeled and diced
2 tbsp olive oil
Juice of 1 lemon
4 oz chukka salad (finished seaweed product)
12 oz lobster meat
4 tbsp crème fraîche
2 cucumbers, peeled and diced
Salt, pepper

Wrap the halved bric dough sheets around 8 large pastry tips and bake at 350 °F for 12 minutes. Combine the diced tuna with ⅓ of the avocados, olive oil and half the lemon juice and season. Take ⅔ of the avocados, mix with the remaining lemon juice and season. Combine lobster meat, crème fraîche and cucumber in a small bowl and season. Take four cones and divide the lobster salad amongst them. For the tuna cones, layer the tuna salad and the marinated avocado alternately into the cones. Top each cone with 1 oz of chukka salad. Serve one tuna cone and one lobster cone together in one metal holder.

4 Scheiben Brickteig, diagonal halbiert
340 g gewürfelter Tunfisch
2 geschälte und gewürfelte Avocados
2 EL Olivenöl
Saft einer Zitrone
120 g Chukka-Salat (Seetang-Salat, fertiges Produkt)
340 g Hummerfleisch
4 EL Crème Fraîche
2 geschälte und gewürfelte Gurken
Salz, Pfeffer

Die halbierten Scheiben Brickteig um 8 große Spritztüllen wickeln und bei 175 °C 12 Minuten backen. Den gewürfelten Tunfisch mit einem Drittel der Avocados, Olivenöl und der Hälfte des Zitronensafts vermengen und würzen. Die restlichen zwei Drittel der Avocados mit dem übrigen Zitronensaft vermischen und würzen. Das Hummerfleisch mit der Crème Fraîche und den Gurken in eine kleine Schüssel geben und würzen. Den Hummersalat auf 4 Blätterteighörnchen verteilen. Bei den Tunfisch-Hörnchen den Tunfischsalat abwechselnd mit der marinierten Avocado schichten. Zum Abschluss auf jedes Hörnchen 30 g Chukka-Salat geben. Je ein Tunfisch-Hörnchen und ein Hummer-Hörnchen zusammen in einem Metallständer servieren.

4 feuilles de brick coupées en diagonale
340 g de thon coupé en dés
2 avocats épluchés et coupés en dés
2 c. à soupe d'huile d'olive
Jus d'1 citron
120 g de salade chukka (salade de varech,
produit préparé)
340 g de chair de homard
4 c. à soupe de crème fraîche
2 concombres épluchés et coupés en dés
Sel, poivre

Enrouler les feuilles de brick autour de 8 embouts et cuire les cornets au four pendant 12 minutes à 175 °C. Mélanger les dés de thon avec un tiers des avocats, l'huile d'olive et la moitié du jus de citron. Mélanger également les deux tiers restants des avocats avec le reste de jus de citron et assaisonner. Dans un plat creux, incorporer la crème fraîche à la chair de homard et aux concombres, puis assaisonner. Répartir la salade de homard dans quatre cornets. Dans le cornet de thon, alterner une couche de salade de thon avec une couche d'avocats marinés. Ajouter enfin 30 g de salade chukka sur chaque cornet. Servir un cornet de chaque sur des présentoirs métalliques.

4 láminas de pasta brick, cortadas por la mitad en diagonal
340 g de atún en dados
2 aguacates pelados y en dados
2 cucharadas de aceite de oliva
Zumo de 1 limón
120 g de ensalada de chuca (ensalada de algas marinas, producto preparado)
340 g de carne de langosta
4 cucharadas de nata fresca espesa
2 pepinos pelados y en dados
Sal, pimienta

Enrolle las mitades de las láminas de pasta brick alrededor de moldes de cucurucho y hornéelos durante 12 minutos a 175 °C. Mezcle los dados de atún con un tercio de los aguacates, aceite de oliva y la mitad del zumo de limón y sazone. Mezcle los dos tercios restantes de aguacate con el zumo de limón sobrante y condimente. Ponga la carne de langosta en un cuenco pequeño junto con la nata fresca espesa y los pepinos y sazone. Reparta la ensalada de langosta entre cuatro cucuruchos. Rellene los cucuruchos de atún alternando una capa de ensalada de atún con otra del avocado marinado. Ponga después en cada cucurucho 30 g de chuca. Sirva los cucuruchos en soportes metálicos de dos conos cada uno.

4 rotoli di pasta yufka tagliati diagonalmente
340 g di tonno spezzettato
2 avocado sbucciati e tagliati a dadini
2 cucchiai di olio di oliva
Il succo di 1 limone
120 g di lattuga di mare (seetang, prodotto pronto)
340 g di polpa di astice
4 cucchiai di crème fraîche
2 cetrioli sbucciati e tagliati a dadini
Sale, pepe

Avvolgere le mezze sfoglie di pasta yufka attorno ad 8 grossi coni e cuocerle in forno a 175 °C per 12 minuti. Mescolare il tonno spezzettato con un terzo degli avocado, l'olio di oliva e la metà del succo di limone e condire. Mescolare gli altri due terzi degli avocado con il restante succo di limone e condire. Mettere in una ciotola la polpa d'astice con la crème fraîche ed i cetrioli e condire. Ripartire l'insalata di astice in 4 coni di pasta yufka. Nei coni destinati al tonno, alternare gli strati di insalata di tonno a strati di avocado marinati. Terminare disponendo su ogni cono 30 g di lattuga di mare. Servire insieme in un portaconi un cono al tonno ed uno all'astice.

Nobu

Design: Rockwell Group | Chef & Owner: Nobu Matsuhisa

4455 Paradise Road | Las Vegas, NV 89109 | Hard Rock Hotel & Casino
Phone: +1 702 693 5090
www.nobumatsuhisa.com
Opening hours: Mon–Sun 6 pm to 11 am
Average price: $ 60
Cuisine: Japanese, Peruvian, sushi

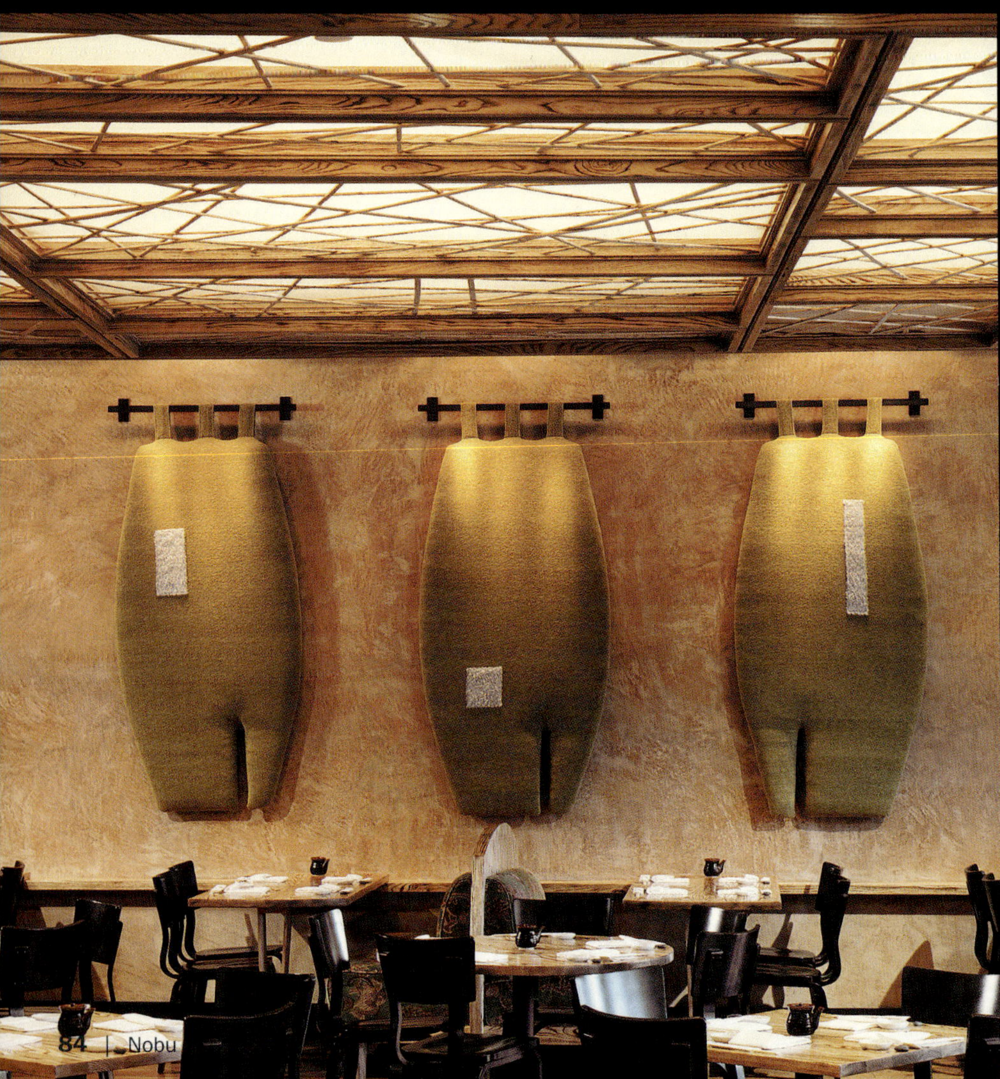

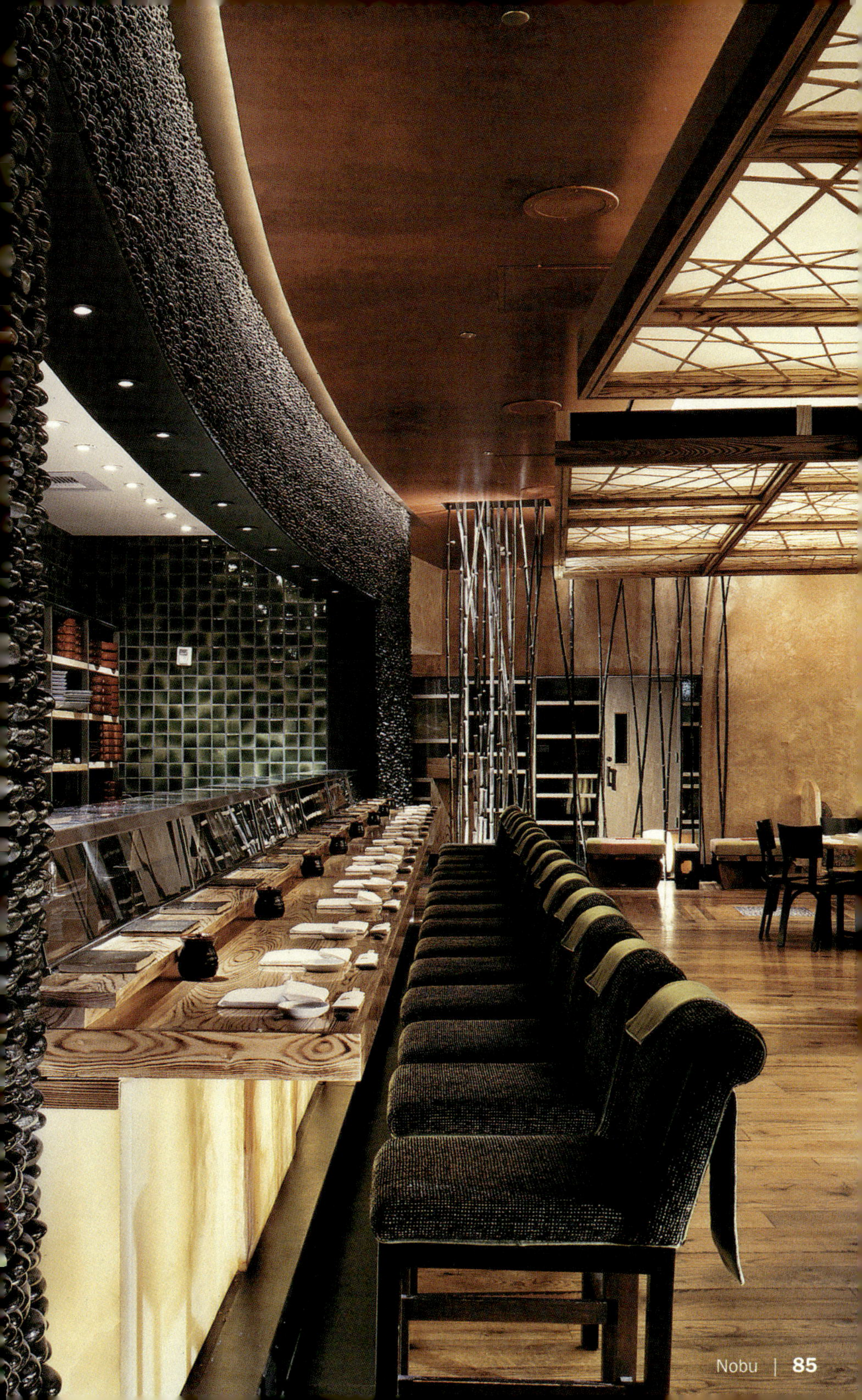

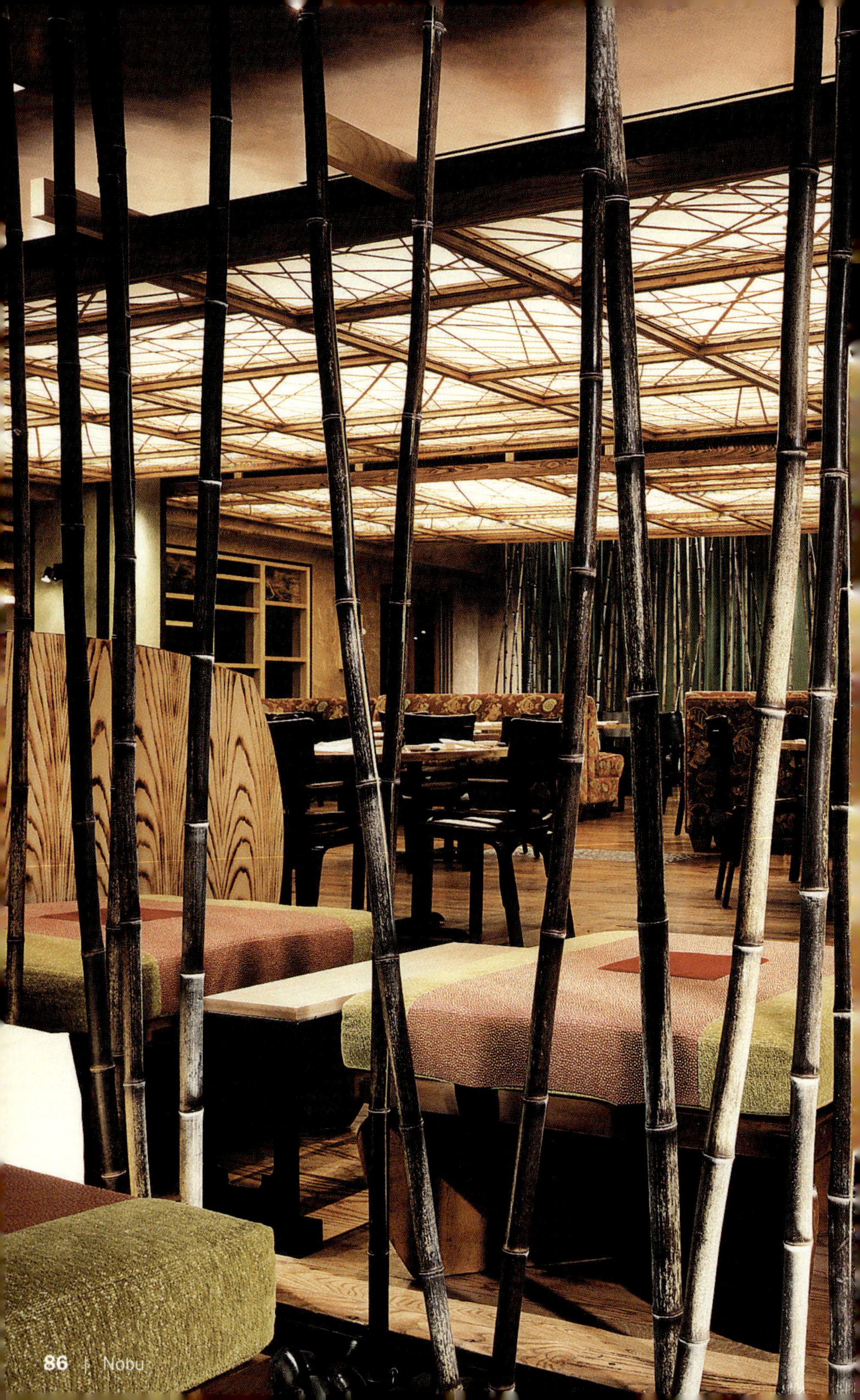

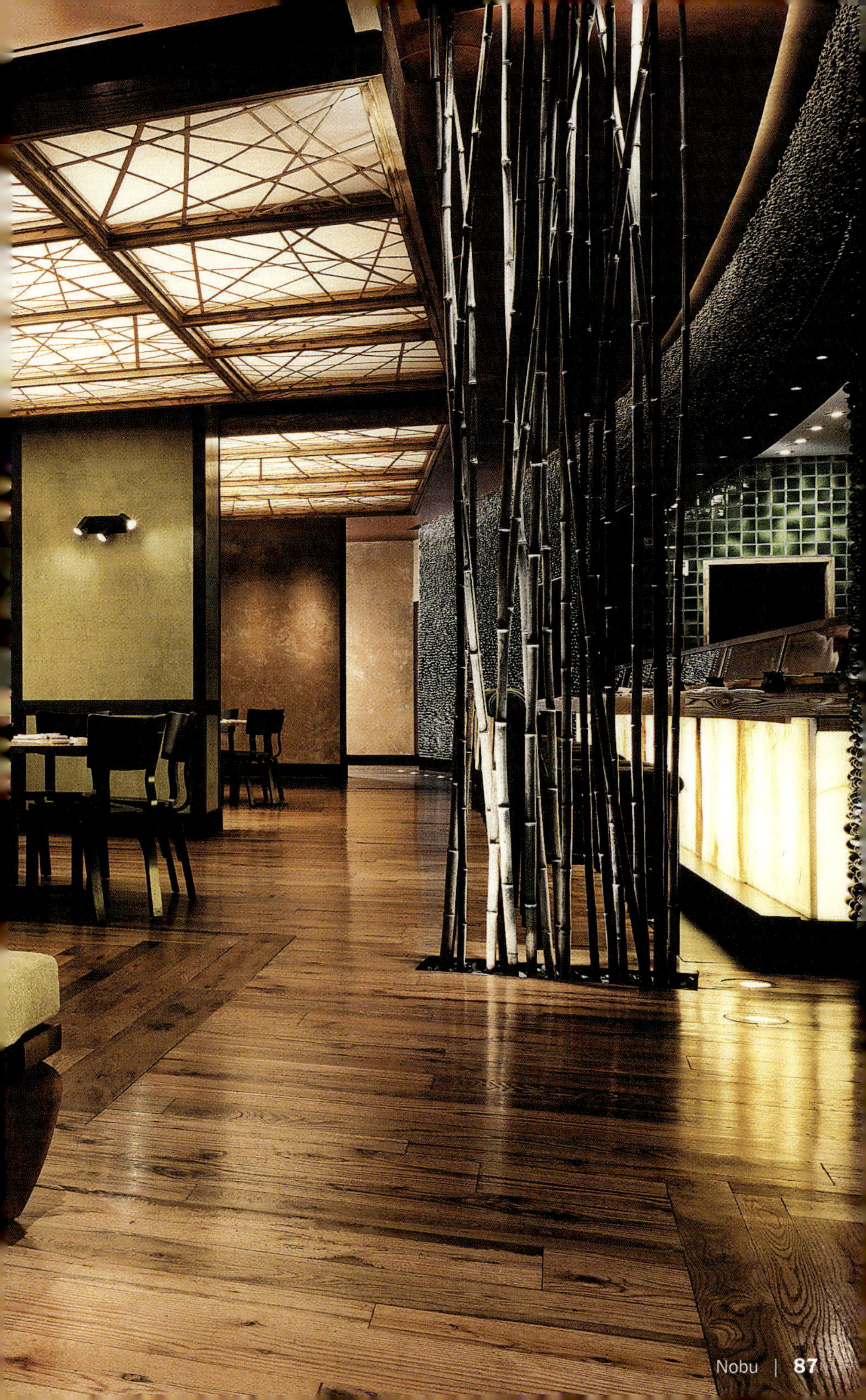

3600 Las Vegas Boulevard S | Las Vegas, NV 89109 | Bellagio Hotel & Casino
Phone: +1 702 693 8181
www.bellagio.com
Opening hours: Daily 11 am to 2 am
Average price: $ 20
Cuisine: Traditional noodle dishes

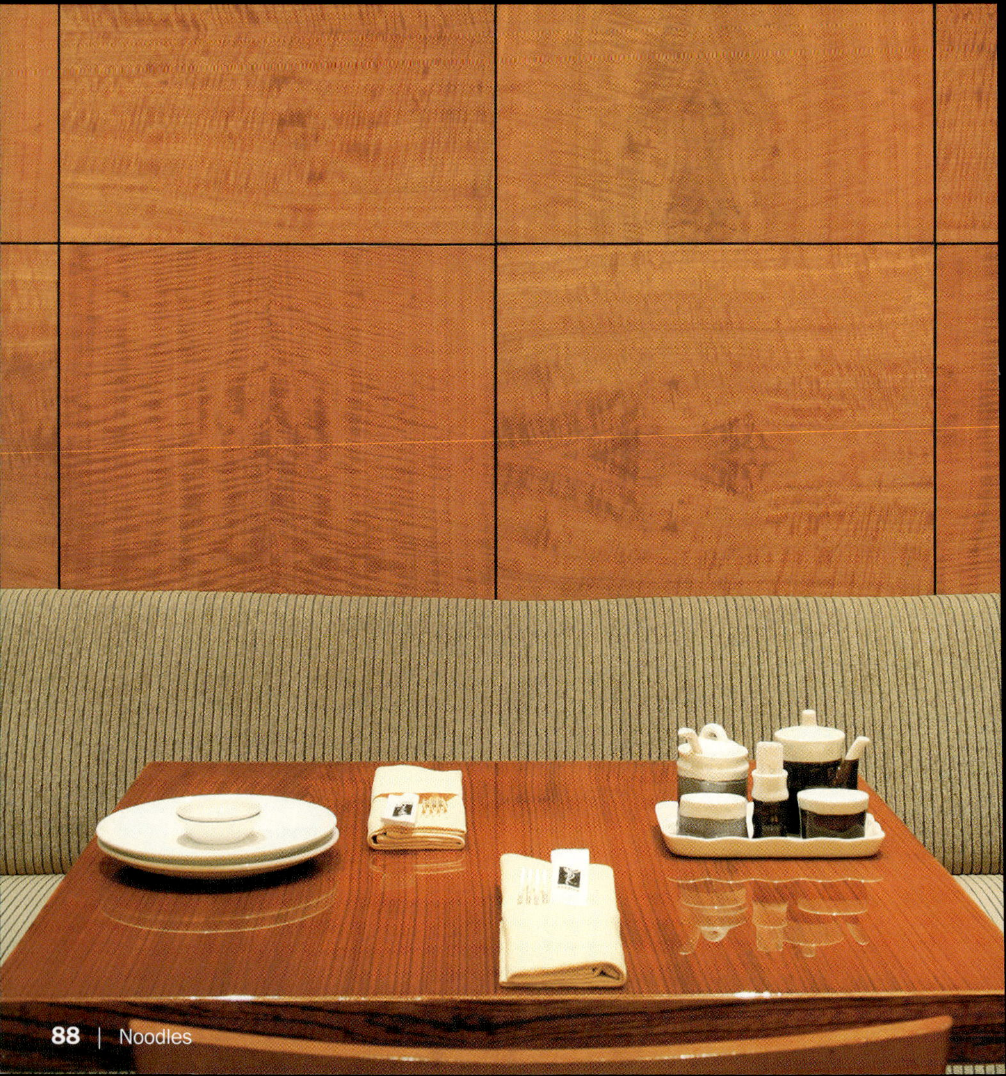

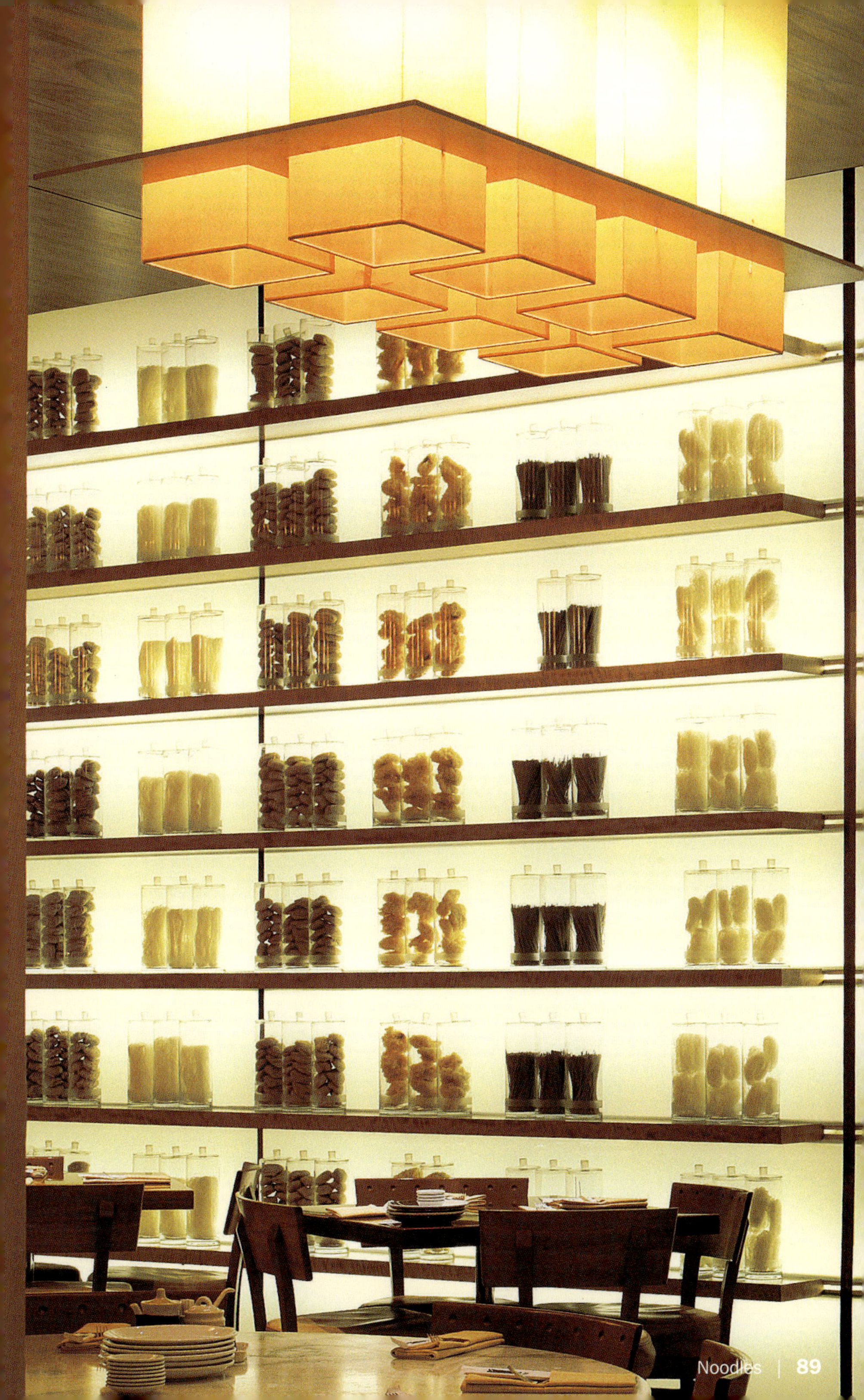

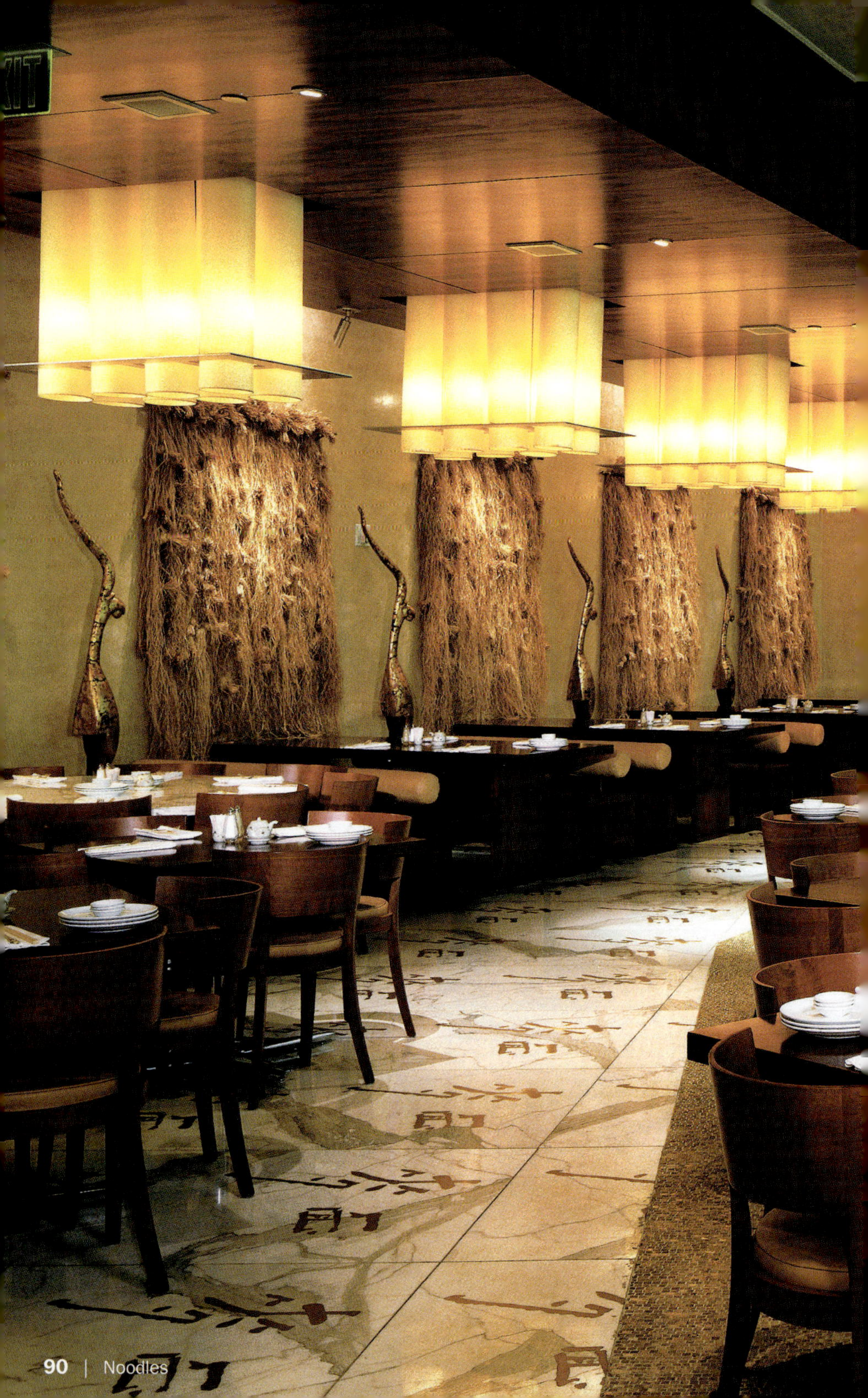

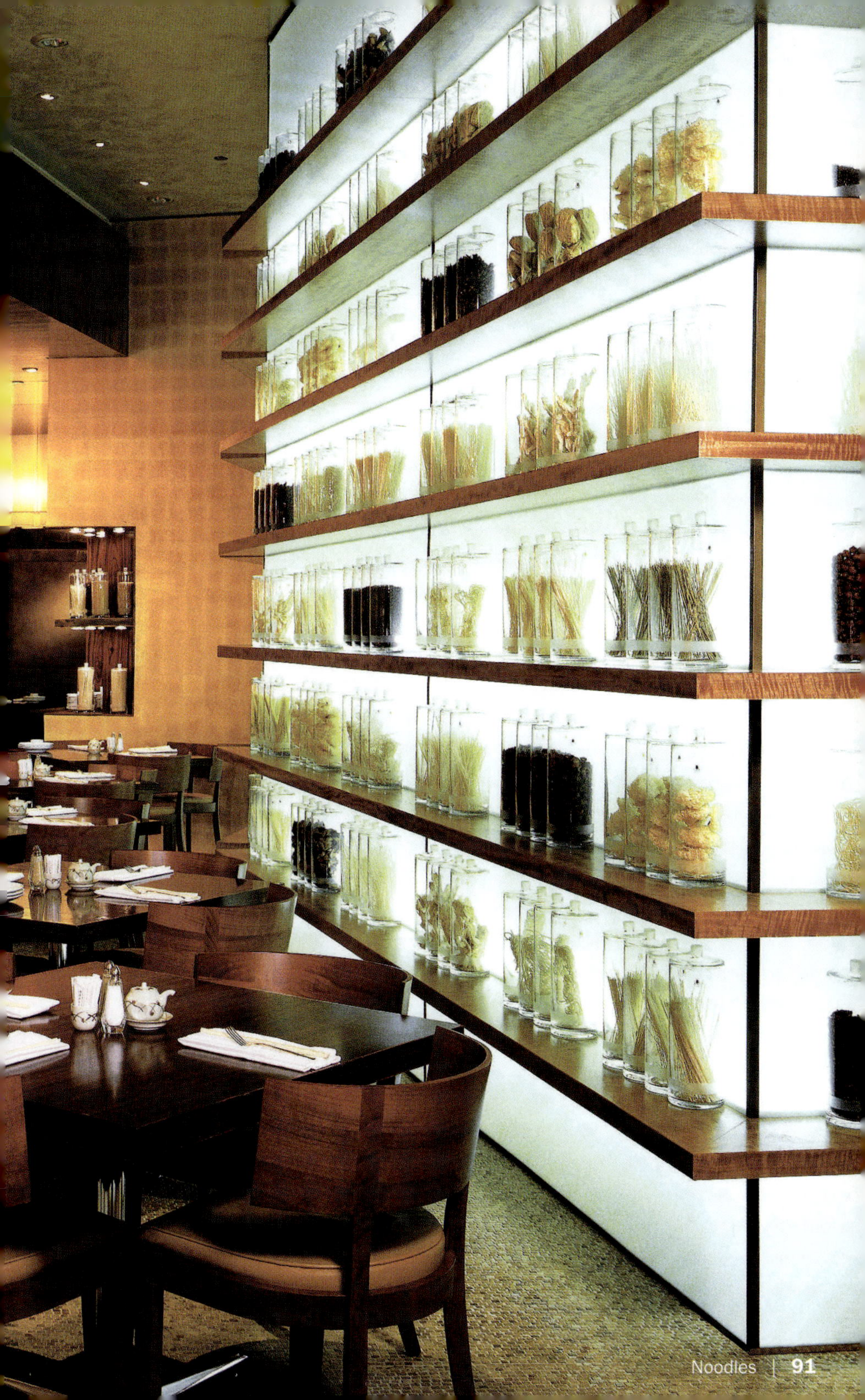

Okada

Design: Hirsch Bedner | Chef: Takashi Yagihashi
Owner: Wynn Las Vegas

3131 Las Vegas Boulevard S | Las Vegas, NV 89109 | Wynn Las Vegas
Phone: +1 702 770 3463
www.wynnlasvegas.com
Opening hours: Sun–Thu 5:30 pm to 10:30 pm, Fri–Sat 5:30 pm to 11:30 pm
Average price: $ 30
Cuisine: Japanese
Special features: Waterfall views

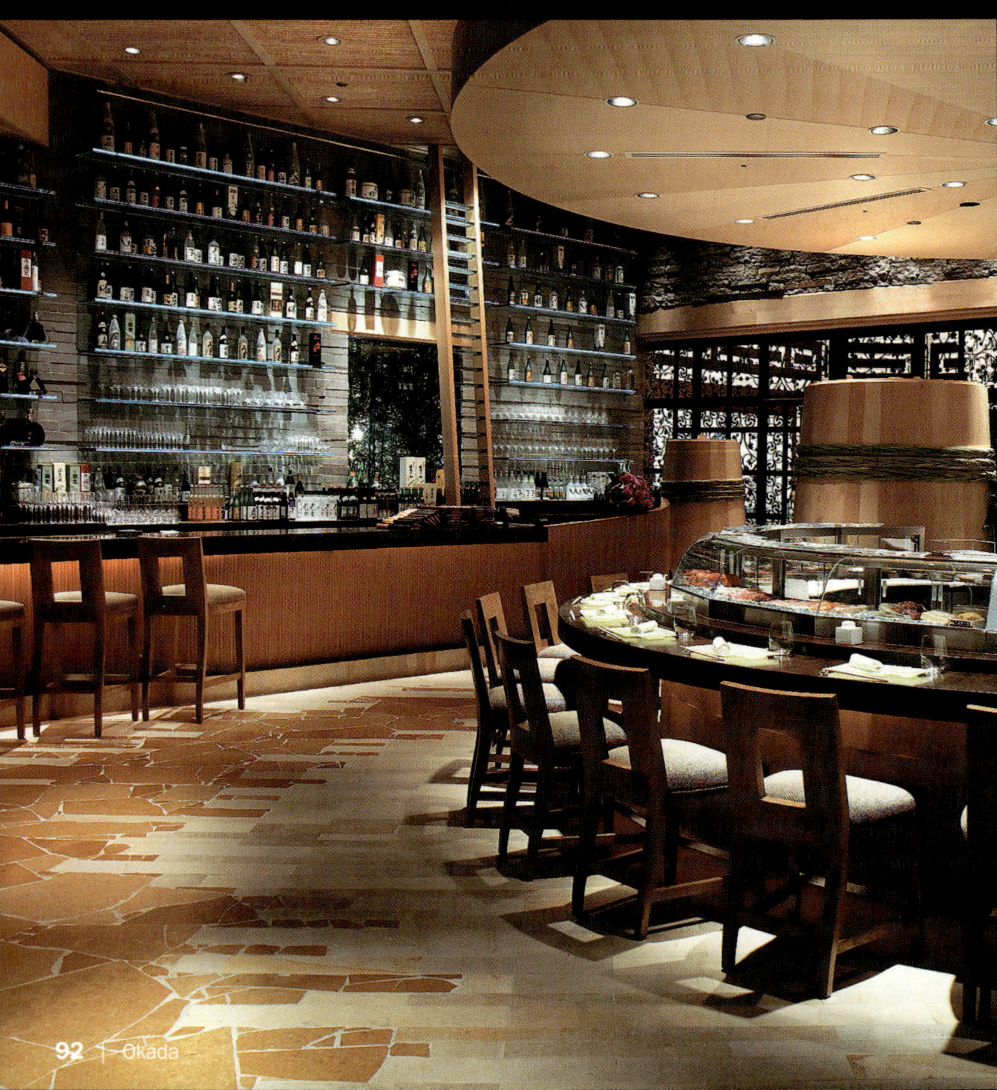

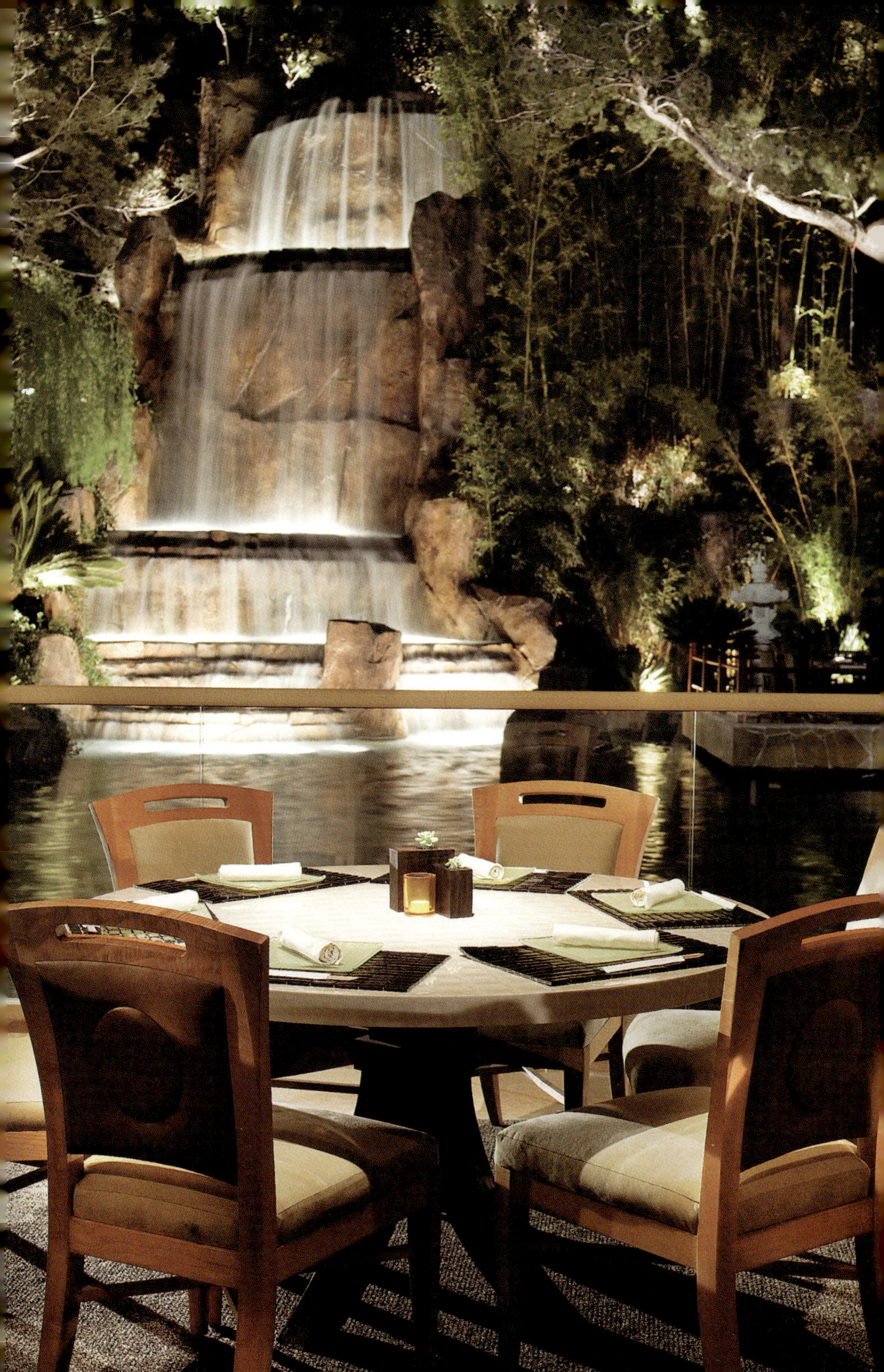

Olives

Design: Jeffrey Beers | Chef & Owner: Todd English

3600 Las Vegas Boulevard S | Las Vegas, NV 89109 | Bellagio Hotel & Casino
Phone: +1 877 234 6358
www.bellagio.com
Opening hours: Daily 11 am to 3 pm and 5 pm to 10:30 pm
Average price: $ 30
Cuisine: Italian, Mediterranean
Special features: Patio seating

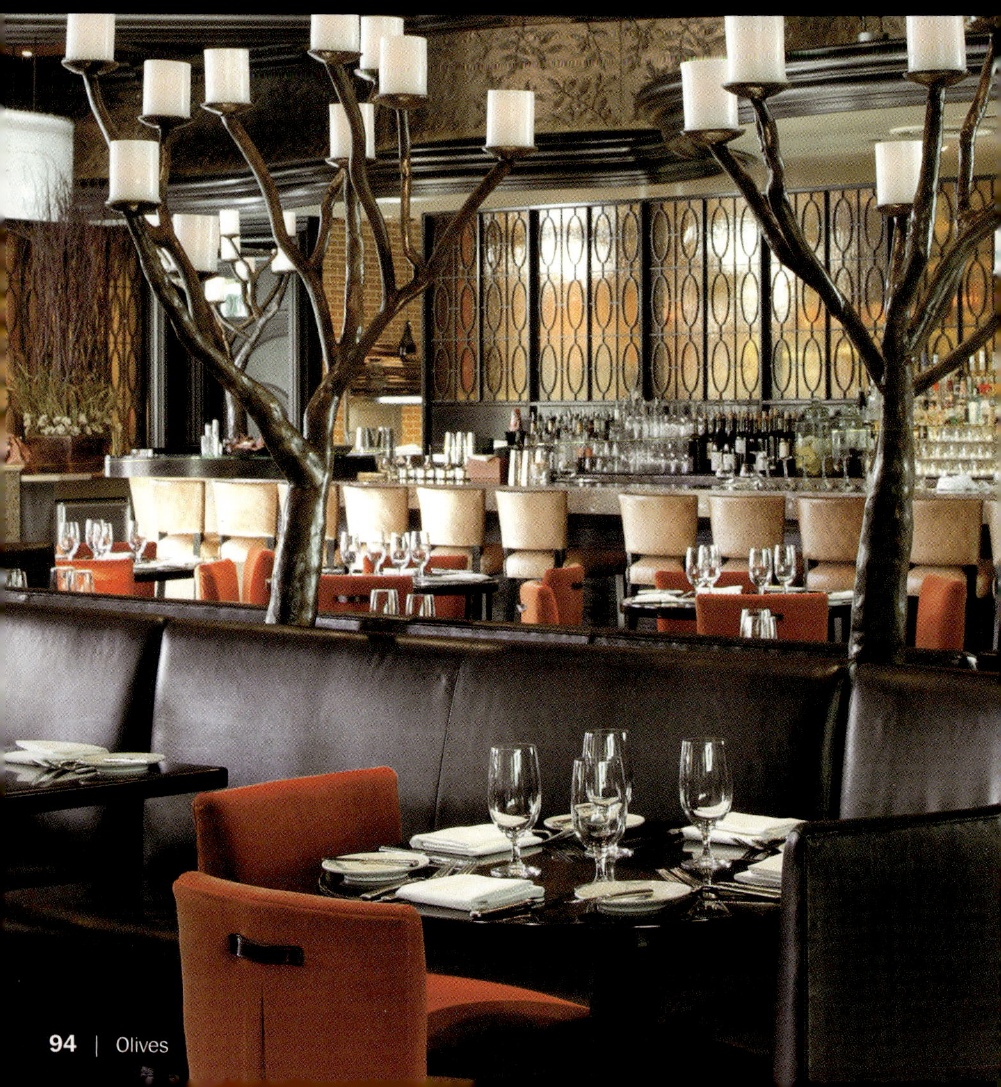

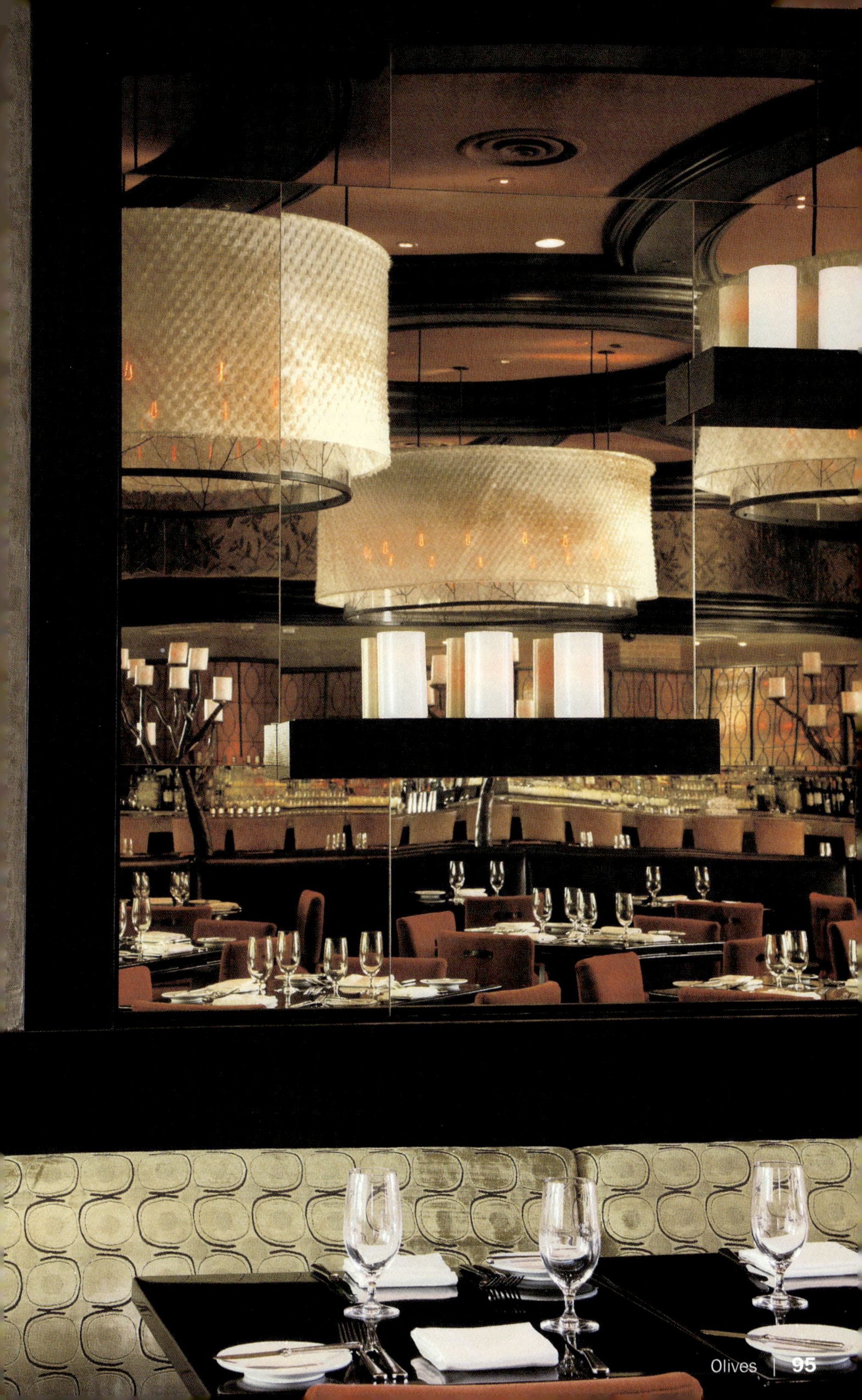

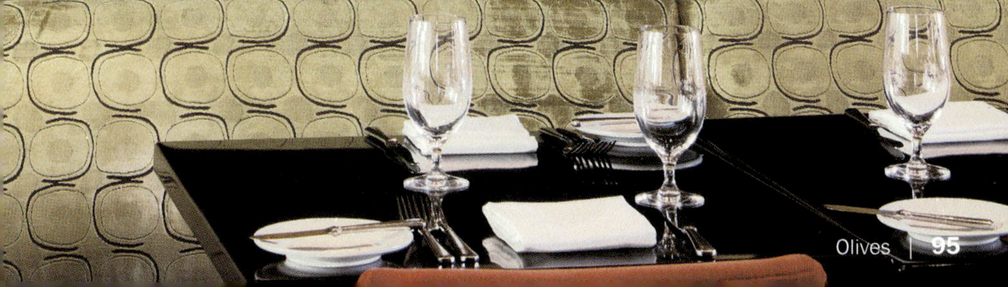

Pearl

Design: Tony Chi | Chef: Kai-Wai Yau
Owner: MGM Grand Hotel & Casino

3799 Las Vegas Boulevard S | Las Vegas, NV 89119 | MGM Grand Hotel & Casino
Phone: +1 702 891 7380
www.mgmgrand.com
Opening hours: Daily 5:30 pm to 10:30 pm
Average price: $ 65
Cuisine: Chinese
Special features: Tableside tea service

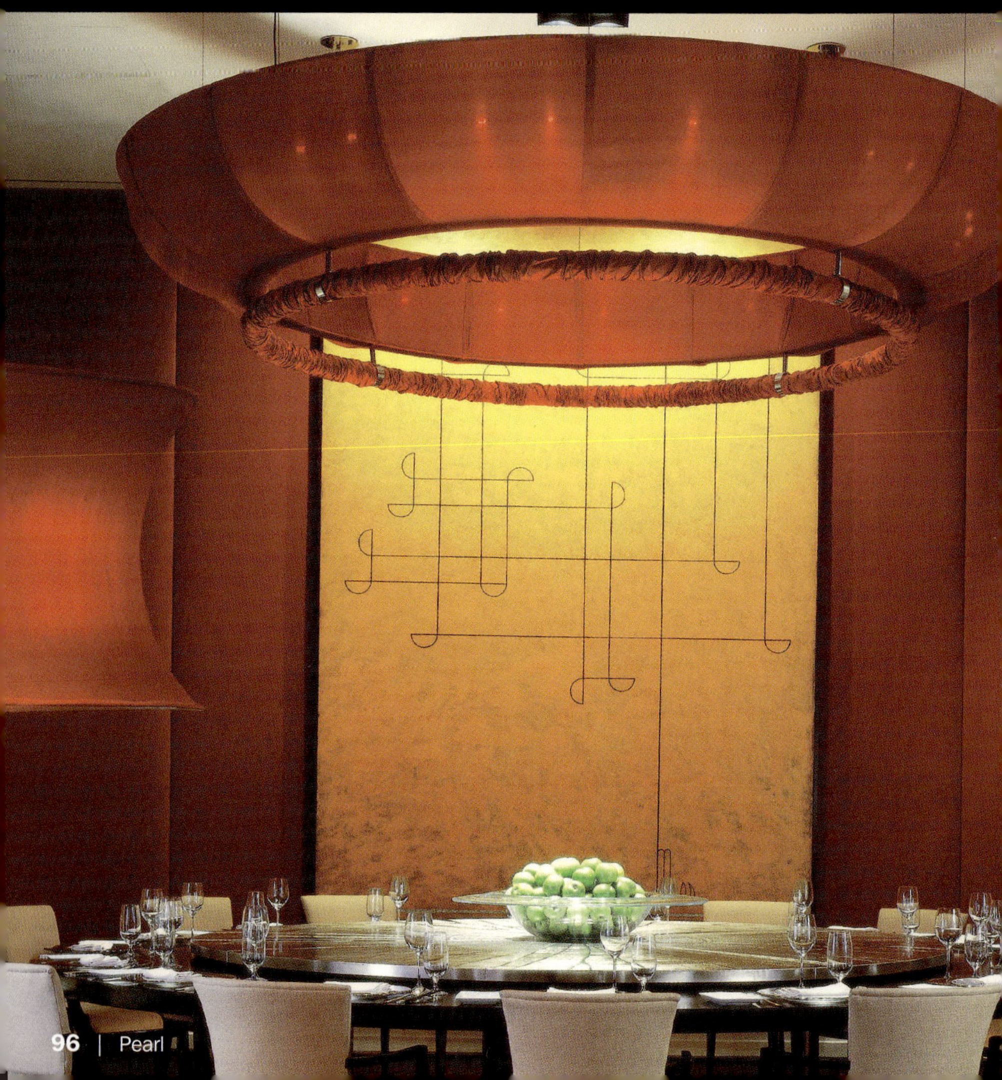

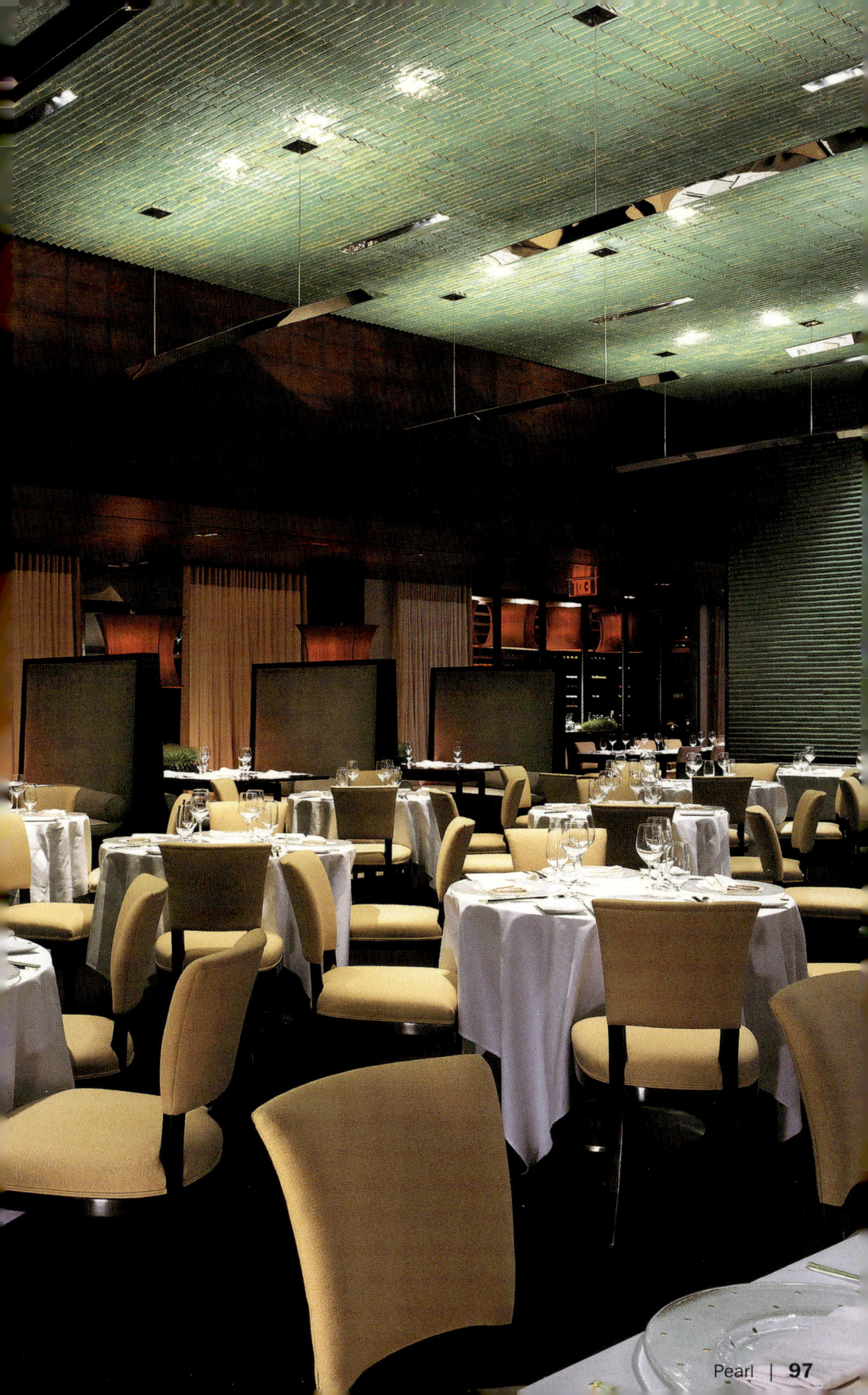

Red Square

Design: Sensei Design | Chef: Michael Schmidt
Owners: Mandalay Bay Resort & Casino, China Grill Management

3950 Las Vegas Boulevard S | Las Vegas, NV 89119 | Mandalay Bay Resort & Casino
Phone: +1 702 632 7407
www.mandalaybay.com
Opening hours: Daily 5 pm to midnight
Average price: $ 31
Cuisine: Russian classics
Special features: Private vodka locker

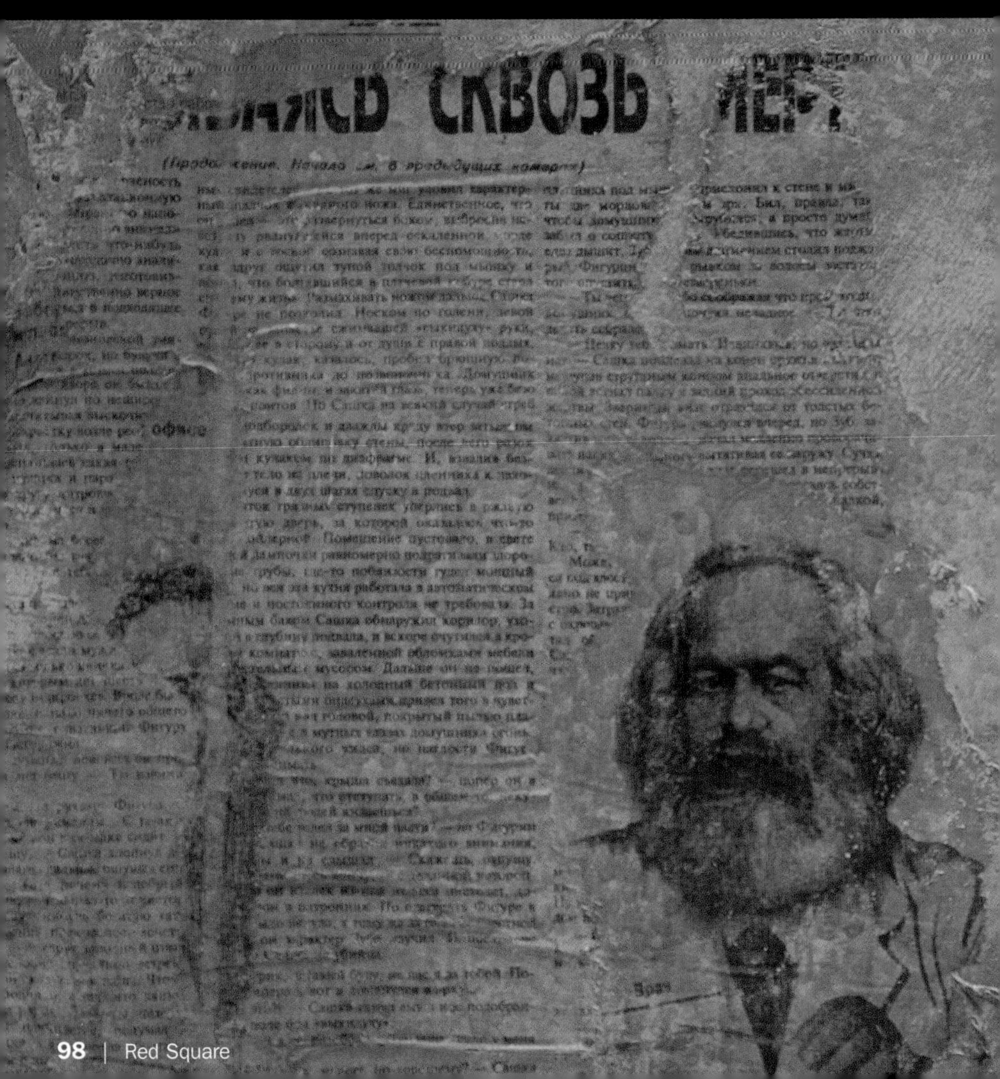

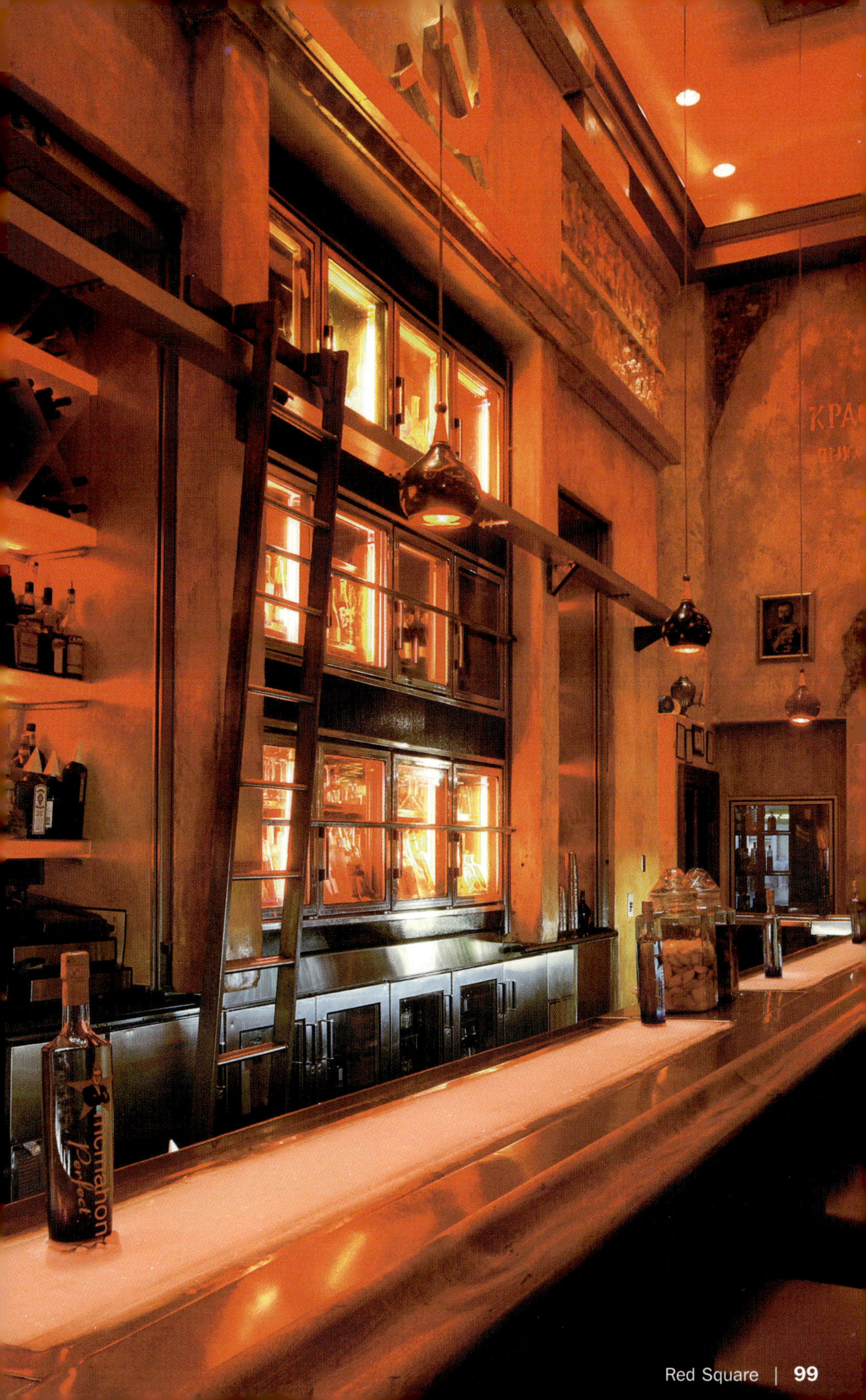

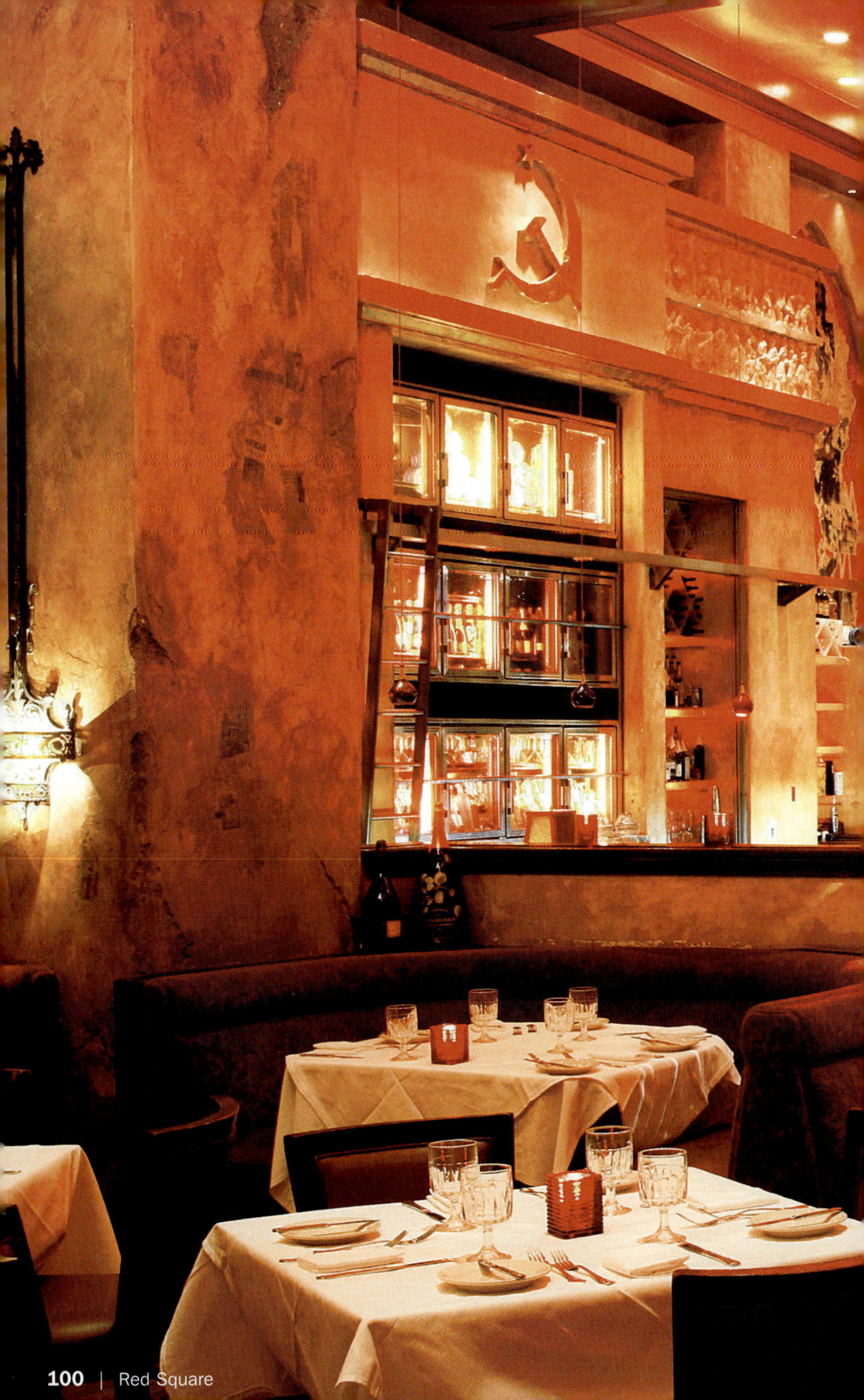

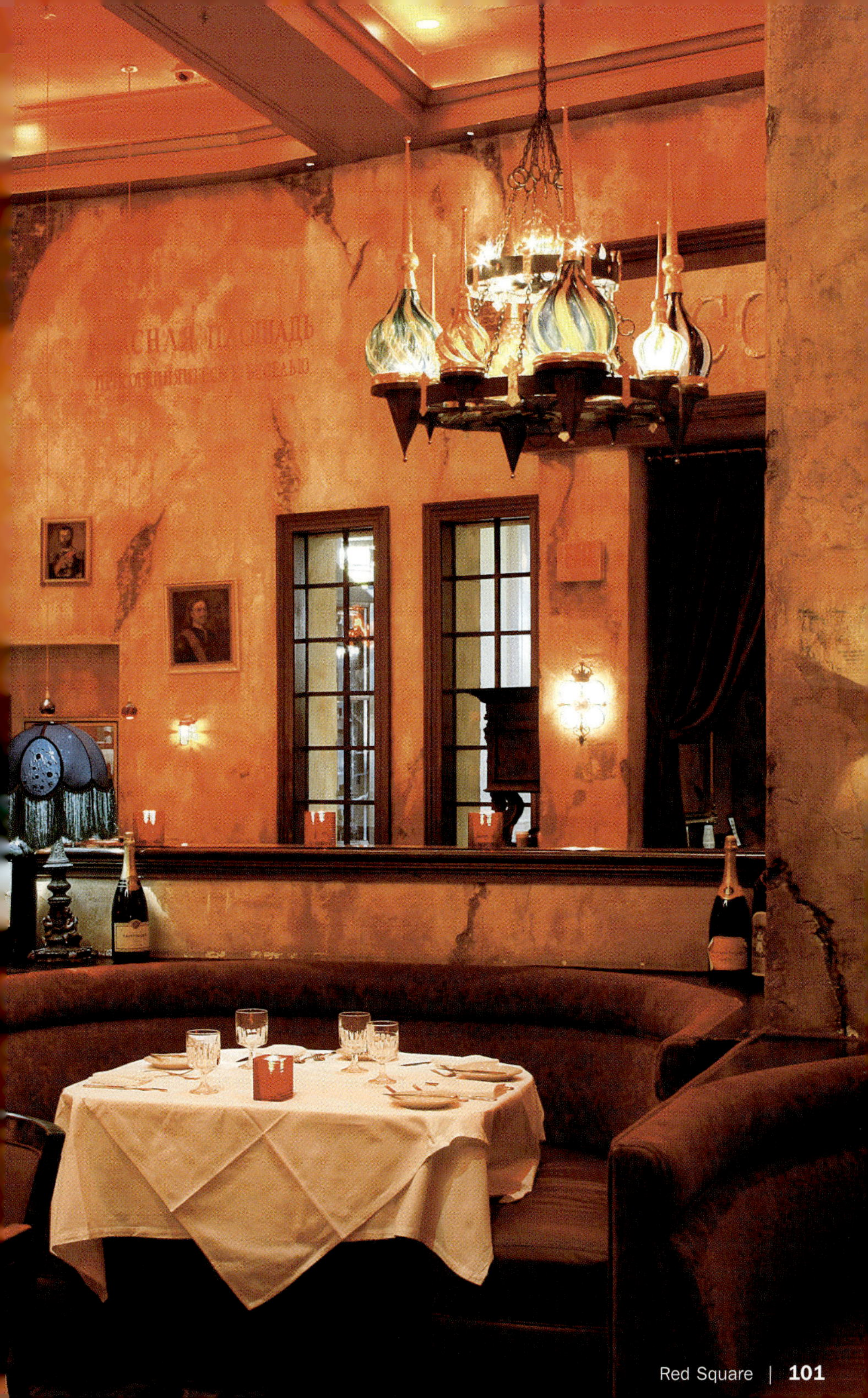

Blackened
Tuna & Foie Gras

Scharf angebratener Tunfisch mit
Gänsestopfleber

Thon rôti & foie gras d'oie

Atún cajún con foie gras

Tonno arrosto con foie gras

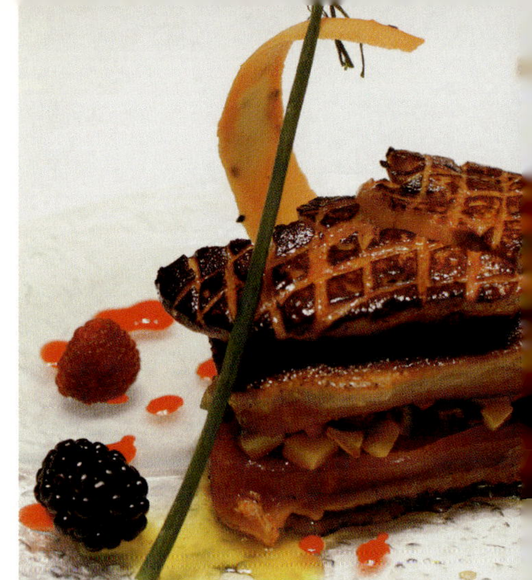

4 pieces of tuna, 7 oz each
2 tbsp Cajun spice mix
2 tbsp soybean oil
1 carrot, cut in julienne and blanched
1 leek, cut in julienne and blanched
4 pieces foie gras, 3 oz each
Salt, pepper
1 tbsp butter
240 ml mixed berry sauce

Chives, raspberries and blackberries for decoration

Coat tuna with Cajun spice and sear in hot oil on both sides. Meanwhile season foie gras and sear in a pan with butter. When tuna is still rare, slice in half lengthwise, place vegetables on tuna and place other half of tuna on top of vegetables. Place foie gras on top of tuna, drizzle sauce around tuna and garnish with raspberries, blackberries, chives.

4 Tunfischstücke, je 200 g
2 EL Cajun-Würzmischung
2 EL Sojabohnenöl
1 in feine Streifen geschnittene und blanchierte Karotte
1 in feine Streifen geschnittene und blanchierte Lauchstange
4 Stück Gänsestopfleber, je 85 g
Salz, Pfeffer
1 EL Butter
240 ml Soße aus gemischten Beeren

Schnittlauch, Himbeeren und Brombeeren zur Dekoration

Den Tunfisch mit Cajun-Gewürz einreiben und in heißem Öl von beiden Seiten scharf anbraten. In der Zwischenzeit die Gänsestopfleber würzen und in einer Pfanne in Butter scharf anbraten. Den Tunfisch nur englisch braten, der Länge nach halbieren, das Gemüse auf eine Hälfte geben und mit der anderen Tunfischhälfte bedecken. Die Gänsestopfleber auf den Tunfisch geben, Soße um den Fisch herum träufeln und mit Himbeeren, Brombeeren und Schnittlauch garnieren.

4 morceaux de thon de 200 g
2 c. à soupe d'épices cajuns
2 c. à soupe d'huile de soja
1 carotte blanchie et coupée en julienne
1 poireau blanchi et coupé en julienne
4 tranches de foie gras d'oie de 85 g
Sel, poivre
1 c. à soupe de beurre
240 ml de sauce aux baies mélangées

Ciboulette, framboises et mûres pour la garniture

Badigeonner le thon du mélange d'épices cajuns et bien le saisir de chaque côté dans de l'huile chaude. Entre-temps, assaisonner les tranches de foie gras et bien les faire revenir dans le beurre dans une poêle. Cuire le thon (saignant), le couper en deux dans le sens de la longueur, disposer les légumes sur une moitié et couvrir avec l'autre moitié. Ajouter la tranche de foie gras dessus, verser la sauce autour du poisson et garnir de framboises, de mûres et de ciboulette.

4 trozos de atún de 200 g cada uno
2 cucharadas de mezcla de especias cajún
2 cucharadas de aceite de soja
1 zanahoria en juliana y escalfada
1 tallo de puerro en juliana y escalfado
4 escalopes de foie gras de 85 g cada uno
Sal, pimienta
1 cucharada de mantequilla
240 ml de salsa de bayas mezcladas

Cebollino, frambuesas y zarzamoras para decorar

Frote el atún con la mezcla de especias cajún y fríalo a fuego fuerte por ambos lados en aceite caliente. En ese tiempo sazone los escalopes de foie gras y fríalos a fuego fuerte en una sartén con mantequilla. Fría ligeramente el atún, de forma que aún siga estando crudo, córtelo después longitudinalmente, coloque la verdura sobre una de las mitades y cúbrala con la otra mitad. Ponga encima el foie gras, vierta alrededor del atún la salsa y decore con el cebollino, las frambuesas y las zarzamoras.

4 tranci di tonno di 200 g ciascuno
2 cucchiai di condimenti misti Cajun
2 cucchiai di olio di semi di soia
1 carota scottata e tagliata a fettine sottili
1 porro scottato e tagliato a fettine sottili
4 foie gras di 85 g ciascuno
Sale, pepe
1 cucchiaio di burro
240 ml di succo di frutti di bosco

Per la guarnizione: erba cipollina, lamponi e more

Strofinare il tonno con i condimenti Cajun e rosolarlo a fuoco vivo nell'olio caldo da entrambi i lati. Nel frattempo condire i foie gras e rosolarli a fuoco vivo in una padella con il burro. Cuocere il tonno al sangue, dimezzarlo nel senso della lunghezza, disporre su una metà le verdure e ricoprire con l'altra metà. Disporre il patè di fegato sul tonno, versarvi intorno il succo di frutti di bosco e guarnire con lamponi, more ed erba cipollina.

Restaurant rm

Design: Class Calder Smith | Chef: Rick Moonen
Owners: Rick Moonen, Mandaly Bay Resort & Casino

3750 Las Vegas Boulevard S | Las Vegas, NV 89119 | Mandalay Bay Resort & Casino
Phone: +1 702 632 9300
www.mandalaybay.com
Opening hours: Daily 6 pm to 10 pm
Average price: $ 150
Cuisine: Seafood
Special featurcs: Downstairs r.bar.cafe

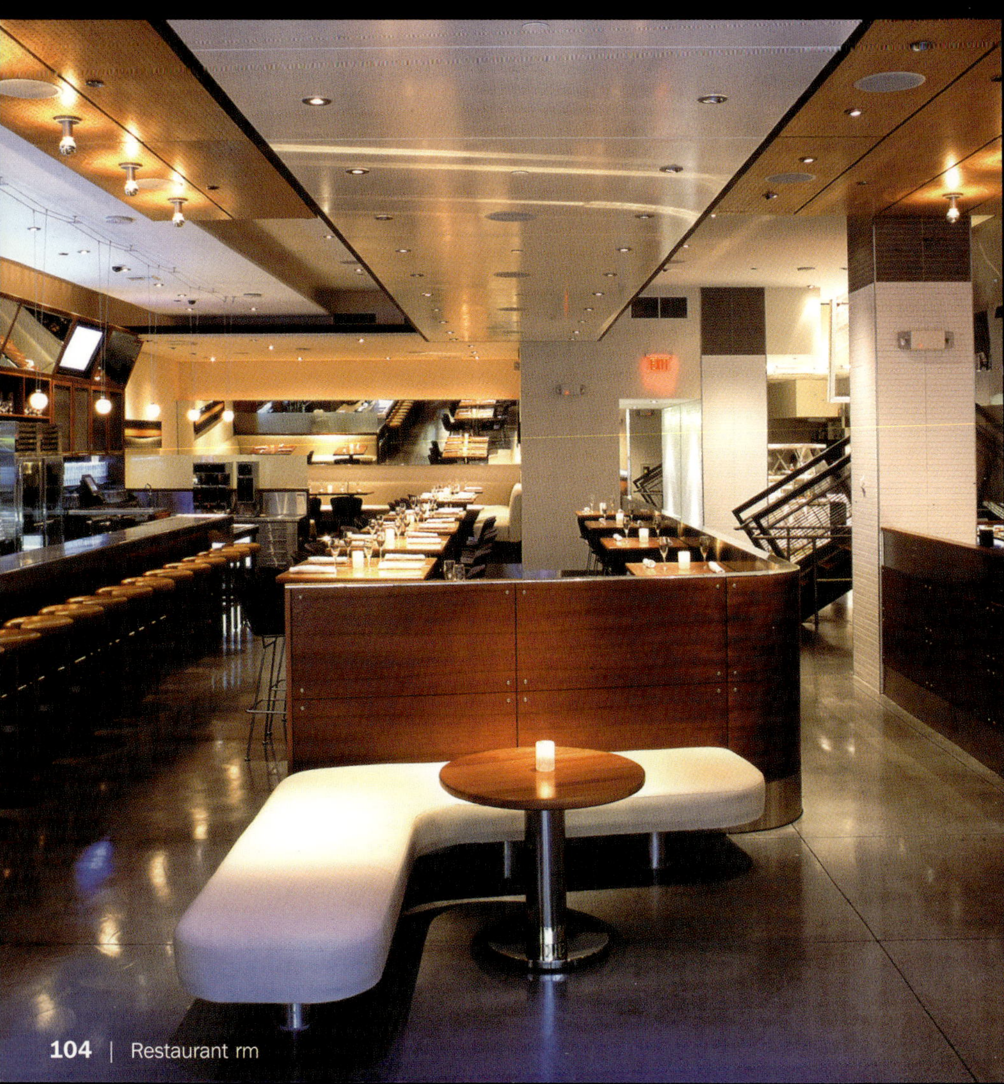

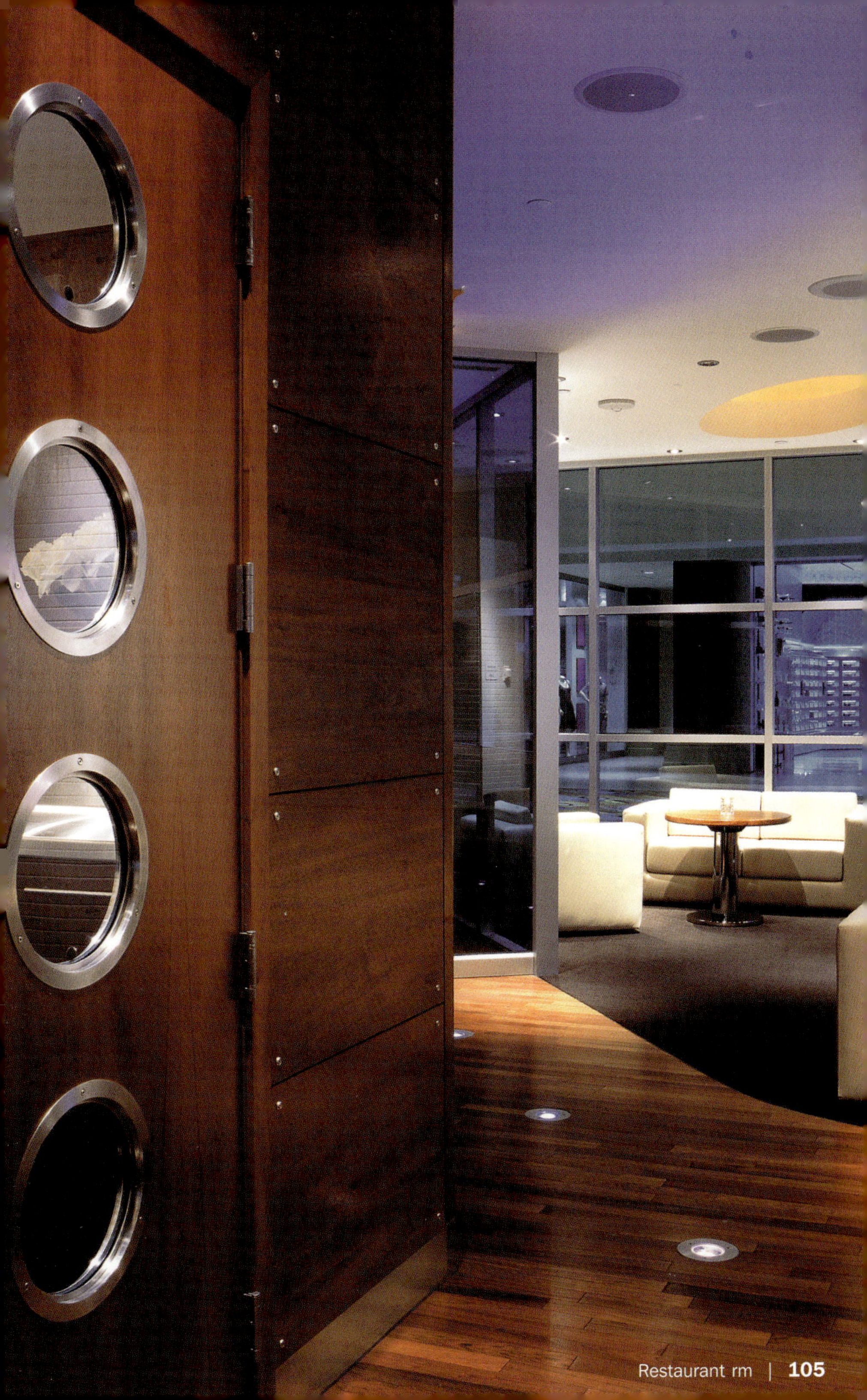

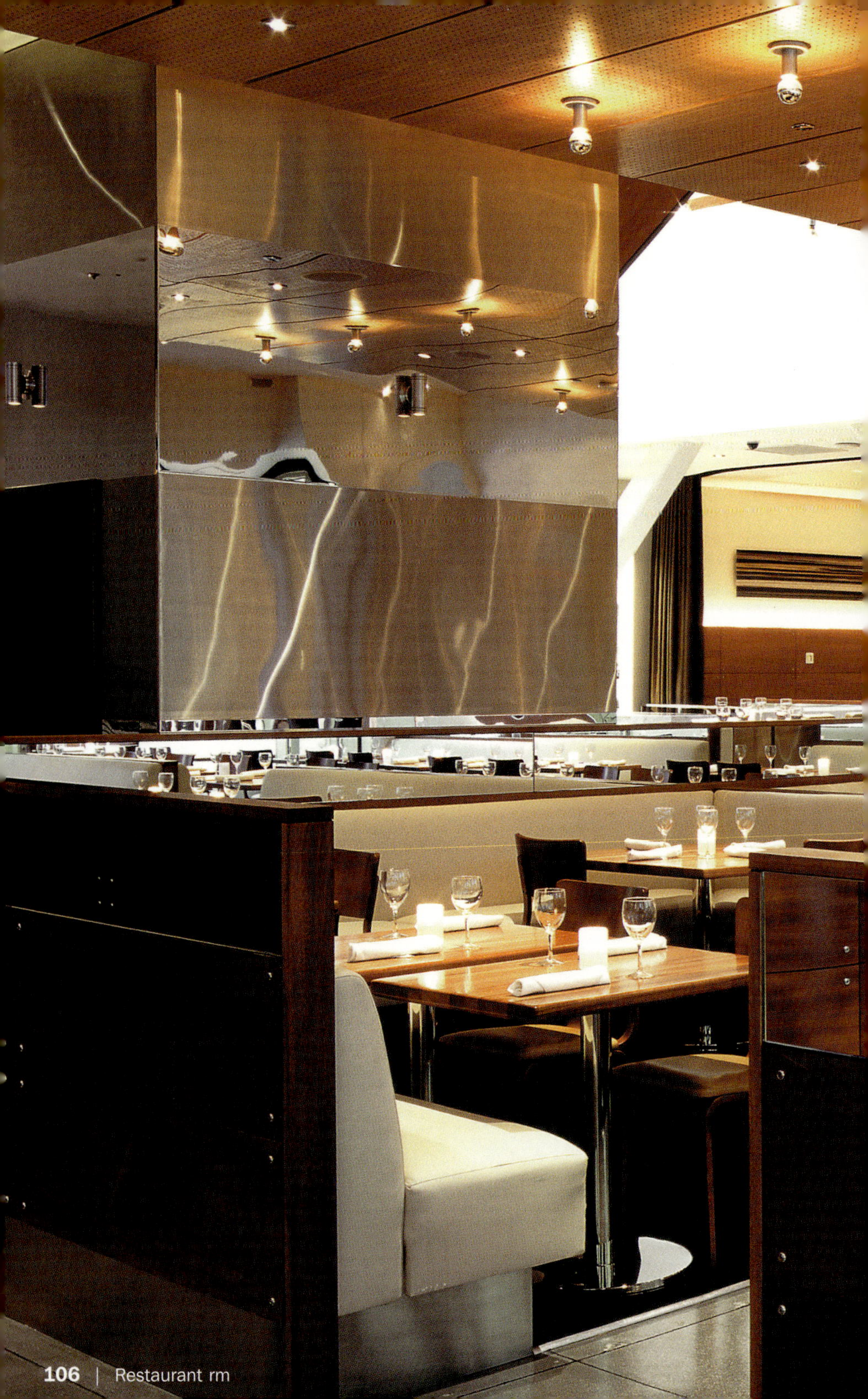

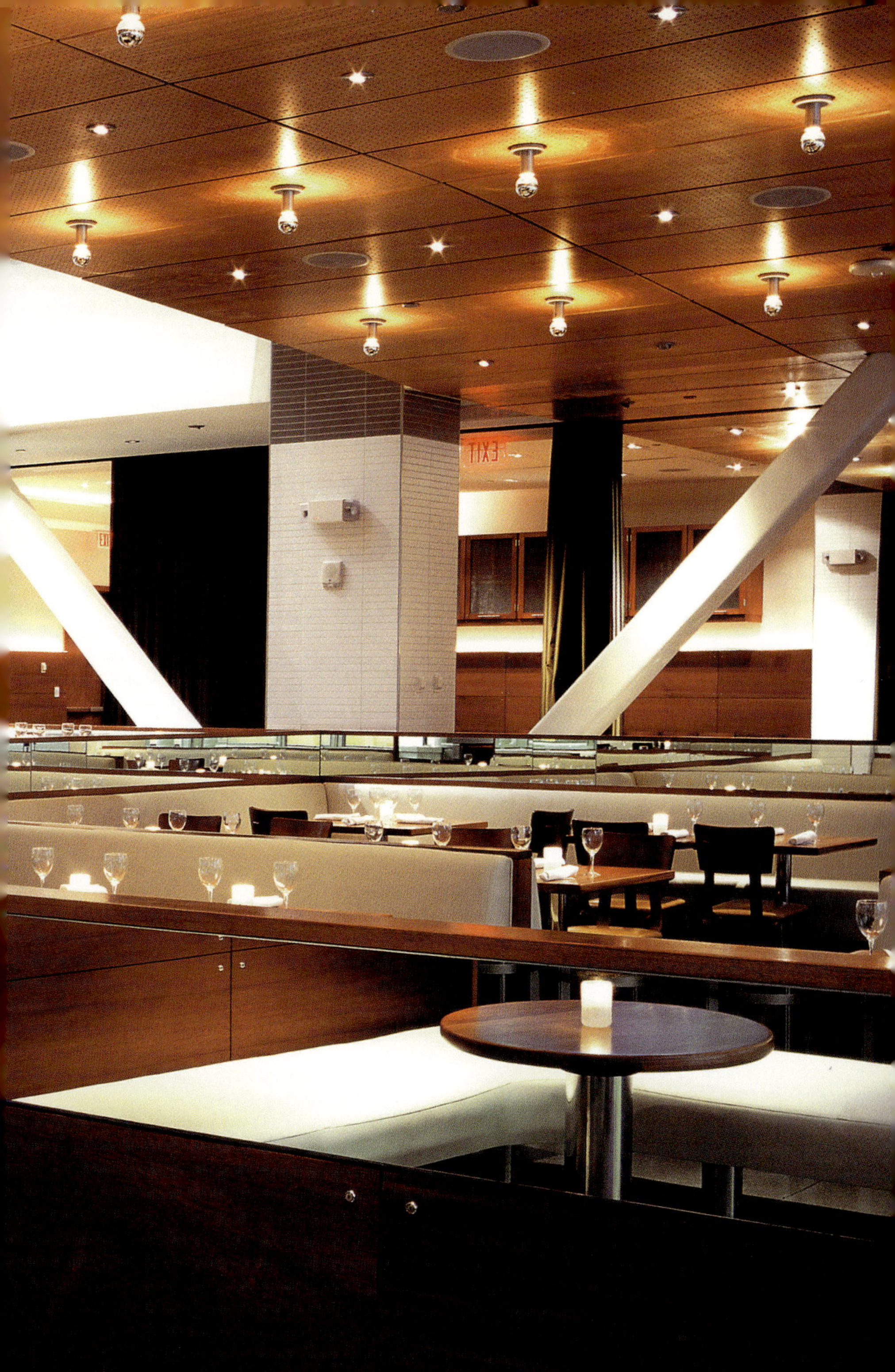

Gnocchi

"Mac 'N' Cheese"

Gnocchi mit Käse

Gnocchis au fromage

Gnocchi con queso

Gnocchi al formaggio

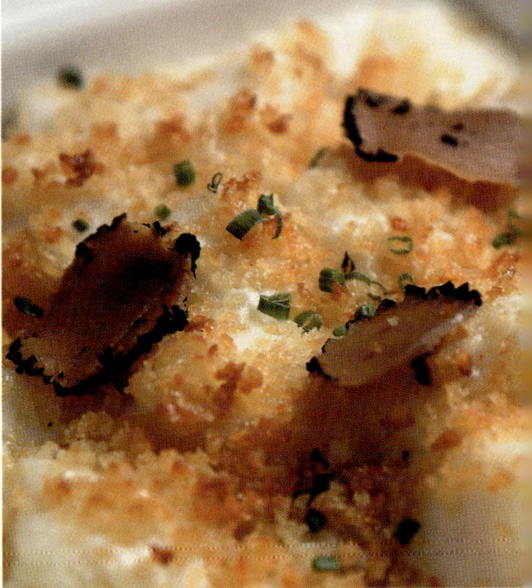

1 lb 5 oz potatoes, peeled and cooked
2 eggs
Salt, pepper, nutmeg
Flour
Mash the potatoes, while they are still hot. Mix with eggs, some flour and seasonings and shape into gnocchi. Boil in salted water until they float to the surface.
3 tbsp butter
4 tbsp flour
300 ml milk
Salt, pepper, nutmeg
2 twigs of thyme and rosemary
Melt butter in a large pot, add flour and sweat. Fill up with milk, add the herbs and bring to a boil. Season with salt, pepper and nutmeg. Boil bechamel sauce for approx. 10 minutes, then strain.

8 oz porcini mushrooms
2 tbsp olive oil
50 ml Brandy
200 ml white wine
150 ml vegetable stock
Salt, pepper
Sautée mushrooms in olive oil, deglaze with Brandy and white wine and fill up with vegetable stock. Simmer until all liquid is evaporated, then season.
7 oz mascarpone
1 black truffle, sliced
4 tbsp breadcrumbs
Chives for decoration
Combine bechamel sauce, mushrooms, mascarpone and truffle and season. Add gnocchi and fill into a baking dish. Sprinkle with breadcrumbs and bake at 360 °F for 15 minutes. Garnish with chives.

600 g geschälte und gekochte Kartoffeln
2 Eier
Salz, Pfeffer, Muskat
Mehl
Die noch heißen Kartoffeln stampfen. Mit den Eiern, etwas Mehl und den Gewürzen vermengen und daraus Gnocchi formen. In Salzwasser kochen, bis sie an die Oberfläche treiben.
3 EL Butter
4 EL Mehl
300 ml Milch
Salz, Pfeffer, Muskat
Je 2 Thymian- und Rosmarinzweige
Die Butter in einem großen Topf schmelzen, Mehl hinzugeben und anschwitzen. Mit Milch auffüllen, Kräuter hinzufügen und zum Kochen bringen. Mit Salz, Pfeffer und Muskat abschmecken. Béchamelsauce ungefähr 10 Minuten lang kochen lassen und dann passieren.

225 g Steinpilze
2 EL Olivenöl
50 ml Brandy
200 ml Weißwein
150 ml Gemüsebrühe
Salz, Pfeffer
Die Pilze in Olivenöl kurz anbraten, mit Brandy und Weißwein ablöschen und mit der Gemüsebrühe auffüllen. Köcheln lassen, bis die ganze Flüssigkeit verdampft ist und dann abschmecken.
200 g Mascarpone
1 schwarzer Trüffel in Scheiben
4 EL Semmelbrösel
Schnittlauch zur Dekoration
Béchamelsoße, Pilze, Mascarpone und Trüffel miteinander vermengen und abschmecken. Die Gnocchi hinzugeben und in eine Auflaufform füllen. Mit Semmelbrösel bestreuen und bei 180 °C 15 Minuten backen. Mit Schnittlauch garnieren.

600 g de pommes de terre épluchées et cuites
2 œufs
Sel, poivre, muscade
Farine
Écraser les pommes de terre encore chaudes. Ajouter les œufs, un peu de farine et l'assaisonnement puis préparer les gnocchis. Les cuire dans l'eau salée jusqu'à ce qu'ils remontent à la surface.
3 c. à soupe de beurre
4 c. à soupe de farine
300 ml de lait
Sel, poivre, muscade
2 branches de thym et 2 de romarin
Faire fondre le beurre dans une grande casserole, ajouter la farine et la faire blondir. Verser le lait, ajouter les herbes et porter le tout à ébullition. Assaisonner avec le sel, le poivre et la muscade. Laisser cuire la sauce béchamel pendant environ 10 minutes, puis filtrer.

225 g de cèpes
2 c. à soupe d'huile d'olive
50 ml de brandy
200 ml de vin blanc
150 ml de bouillon de légumes
Sel, poivre
Faire revenir brièvement les champignons, mouiller avec le brandy et le vin blanc, puis verser le bouillon de légumes. Laisser mijoter jusqu'à ce que tout le liquide se soit évaporé, puis assaisonner.
200 g de mascarpone
1 truffe noire en tranches
4 c. à soupe de chapelure
Ciboulette pour la garniture
Mélanger la sauce béchamel, les champignons, le mascarpone et la truffe, puis assaisonner. Ajouter les gnocchis et disposer le mélange dans un plat à gratin. Saupoudrer de chapelure et cuire au four pendant 15 minutes à 180 °C. Garnir de ciboulette.

600 g de patatas peladas y cocidas
2 huevos
Sal, pimienta, nuez moscada
Harina
Machaque las patatas aún calientes. Mezcle el puré con los huevos y las especias y forme los gnocchi. Cuézalos en agua con sal hasta que floten en la superficie.
3 cucharadas de mantequilla
4 cucharadas de harina
300 ml de leche
Sal, pimienta, nuez moscada
2 ramitos de tomillo y de romero
Derrita la mantequilla en una cazuela grande, añada la harina y fríala brevemente. Añada la leche, las hierbas y lleve la mezcla a ebullición. Sazone con sal, pimienta y nuez moscada. Deje que hierva la besamel durante 10 minutos y cuélela después.

225 g de boletos
2 cucharadas de aceite de oliva
50 ml de brandy
200 ml de vino blanco
150 ml de caldo de verdura
Sal, pimienta
Sofría brevemente los boletos en aceite de oliva, incorpore después el brandy y el vino y añada el caldo de verdura. Deje que hierva hasta que el líquido se haya evaporado, condimente después.
200 g de queso mascarpone
1 trufa negra en láminas
4 cucharadas de migas de pan
Cebollino para decorar
Mezcle la besamel, los boletos, el mascarpone y la trufa y condimente. Añada los gnocchi y ponga después la mezcla en un molde para horno. Esparza por encima las migas de pan y hornee durante 15 minutos a 180 °C. Decore con el cebollino.

600 g di patate sbucciate e bollite
2 uova
Sale, pepe, noce moscata
Farina
Schiacciare le patate ancora calde. Incorporarvi le uova e gli aromi e ricavare degli gnocchi. Cuocerli in acqua salata finché non verranno a galla.
3 cucchiai di burro
4 cucchiai di farina
300 ml di latte
Sale, pepe, noce moscata
2 ramoscelli di timo e 2 di rosmarino
Sciogliere il burro in una grossa pentola, unire la farina ed imbiondirla. Ricoprire con il latte, aggiungere le erbe e portare a cottura. Assaggiare la besciamella e condirla con sale, pepe e noce moscata. Lasciar cuocere per circa 10 minuti, quindi passare con il passaverdura.

225 g di funghi porcini
2 cucchiai di olio di oliva
50 ml di brandy, 200 ml di vino bianco
150 ml di fondo di verdure
Sale, pepe
Rosolare brevemente i funghi nell'olio di oliva, bagnare con il brandy ed il vino bianco e ricoprire con il brodo di verdure. Lasciar cuocere lentamente finché tutto il liquido sia evaporato, assaggiare e regolare il condimento.
200 g di mascarpone
1 tartufo nero tagliato a fette
4 cucchiai di pangrattato
Per la guarnizione: erba cipollina
Mescolare la besciamella, i funghi, il mascarpone ed il tartufo, assaggiare e regolare il condimento. Unire gli gnocchi e mettere il tutto in una pirofila. Cospargere di pangrattato e cuocere in forno a 180 °C per 15 minuti. Guarnire con erba cipollina.

Sensi

Design: Super Potato | Chef: Martin Heierling
Owners: Martin Heierling, Bellagio Hotel & Casino

3600 Las Vegas Boulevard S | Las Vegas, NV 89109 | Bellagio Hotel & Casino
Phone: +1 702 693 7223
www.bellagio.com
Opening hours: Daily 11 am to 2:30 pm and 5 pm to 10:30 pm
Average price: Lunch $ 18, dinner $ 32
Cuisine: Italian, Asian, seafood classics
Special features: Open, central kitchen

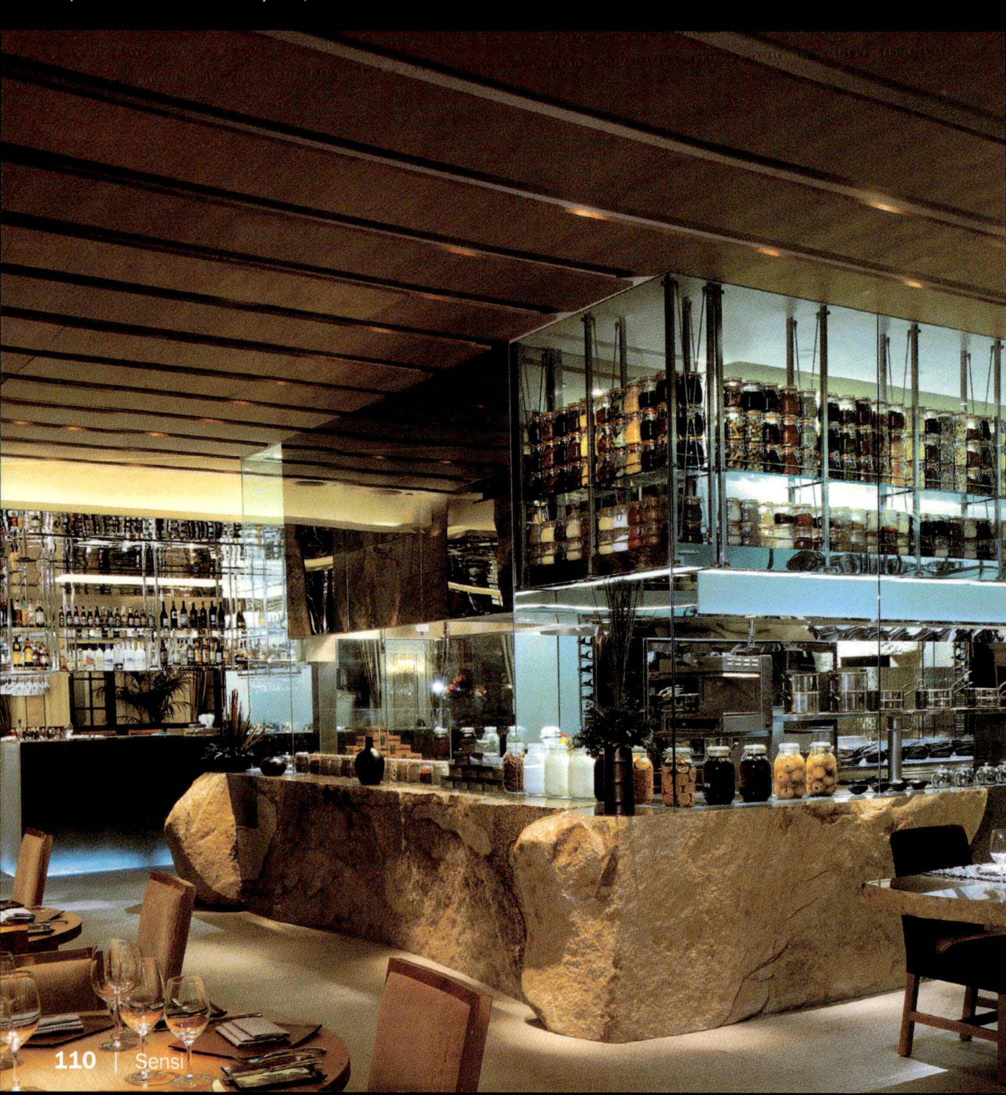

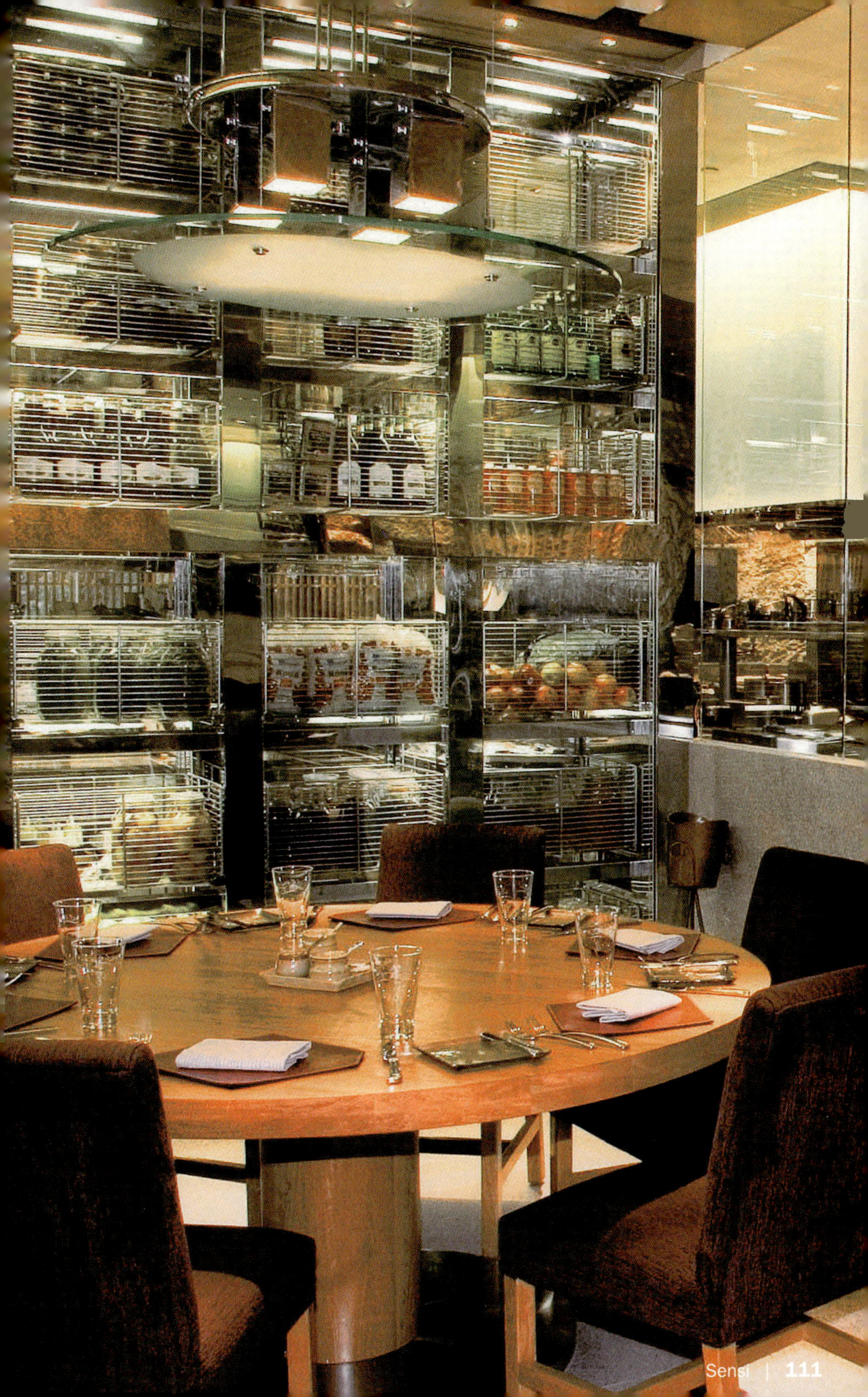

Baby Loup de Mer **with Cippolini Onions**

Junger Seewolf mit Cippolini-Zwiebeln

Jeune loup de mer aux oignons cippolini

Lubina joven con cebollas cippolini

Lupo di mare giovane con cipollini

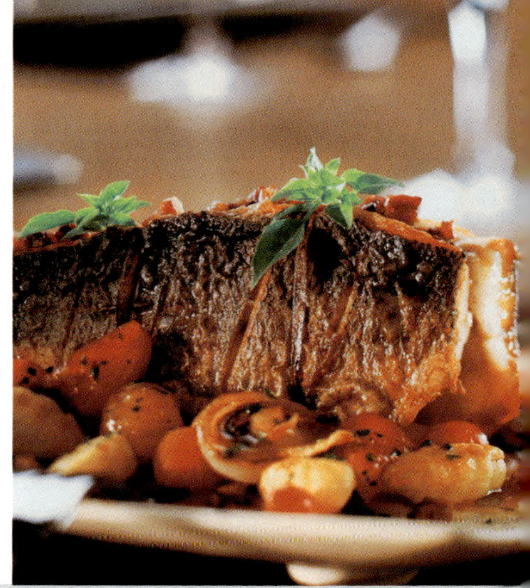

4 whole baby loup de mer, 14 oz each
Salt, pepper
Flour for dusting
4 tbsp olive oil
1 lb cippolini onions, peeled
100 ml olive oil
3 tsp sugar
100 ml balsamic vinegar
4 fennel, cleaned and quartered
2 tbsp olive oil
3 tbsp brown sugar
200 ml white wine
2 bay leaves
2 twigs of thyme
8 yellow and 8 red cherry tomatoes
1 tbsp olive oil
1 tsp rosemary and thyme each, chopped
4 slices pancetta, diced and roasted

Cut the cherry tomatoes in half, mix with olive oil and herbs and dry for one hour at 300 °F in the oven. Sautée onions in olive oil, add sugar and deglaze with vinegar. Take off the stove and marinate for at least 2 hours. Sweat the fennel quarters in oil, caramelize with brown sugar and deglaze with wine. Add herbs, season and braise at 390 °F for 20 minutes. Cut head and fins off the fish, remove the backbone carefully, so the two fillets are still connected. Season, dust with flour and sear in hot oil from both sides. Place the marinated onions with the fish in an ovenproof dish and bake at 390 °F for 10 minutes. Arrange the fennel quarters around the fish and decorate with dried tomatoes and pancetta cubes.

4 Stück junger Seewolf, ganz, je 400 g
Salz, Pfeffer
Mehl zum Bestäuben
4 EL Olivenöl
450 g geschälte Cippolini-Zwiebeln
100 ml Olivenöl
3 TL Zucker
100 ml Balsamico-Essig
4 geputzte und geviertelte Fenchelknollen
2 EL Olivenöl
3 EL brauner Zucker
200 ml Weißwein
2 Lorbeerblätter
2 Thymianzweige
8 gelbe und 8 rote Kirschtomaten
1 EL Olivenöl
Je 1 TL gehackter Rosmarin und Thymian
4 Scheiben gewürfeltes und geröstetes Pancetta

Die Kirschtomaten halbieren, mit Olivenöl und den Kräutern vermengen und 1 Stunde lang bei 150 °C im Ofen trocknen lassen. Zwiebeln in Olivenöl anbraten, Zucker hinzugeben und mit Essig ablöschen. Vom Herd nehmen und mindestens 2 Stunden lang durchziehen lassen. Fenchel in Öl anschwitzen, mit braunem Zucker karamellisieren lassen und mit Wein ablöschen. Kräuter hinzufügen, abschmecken und bei 200 °C 20 Minuten lang schmoren. Den Fisch von Kopf und Flossen befreien. Vorsichtig entgräten, so dass die beiden Filets noch miteinander verbunden sind. Würzen, in Mehl wenden und in heißem Öl von beiden Seiten scharf anbraten. Den Fisch zusammen mit den marinierten Zwiebeln in ein feuerfestes Gefäß geben und im Backofen 10 Minuten lang bei 200°C garen. Die Fenchelviertel um den Fisch herum anrichten und mit getrockneten Tomaten und Pancettawürfeln garnieren.

4 jeunes loups de mer de 400 g
Sel, poivre
Farine pour saupoudrer
4 c. à soupe d'huile d'olive
450 g d'oignons cippolini épluchés
100 ml d'huile d'olive
3 c. à café de sucre
100 ml de vinaigre balsamique
4 bulbes de fenouil lavés et coupés en quatre
2 c. à soupe d'huile d'olive
3 c. à soupe de sucre brun
200 ml de vin blanc
2 feuilles de laurier
2 branches de thym
8 tomates cerises jaunes et 8 rouges
1 c. à soupe d'huile d'olive
1 c. à café de romarin haché et 1 de thym haché
4 tranches de pancetta grillées et coupées en dés

Couper les tomates cerises en deux, ajouter l'huile d'olive et les herbes et les laisser sécher au four pendant 1 heure à 150 °C. Faire revenir les oignons dans l'huile d'olive, ajouter le sucre et mouiller de vinaigre. Ôter du feu et laisser mariner pendant au moins 2 heures. Faire blondir le fenouil dans l'huile, puis le caraméliser avec du sucre brun et le mouiller de vin. Ajouter les herbes, assaisonner et le cuire à l'étuvée pendant 20 minutes à 200 °C. Ôter la tête et les nageoires du poisson. Enlever prudemment les arêtes, de sortes que les deux filets restent joints. Les assaisonner et les rouler dans la farine, puis bien les saisir dans l'huile chaude de chaque côté. Disposer le poisson et les oignons marinés dans un plat résistant à la chaleur et laisser cuire au four pendant 10 minutes à 200 °C. Disposer les quartiers de fenouil autour du poisson et garnir de tomates séchées et de dés de pancetta.

4 lubinas jóvenes enteras de 400 g cada una
Sal, pimienta
Harina para espolvorear
4 cucharadas de aceite de oliva
450 g de cebollas cippolini peladas
100 ml de aceite de oliva
3 cucharaditas de azúcar
100 ml de vinagre balsámico
4 bulbos de hinojo limpios y en cuartos
2 cucharadas de aceite de oliva
3 cucharadas de azúcar moreno
200 ml de vino blanco
2 hojas de laurel
2 ramitas de tomillo
8 tomates cereza amarillos y 8 rojos
1 cucharada de aceite de oliva
1 cucharadita de romero y de tomillo picados
4 lonchas de panceta en dados y asadas

Corte los tomates en mitades, mézclelos con el aceite de oliva y las hierbas y deje que se sequen durante 1 hora a 150 °C en el horno. Rehogue las cebollas en aceite de oliva, añada el azúcar y vierta dentro el vinagre. Quite las cebollas del fuego y déjelas marinar durante 2 horas como mínimo. Rehogue el hinojo en el aceite, caramelícelo con el azúcar moreno y añada el vino. Añada las hierbas, sazone y déjelo estofar a fuego lento durante 20 minutos a 200 °C. Quite la cabeza y las aletas al pescado. Quite con cuidado la espina de modo que los dos filetes queden unidos. Sazónelos, rebócelos en harina y fríalos a fuego fuerte en aceite caliente. Ponga el pescado y las cebollas marinadas en un recipiente resistente al fuego y ase los ingredientes en el horno durante 10 minutos a 200 °C. Reparta los cuartos de hinojo alrededor del pescado y decore con los tomates secos y los dados de panceta.

4 lupi di mare giovani di 400 g ciascuno
Sale, pepe
Farina per spolverare
4 cucchiai di olio di oliva
450 g di cipollini sbucciati
100 ml di olio di oliva
3 cucchiaini di zucchero
100 ml di aceto balsamico
4 bulbi di finocchio puliti e tagliati in quattro
2 cucchiai di olio di oliva
3 cucchiai di zucchero bruno
200 ml di vino bianco
2 foglie di alloro
2 ramoscelli di timo
8 pomodorini gialli e 8 pomodorini rossi
1 cucchiaio di olio di oliva
1 cucchiaino di rosmarino ed 1 cucchiaino di timo tritati
4 fette di pancetta tagliata a dadini e abbrustolita

Tagliare a metà i pomodorini, unire l'olio di oliva e le erbe e lasciar asciugare in forno per 1 ora a 150 °C. Imbiondire la cipolla nell'olio di oliva, aggiungere lo zucchero e bagnarla con l'aceto. Toglierla dal fuoco e lasciarla macerare per almeno 2 ore. Rosolare il finocchio nell'olio, caramellarlo con lo zucchero bruno e bagnarlo con il vino. Unire le erbe, regolare il condimento e cuocere a 200 °C per 20 minuti. Privare il pesce della testa e delle pinne e diliscarlo con cura, in modo che i filetti restino attaccati. Condirlo, infarinarlo, e rosolarlo a fuoco vivo nell'olio caldo da entrambi i lati. Disporre il pesce in una pirofila con le cipolle marinate e cuocerlo in forno a 200 °C per 10 minuti. Disporre i quarti di finocchio intorno al pesce e guarnire con i pomodori secchi e i dadini di pancetta.

Shibuya

Design: Yabu Pushelberg | Chef: Stephane Chevet
Owner: MGM Grand Hotel & Casino

3799 Las Vegas Boulevard S | Las Vegas, NV 89109 | MGM Grand Hotel & Casino
Phone: +1 702 891 3001
www.mgmgrand.com
Opening hours: Sun–Thu 5:30 pm to 10:30 pm, Fri–Sat 5:30 pm to 11 pm
Average price: Sushi $ 12, a la carte $ 28, teppan $ 96
Cuisine: Modern Japanese
Special features: Widest sake selection this side of the Pacific

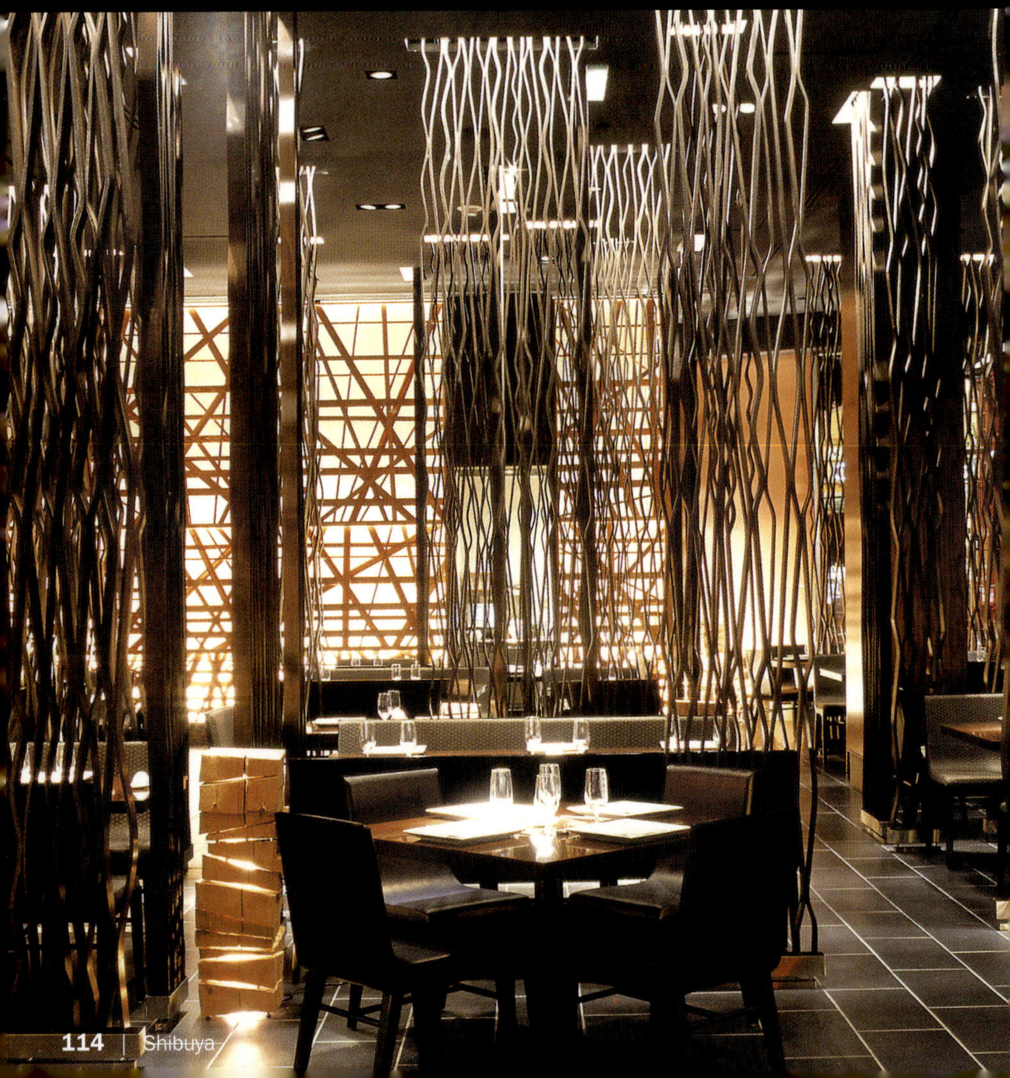

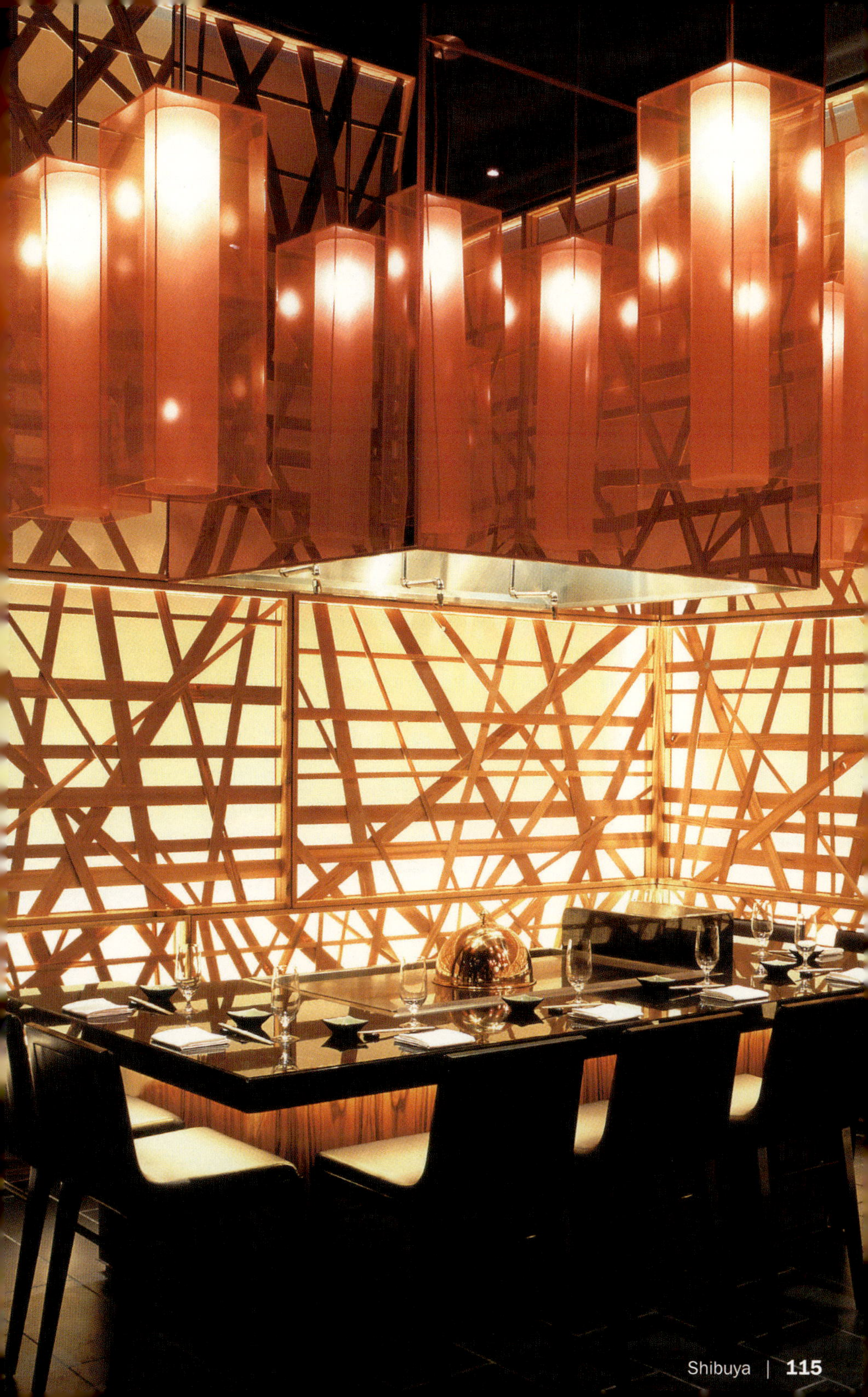

Tuna Tartar

Tunfischtartar
Tartare de thon
Tartar de atún
Tonno alla tartara

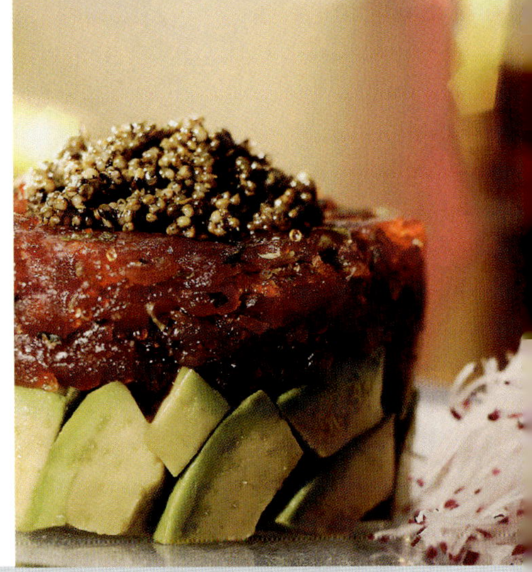

12 oz tuna, ground
2 tbsp spring onions, finely chopped
2 tbsp chives, finely chopped
1 tsp soy sauce
1 tsp mirin (sweet rice wine)
1 tsp lemon juice
1 tsp tarragon oil
Salt, pepper

2 avocados, diced
2 tsp lemon juice
Salt

Decoration:
4 tsp tobiko (flying fish roe)
4 tbsp red radish, in julienne
Fried tofu skins

Combine tuna, spring onions and chives in a small bowl and season with spices, salt and pepper. Marinate the avocado cubes with lemon juice and salt. Divide the marinated avocados onto four metal rings, repeat the same procedure with the tuna tartar. Place one ring on each plate, remove the ring carefully and top the tartar with tobiko. Garnish with red radish and fried tofu skins.

340 g gehackter Tunfisch
2 EL fein gehackte Frühlingszwiebeln
2 EL fein gehackter Schnittlauch
1 TL Sojasoße
1 TL Mirin (süßer Reiswein)
1 TL Zitronensaft
1 TL Estragonöl
Salz, Pfeffer

2 gewürfelte Avocados
2 TL Zitronensaft
Salz

Für die Dekoration:
4 TL Tobiko (Rogen des Fliegenfisches)
4 EL in feine Streifen geschnittene Radieschen
Gebratene Tofuhäute

Tunfisch, Frühlingszwiebeln und Schnittlauch in einer kleinen Schüssel vermengen und mit den Gewürzen, Salz und Pfeffer abschmecken. Die Avocadowürfel mit Zitronensaft und Salz marinieren. Die marinierten Avocados in vier Metallringe geben und ebenso mit dem Tunfischtartar verfahren. Jeden Ring auf einen Teller geben, den Ring vorsichtig abheben und etwas Tobiko oben auf das Tartar geben. Mit Radieschen und gebratenen Tofuhäuten garnieren.

340 g de thon haché
2 c. à soupe d'oignons de printemps émincés
2 c. à soupe de ciboulette finement hachée
1 c. à café de sauce de soja
1 c. à café de mirin (vin de riz doux)
1 c. à café de jus de citron
1 c. à café d'huile d'estragon
Sel, poivre

2 avocats coupés en dés
2 c. à café de jus de citron
Sel

Pour la garniture :
4 c. à café de tobiko (œufs de poisson volant)
4 c. à soupe de radis coupés en julienne
Poches de tofu cuites

Mélanger le thon, les oignons de printemps et la ciboulette dans un petit plat creux, puis assaisonner avec les épices, le sel et le poivre. Laisser mariner les dés d'avocat dans le jus de citron et le sel. Disposer les avocats marinés dans des anneaux en métal et procéder de la même manière avec le tartare de thon. Poser chaque anneau sur une assiette, l'ôter précautionneusement, et ajouter un peu de tobiko sur le tartare. Garnir de radis et de poches de tofu.

340 g de atún picado
2 cucharadas de cebolletas finamente picadas
2 cucharadas de cebollinos finamente picados
1 cucharadita de salsa de soja
1 cucharadita de mirin (vino de arroz dulce)
1 cucharadita de zumo de limón
1 cucharadita de estragón
Sal, pimienta

2 aguacates en dados
2 cucharaditas de zumo de limón
Sal

Para decorar:
4 cucharaditas de tobiko (huevas de pez volador)
4 cucharadas de rabanitos en juliana
Pieles de tofu fritas

Ponga el atún, las cebolletas y el cebollino en un cuenco pequeño y sazone con las especias, la sal y la pimienta. Marine los dados de aguacate con el zumo de limón y la sal. Reparta el aguacate marinado en cuatro anillos metálicos, proceda del mismo modo con el tartar de atún. Coloque cada anillo en un plato, retire cuidadosamente el anillo y coloque encima del tartar un poco de tobiko. Decore con rabanitos y las pieles fritas de tofu.

340 g di tonno tritato
2 cucchiai di cipollotti finemente tritati
2 cucchiai di erba cipollina finemente tritata
1 cucchiaino di salsa di soia
1 cucchiaino di mirin (vino di riso dolce)
1 cucchiaino di succo di limone
1 cucchiaino di olio di dragoncello
Sale, pepe

2 avocado tagliati a dadini
2 cucchiaini di succo di limone
Sale

Per la guarnizione:
4 cucchiaini di tobiko (uova di pesce volante)
4 cucchiai di ravanelli tagliati a julienne
Fogli di tofu arrostiti

Mettere il tonno, i cipollotti e l'erba cipollina in una ciotola e condire con gli aromi, sale e pepe. Marinare i dadini di avocado in succo di limone e sale e disporli quindi in quattro anelli di metallo. Ripetere l'operazione con il tonno. Disporre gli anelli nei piatti, quindi toglierli delicatamente e cospargere il tonno con un po' di tobiko. Guarnire con i ravanelli ed i fogli di tofu arrostiti.

Simon kitchen & bar

Design: Yabu Pushelberg | Chef & Owner: Kerry Simon

4455 Paradise Road | Las Vegas, NV 89109 | Hard Rock Hotel & Casino
Phone: +1 702 693 4440
www.kerrysimon.com
Opening hours: Mon–Fri 11 am to 2 pm, Sun–Thu 6 pm to 10:30 pm, Fri–Sat 6 pm to 11:30 pm
Average price: $ 60
Cuisine: American eclectic comfort food

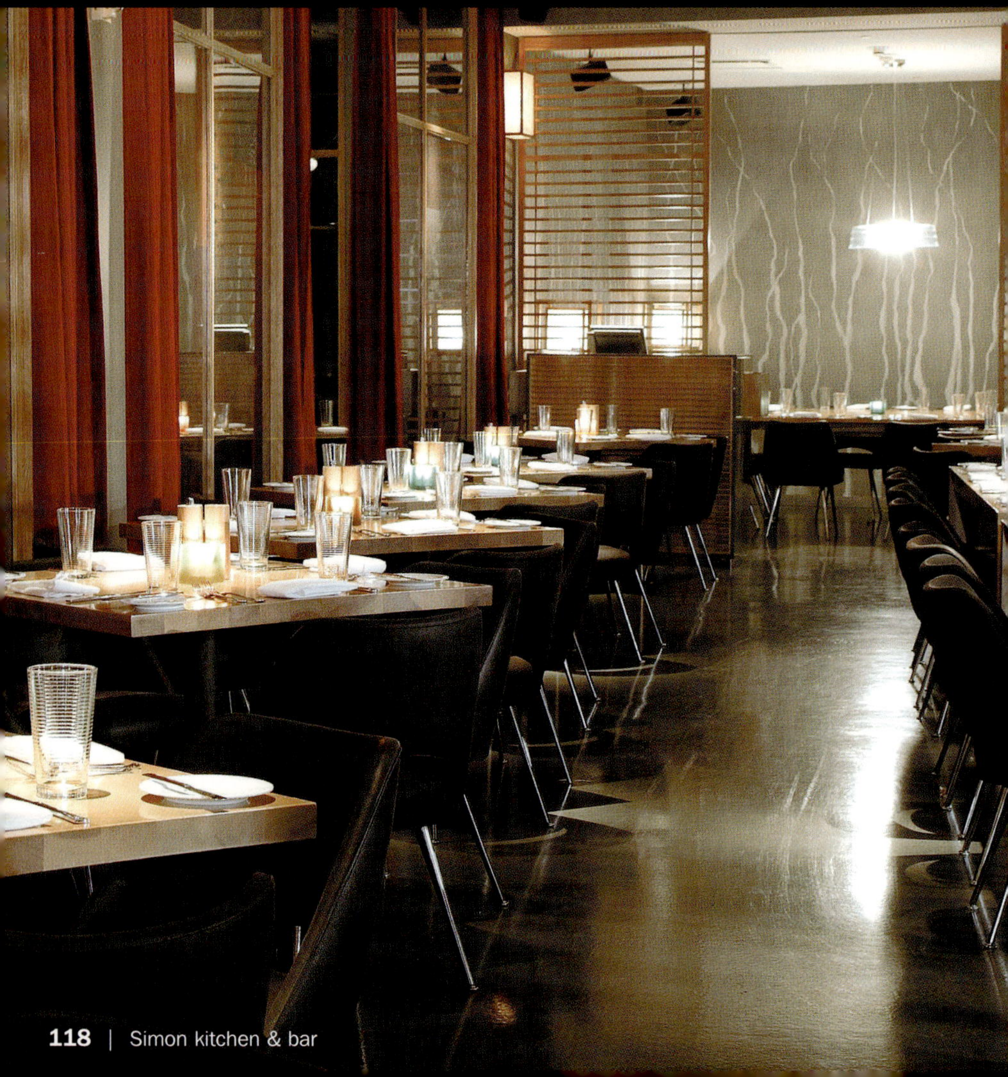

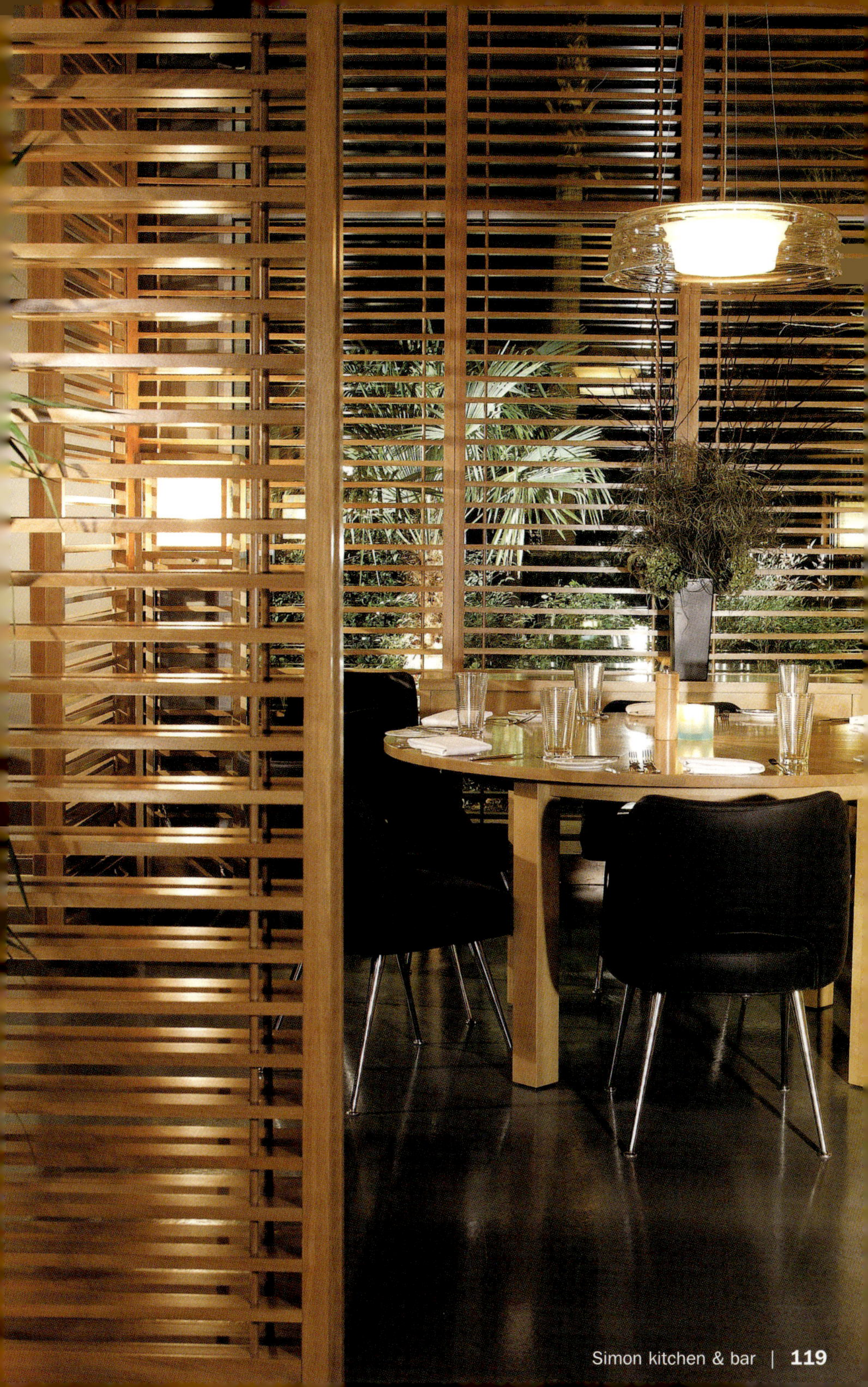

Sushi Roku

Design: Dodd Mitchell | Chef: Yoghi Nakazawa
Owner: Innovative Dining Group

3500 Las Vegas Boulevard S | Las Vegas, NV 89109 | The Forum Shops of Caesars
Phone: +1 702 733 7373
www.sushiroku.com
Opening hours: Sun–Thu noon to 10:30 pm, Fri–Sat noon to midnight
Average price: $ 27
Cuisine: Sushi, Asian fusion
Special features: View of the strip, private dining room

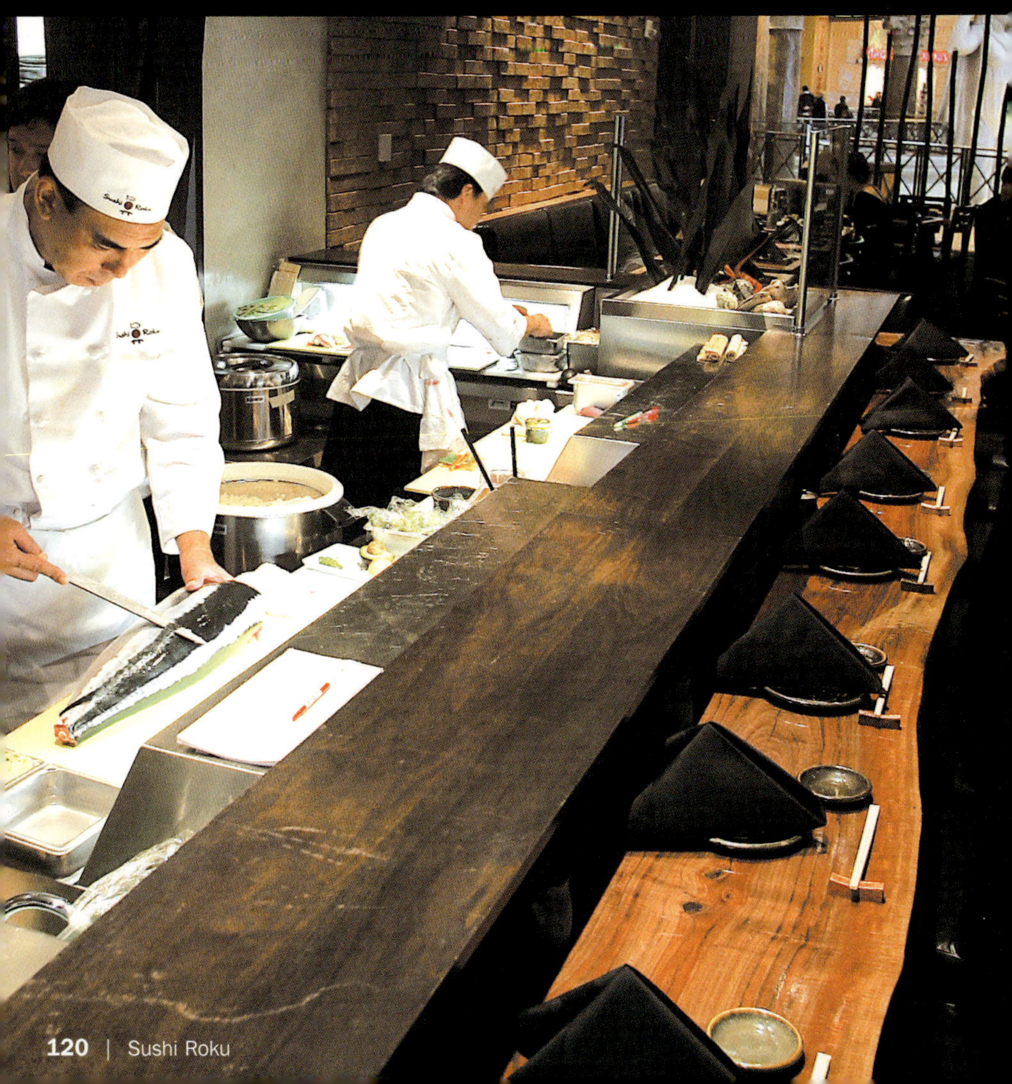

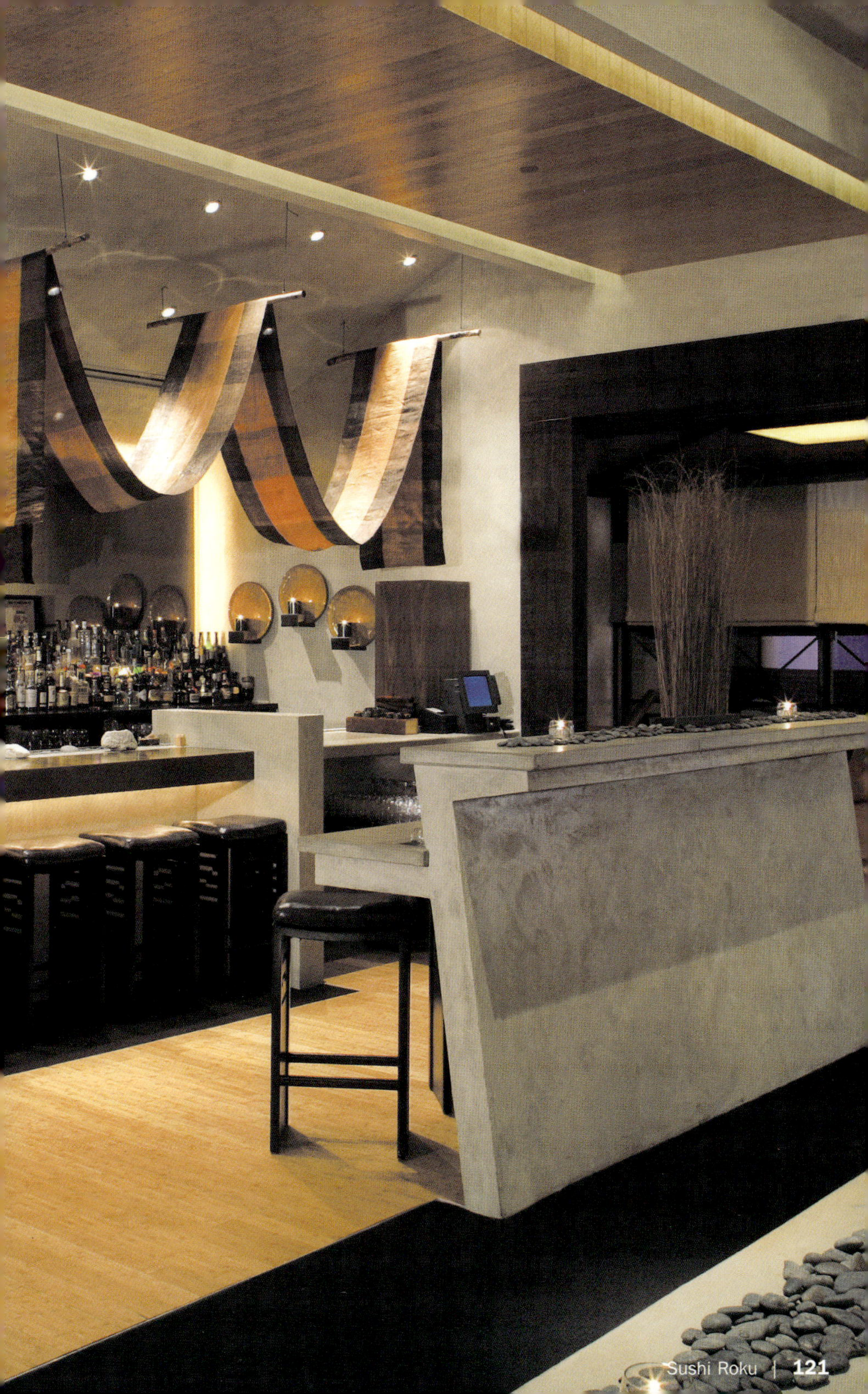

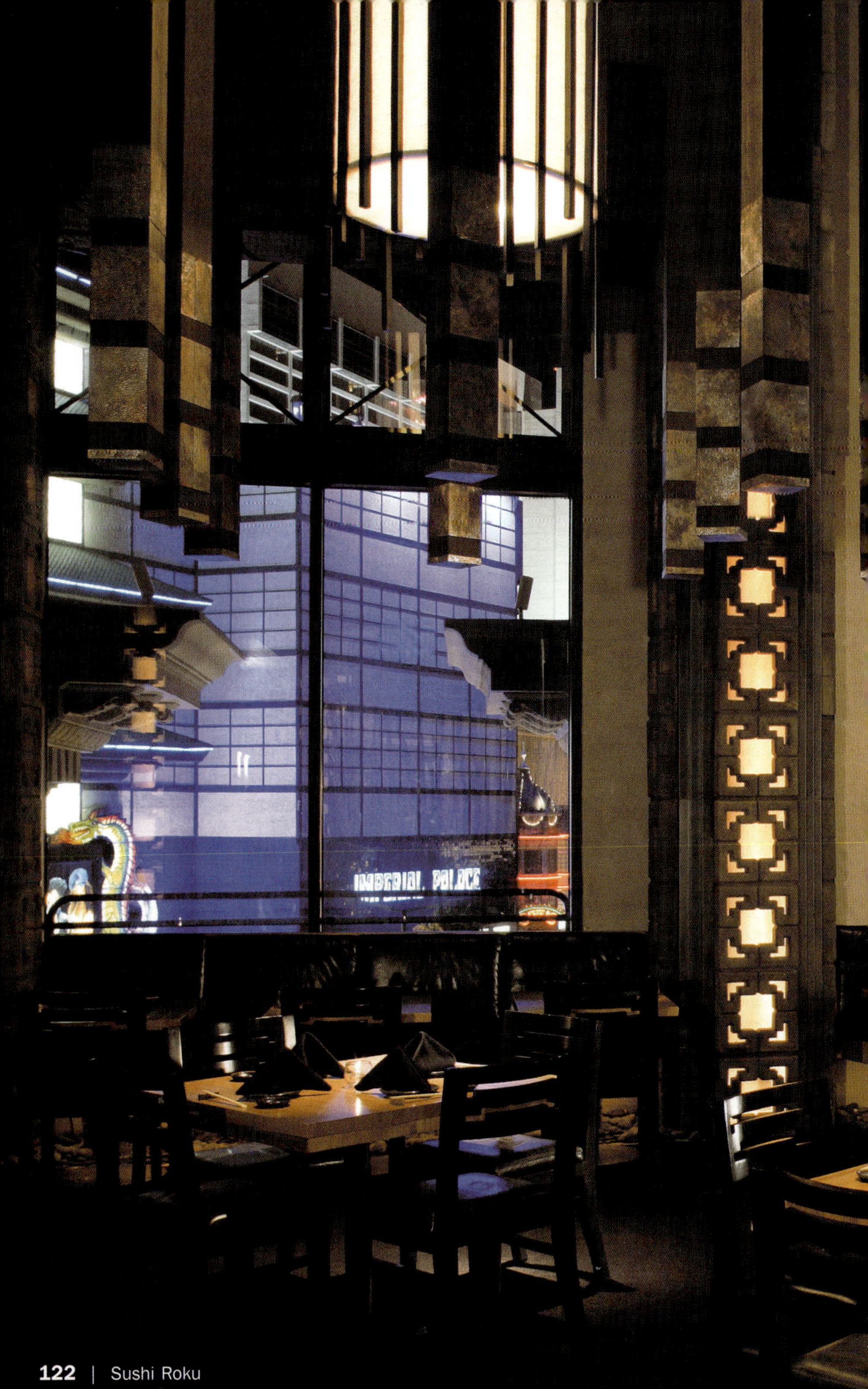

IMPERIAL PALACE

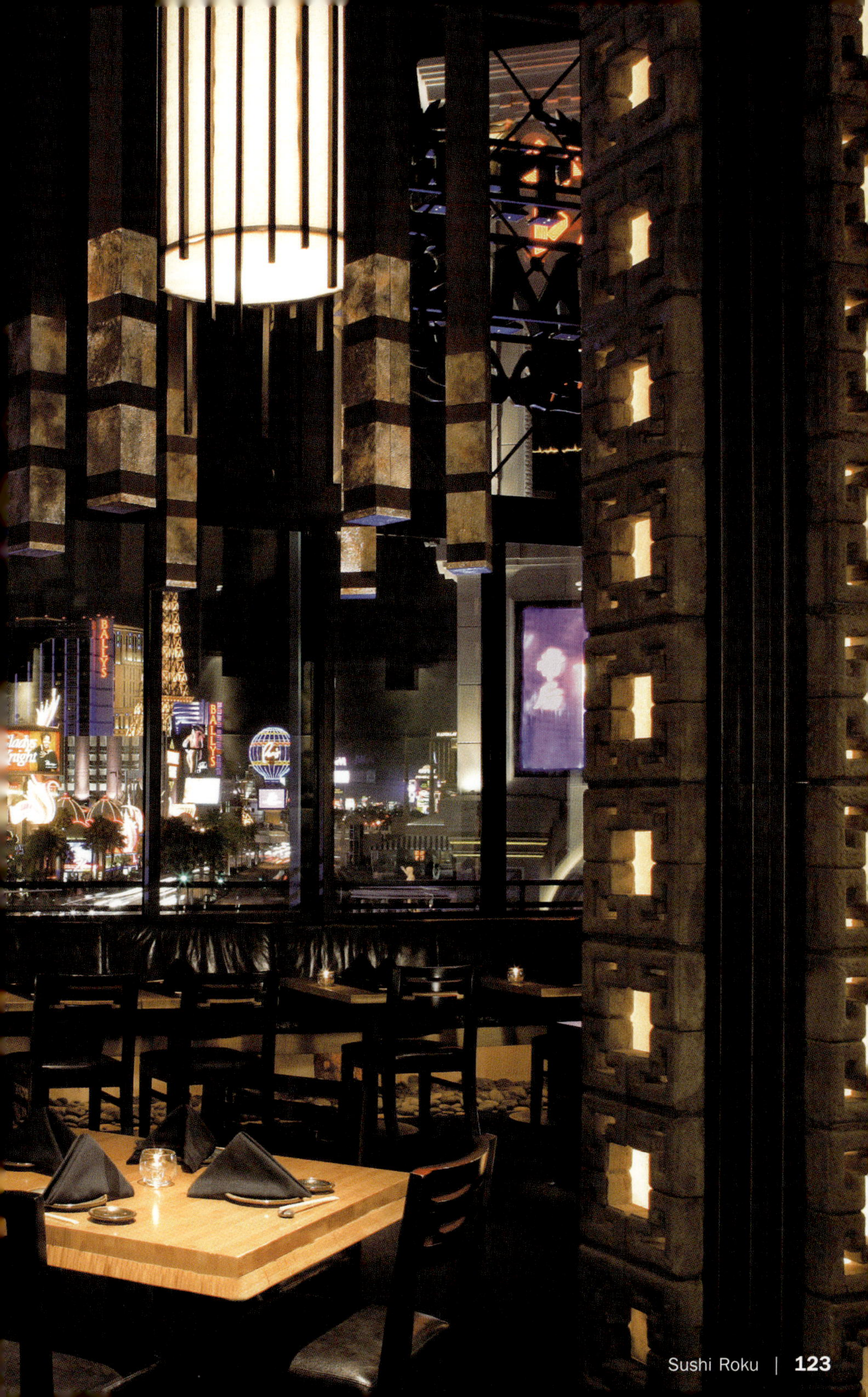

Braised Chilean Sea Bass

Geschmorter chilenischer Wolfsbarsch

Mérou du Chili braisé

Lubina chilena estofada

Spigola cilena in stufato

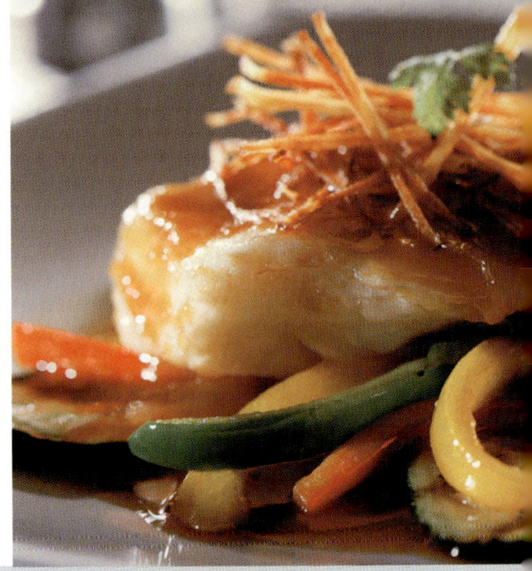

4 Chilean sea bass fillets, 6 oz each
200 ml sake
200 ml mirin (sweet rice wine)
Salt, pepper
4 slices miso, 2 oz each
1 red, green and yellow bell pepper, sliced
2 large onions, sliced
2 zucchini, sliced
2 tbsp vegetable oil
4 tbsp soy sauce
2 tbsp butter
Fried carrot juliennes and thai basil for decoration

Place the fish in a pot, season and cover with sake and mirin. Bring to a boil, then place in a preheated 320 °F oven and stew for 8 minutes. In the meantime sautée the vegetables in oil until tender. Season with salt and pepper. When the fish is done, remove from the pot, place one slice of miso on each fish and brown under a grill. Stir the soy sauce and butter into the fish sauce and season if necessary. Divide the vegetables onto four plates, place 1 fish fillet on each plate, drizzle with sauce and garnish with fried carrot juliennes and thai basil.

4 chilenische Wolfsbarsch-Filets, je 170 g
200 ml Sake
200 ml Mirin (süßer Reiswein)
Salz, Pfeffer
4 Scheiben Miso, je 60 g
Je 1 in Streifen geschnittene rote, grüne und gelbe Paprika
2 große, in Ringe geschnittene Zwiebeln
2 in Scheiben geschnittene Zucchini
2 EL Pflanzenöl
4 EL Sojasoße
2 EL Butter
Gebratene feine Karottenstreifen und Thai-Basilikum zur Dekoration

Den Fisch in einen Bräter geben, würzen und mit Sake und Mirin bedecken. Zum Kochen bringen und dann 8 Minuten im auf 160 °C vorgeheizten Backofen schmoren lassen. In der Zwischenzeit das Gemüse in Öl kurz anbraten, bis es weich ist. Mit Salz und Pfeffer würzen. Wenn der Fisch gar ist, aus dem Bräter nehmen, eine Scheibe Miso auf jeden Fisch legen und unter dem Grill bräunen. Sojasoße und Butter in die Fischsoße einrühren und bei Bedarf würzen. Das Gemüse auf vier Teller verteilen, 1 Fischfilet auf jeden Teller geben, mit der Soße beträufeln und mit den gebratenen feinen Karottenstiften und dem Thai-Basilikum garnieren.

4 filets de mérou du Chili de 170 g
200 ml de saké
200 ml de mirin (vin de riz doux)
Sel, poivre
4 tranches de miso de 60 g
1 poivron rouge, 1 vert et 1 jaune coupés en julienne
2 gros oignons coupés en rondelles
2 courgettes coupées en rondelles
2 c. à soupe d'huile végétale
4 c. à soupe de sauce de soja
2 c. à soupe de beurre
Julienne de carottes cuites et basilic thaï pour la garniture

Placer le poisson dans une cocotte, assaisonner et couvrir de saké et de mirin. Faire cuire, puis laisser braiser au four préchauffé 8 minutes à 160 °C. Entre-temps, faire brièvement revenir les légumes dans l'huile de sorte qu'ils ramollissent. Saler et poivrer. Ôter le poisson de la cocotte quand il est cuit, poser une tranche de miso sur chaque poisson et faire cuire au gril. Mélanger la sauce de soja et le beurre avec la sauce de poisson et relever l'assaisonnement si nécessaire. Répartir les légumes sur quatre assiettes, disposer un filet de poisson sur chacune, arroser de sauce et garnir avec la julienne de carottes et le basilic thaï.

4 filetes de lubina chilena de 170 g cada uno
200 ml de sake
200 ml de mirin (vino de arroz dulce)
Sal, pimienta
4 lonchas de miso de 60 g cada una
1 pimiento rojo, verde y amarillo cortados en tiras
2 cebollas cortadas en anillos
2 calabacines cortados en rodajas
2 cucharadas de aceite vegetal
4 cucharadas de salsa de soja
2 cucharadas de mantequilla
Finas tiras de zanahoria fritas y albahaca thai para decorar

Coloque el pescado en una sartén profunda, condiméntelo y cúbralo con sake y mirin. Lleve a ebullición y deje que se siga estofando en un horno precalentado durante 8 minutos a 160 °C. Mientras, saltee brevemente la verdura en aceite hasta que esté tierna. Salpimiente. Cuando el pescado esté hecho sáquelo de la sartén, ponga una loncha de miso sobre cada pescado y dórelos debajo de la parrilla. Disuelva la salsa de soja y la mantequilla en el caldo de pescado y condimente si fuera necesario. Reparta la verdura entre cuatro platos, coloque 1 filete de pescado en cada plato, vierta por encima la salsa y decore con las tiras fritas de zanahoria y la albahaca thai.

4 filetti di spigola cilena di 170 g ciascuno
200 ml di sake
200 ml di mirin (vino di riso dolce)
Sale, pepe
4 fette di miso di 60 g ciascuna
1 peperone rosso, 1 peperone verde ed 1 peperone giallo tagliati a listarelle
2 grosse cipolle tagliate ad anelli
2 zucchini tagliati a fettine
2 cucchiai di olio vegetale
4 cucchiai di salsa di soia
2 cucchiai di burro
Per la guarnizione: julienne di carota arrostite e basilico tailandese

Mettere il pesce in una teglia, condirlo e ricoprirlo con il sake e il mirin. Portare a cottura, quindi farlo cuocere per 8 minuti nel forno già caldo a 160 °C. Nel frattempo, rosolare brevemente le verdure nell'olio finché siano tenere, salare e pepare. Quando sarà cotto, estrarre il pesce dalla teglia, disporre una fetta di miso su ogni filetto e passarlo sotto il grill finché sarà dorato. Unire la salsa di soia ed il burro al sugo del pesce e, se necessario, condire. Ripartire le verdure in quattro piatti, disporre 1 filetto di pesce su ogni piatto, pillottare con la salsa e guarnire con julienne di carota arrostite e basilico tailandese.

Tao

Design: Thomas Schoos, Studio Gaia | Chef: Sam Hazen
Owners: Marc Packer, Rich Wolf

3377 Las Vegas Boulevard S | Las Vegas, NV 89109 | Venetian Resort Hotel Casino
Phone: +1 702 388 8383
www.taolasvegas.com
Opening hours: Mon–Tue 11 am to midnight, Wed–Fri 11 am to 1 am
Sat 5 pm to 1 am, Sun 5 pm to midnight
Average price: $ 20
Cuisine: Pan-Asian
Special features: Restaurant and nightclub

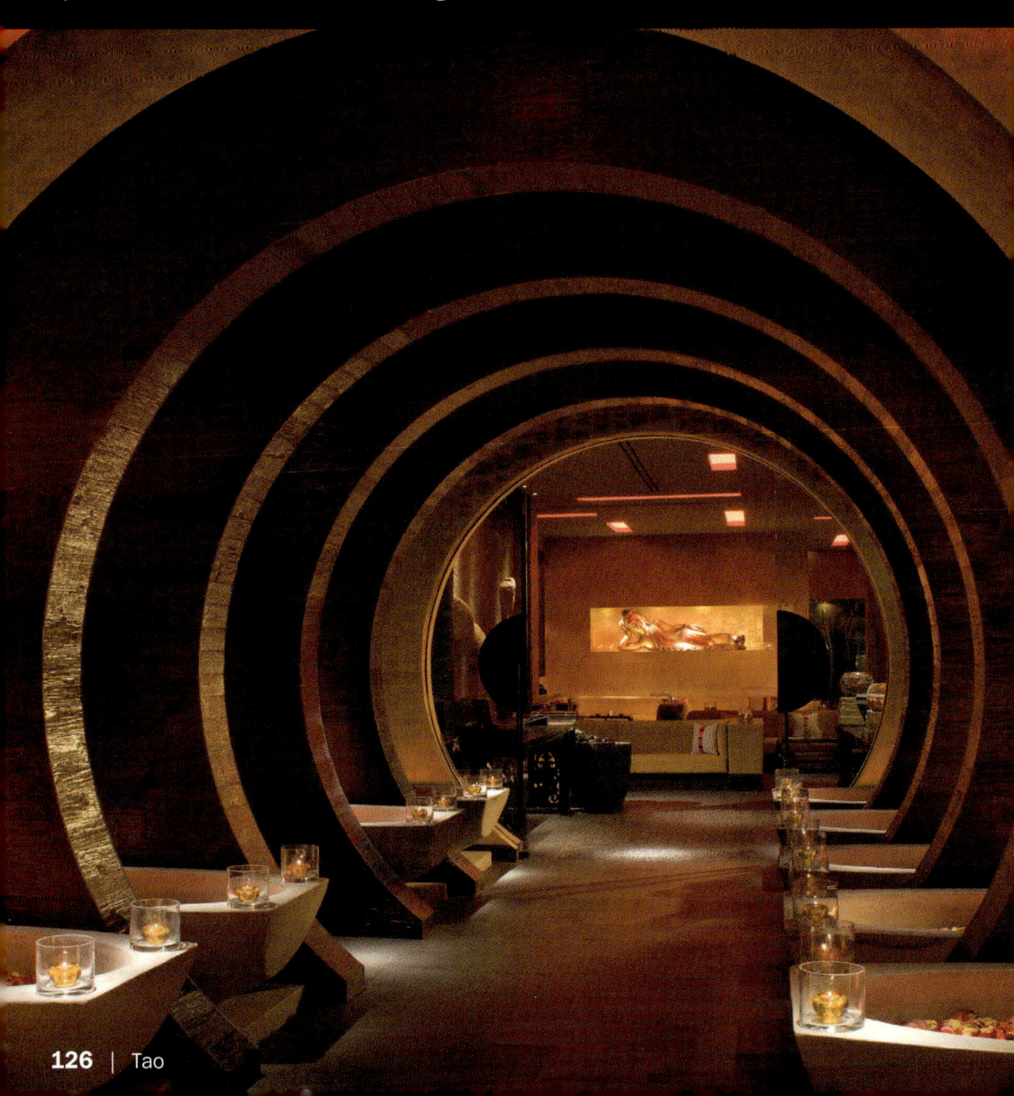

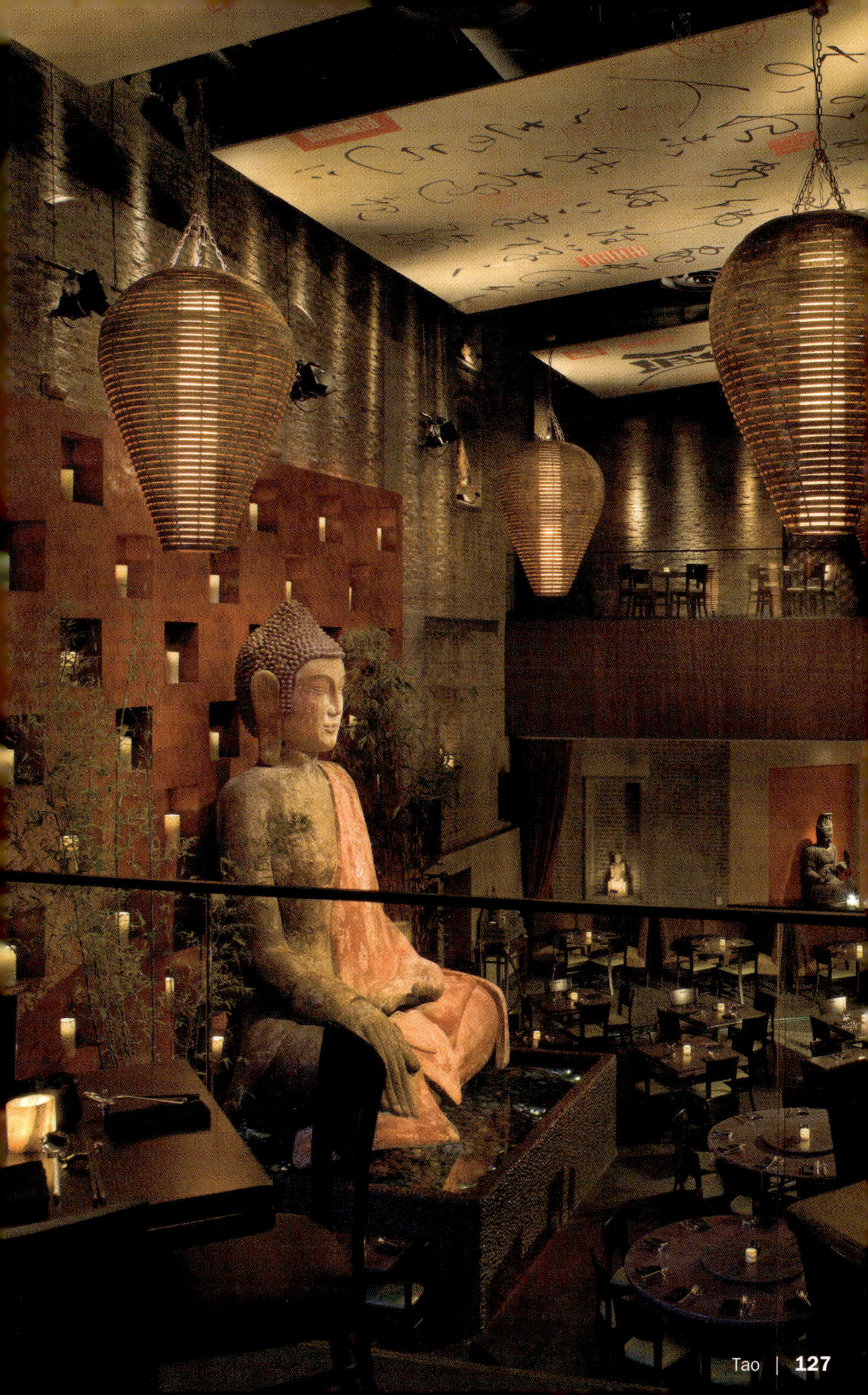

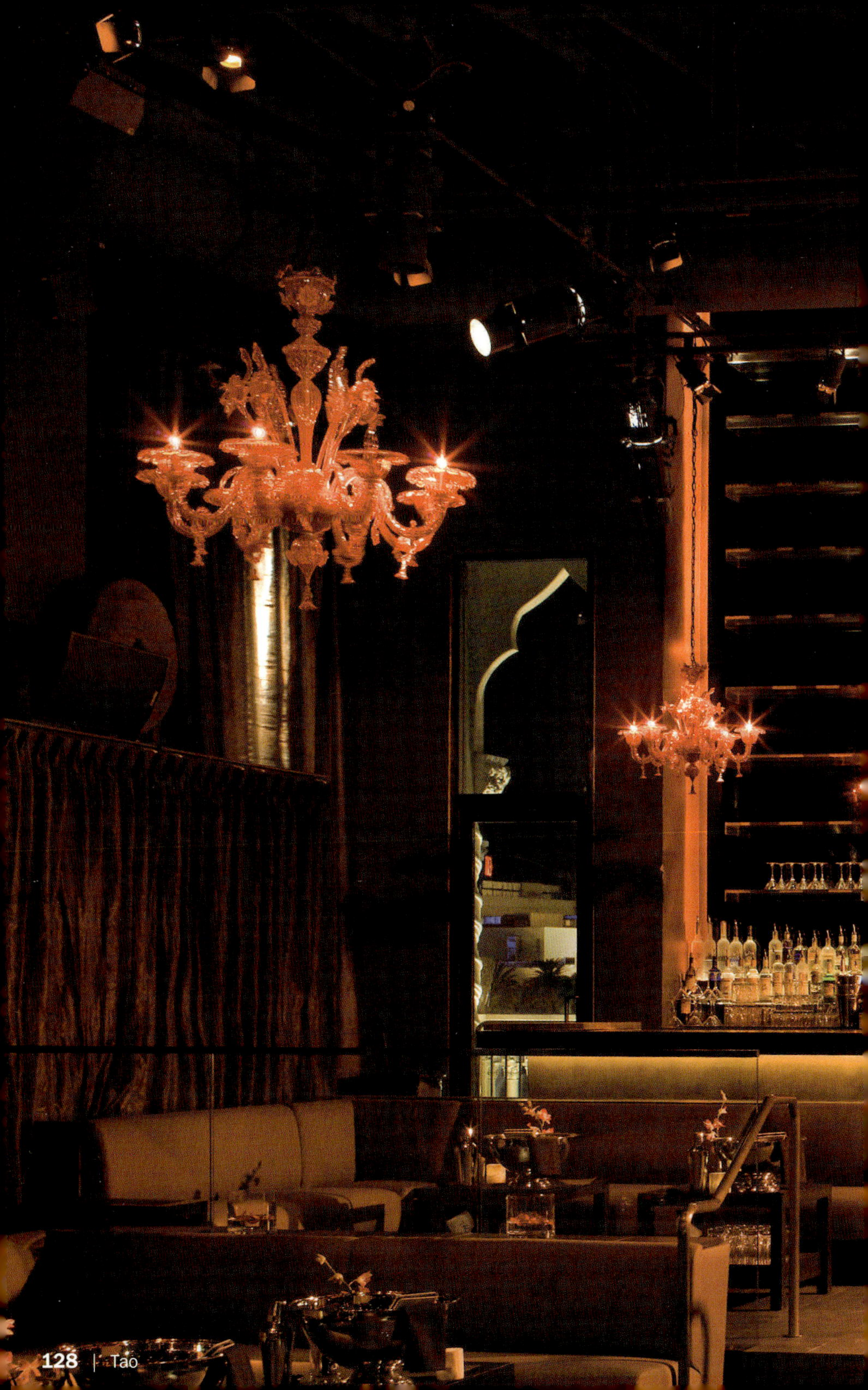

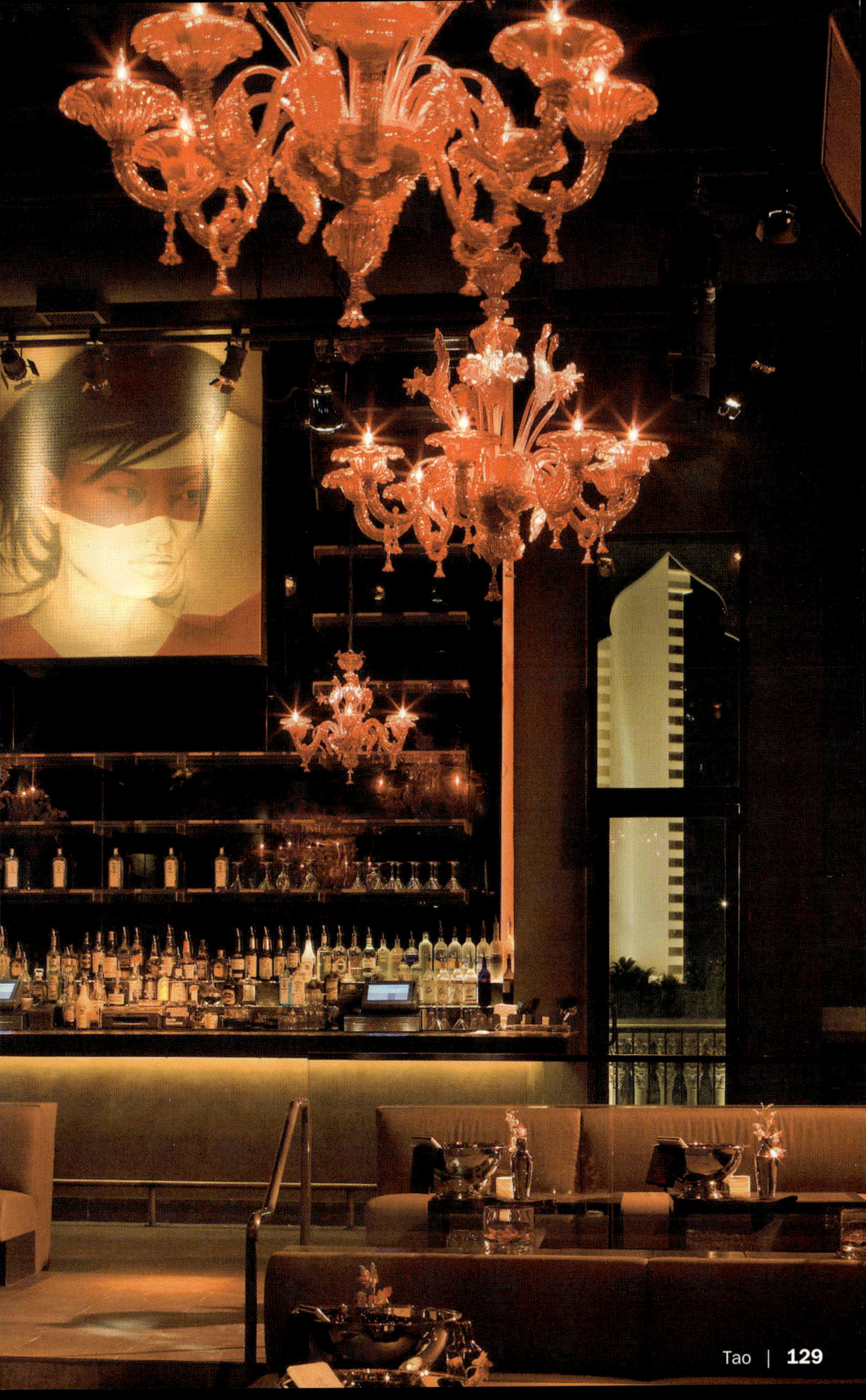

Wolfgang Puck Bar & Grill

Design: tonychi&associates | Chef: Marc Djozjia, David Robins
Owner: Wolfgang Puck

3799 Las Vegas Boulevard S | Las Vegas, NV 89109 | MGM Grand Hotel & Casino
Phone: +1 702 891 3000
www.wolfgangpuck.com
Opening hours: Mon–Thu 11:30 am to 10:30 pm, Fri–Sat 11:30 am to 11:30 pm
Average prize: $ 24
Cuisine: Contemporary bar and grill
Special features: Homemade desserts

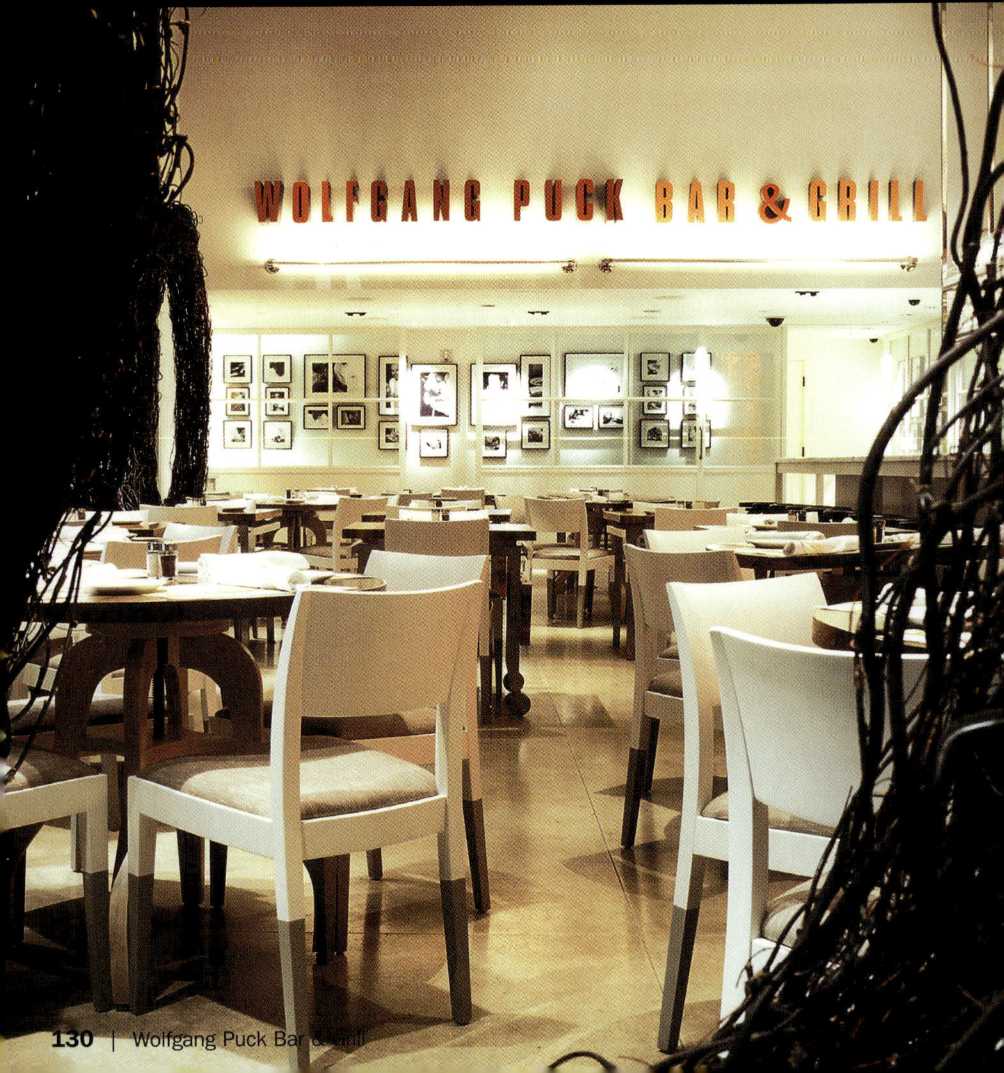

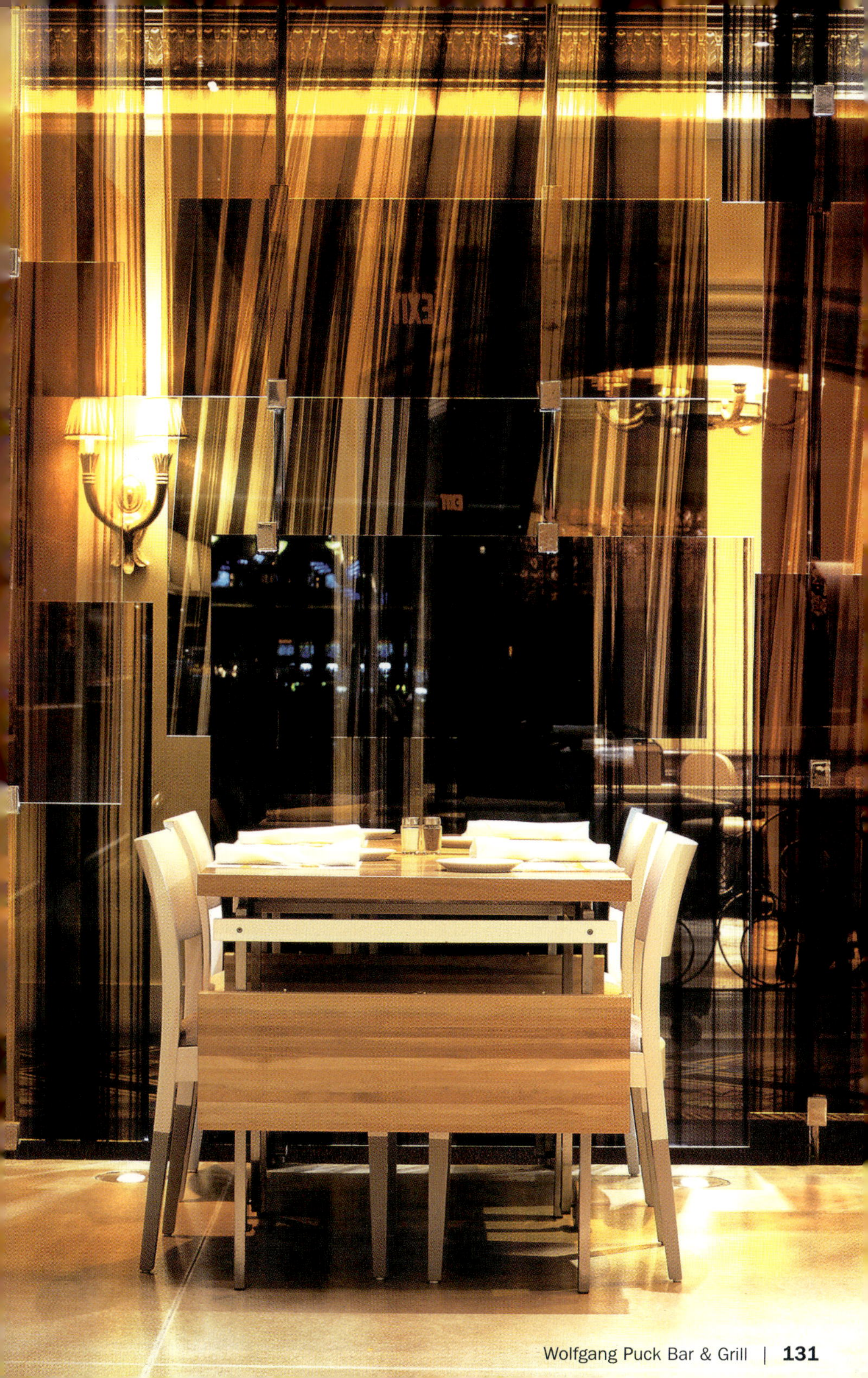

Focaccia

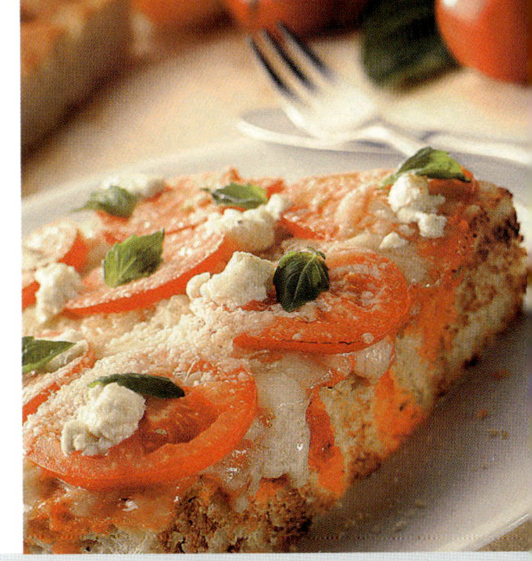

1 lb flour
1 tsp salt
1 shallot, diced
1 tsp rosemary, chopped
2 oz fresh yeast
250 ml warm water
2 tbsp olive oil
2 tbsp soft butter
Combine flour, salt, shallot and rosemary in a large bowl. Dissolve yeast in warm water and stir in the flour mixture. Knead for 5 minutes, then add olive oil and butter. Knead for another 5 minutes and let the dough rest for 30 minutes.

2 cans crushed tomatoes
2 cloves of garlic, chopped

2 tbsp tomato paste
2 tbsp parsley, chopped
2 tbsp basil, chopped
Sugar, salt and pepper
Combine all ingredients and season.
4 tomatoes, sliced
8 oz mozzarella cheese
1 bunch of basil
Place the dough on a round cake pan and let it rise for another 30 minutes. Drizzle with olive oil and salt and bake at 425 °F for 12 minutes. Spoon the tomato sauce evenly over the dough, top with tomato slices and mozzarella and bake at 400 °F until the cheese has melted and the bread is crisp. Garnish with basil juliennes.

450 g Mehl
1 TL Salz
1 gewürfelte Schalotte
1 TL gehackter Rosmarin
55 g frische Hefe
250 ml warmes Wasser
2 EL Olivenöl
2 EL weiche Butter
Mehl mit Salz, Schalotte und Rosmarin in einer großen Schüssel vermischen. Die Hefe in warmem Wasser auflösen und unter die Mischung rühren. 5 Minuten lang durchkneten, dann das Olivenöl und die Butter hinzufügen. Weitere 5 Minuten lang kneten und den Teig dann 30 Minuten ruhen lassen.

2 Dosen zerstoßene Tomaten
2 gehackte Knoblauchzehen

2 EL Tomatenmark
2 EL gehackte Petersilie
2 EL gehacktes Basilikum
Zucker, Salz und Pfeffer
Alle Zutaten miteinander vermischen und abschmecken.
4 in Scheiben geschnittene Tomaten
225 g Mozzarella
1 Bund Basilikum
Teig in eine runde Backform geben und weitere 30 Minuten gehen lassen. Salzen, mit Olivenöl beträufeln und 12 Minuten bei 220 °C backen. Die Tomatensoße gleichmäßig auf dem Teig verteilen, mit Tomatenscheiben und Mozzarella belegen und bei 200 °C backen, bis der Käse geschmolzen und das Brot knusprig ist. Mit feinen Basilikumstreifen garnieren.

450 g de farine
1 c. à café de sel
1 échalote coupée en dés
1 c. à café de romarin haché
55 g de levure fraîche
250 ml d'eau chaude
2 c. à soupe d'huile d'olive
2 c. à soupe de beurre mou
Dans un grand plat creux, mélanger la farine, le sel, l'échalote et le romarin. Diluer la levure dans l'eau chaude et incorporer le liquide au mélange en remuant. Pétrir la pâte pendant 5 minutes, puis incorporer l'huile d'olive et le beurre. Pétrir pendant 5 minutes encore, puis laisser reposer la pâte 30 minutes.

2 boites de tomates écrasées
2 gousses d'ail hachées

2 c. à soupe de concentré de tomate
2 c. à soupe de persil haché
2 c. à soupe de basilic haché
Sucre, sel et poivre
Mélanger tous les ingrédients, puis assaisonner.
4 tomates coupées en rondelles
225 g de mozzarella
1 bouquet de basilic
Disposer la pâte dans un moule rond allant au four et laisser reposer 30 minutes. Saler, arroser d'huile d'olive et cuire au four à 220 °C. Répartir régulièrement la sauce à la tomate sur la pâte, couvrir avec les rondelles de tomates et la mozzarella, puis cuire au four à 200 °C jusqu'à ce que le fromage fonde. Le pain doit être croustillant. Garnir de basilic finement coupé.

450 g de harina
1 cucharadita de sal
1 chalote en dados
1 cucharadita de romero picado
55 g de levadura fresca
250 ml de agua caliente
2 cucharadas de aceite de oliva
2 cucharadas de mantequilla blanda
Ponga la harina con la sal, el chalote y el romero en un cuenco grande. Disuelva la levadura en agua caliente, añádala al cuenco y remueva. Amase la mezcla durante 5 minutos e incorpore después el aceite de oliva y la mantequilla. Siga amasando la pasta durante 5 minutos más y déjela reposar durante 30 minutos.

2 latas de tomate triturado
2 dientes de ajo picados

2 cucharadas de concentrado de tomate
2 cucharadas de perejil picado
2 cucharadas de albahaca picada
Azúcar, sal y pimienta
Mezcle todos los ingredientes y condimente.
4 tomates en rodajas
225 g de queso mozzarella
1 manojo de albahaca
Ponga la masa en un molde redondo y deje que repose durante 30 minutos. Sazone con sal, vierta por encima el aceite de oliva y hornee durante 12 minutos a 220 °C. Reparta el tomate triturado de forma uniforme sobre la masa, ponga después encima las rodajas de tomate y el queso mozzarella y hornee a 200 °C hasta que el queso se haya fundido y el pan esté crujiente. Decore con tiras de albahaca.

450 g di farina
1 cucchiaino di sale
1 scalogno tagliato a dadini
1 cucchiaino di rosmarino tritato
55 g di lievito fresco
250 ml di acqua calda
2 cucchiai di olio di oliva
2 cucchiai di burro morbido
Mettere la farina, il sale, lo scalogno ed il rosmarino in una grossa ciotola. Sciogliere il lievito in acqua calda ed incorporarlo al composto. Impastare per 5 minuti, quindi unire l'olio di oliva ed il burro. Lavorare per altri 5 minuti e lasciar riposare l'impasto per 30 minuti.

2 scatole di pomodori a pezzetti
2 spicchi d'aglio tritati

2 cucchiai di pasta di pomodoro
2 cucchiai di prezzemolo tritato
2 cucchiai di basilico tritato
Zucchero, sale e pepe
Mescolare tutti gli ingredienti, assaggiare e regolare il condimento.
4 pomodori tagliati a fette
225 g di mozzarella
1 mazzetto di basilico
Mettere l'impasto in uno stampo rotondo e lasciarlo riposare per 30 minuti. Salare, spennellare con olio di oliva e cuocere in forno a 220 °C per 12 minuti. Versare uniformemente la salsa di pomodoro sulla focaccia, distribuirvi sopra le fette di pomodoro e la mozzarella e cuocere in forno a 200 °C, finché il formaggio si sarà sciolto e la focaccia croccante. Guarnire con striscioline di basilico.

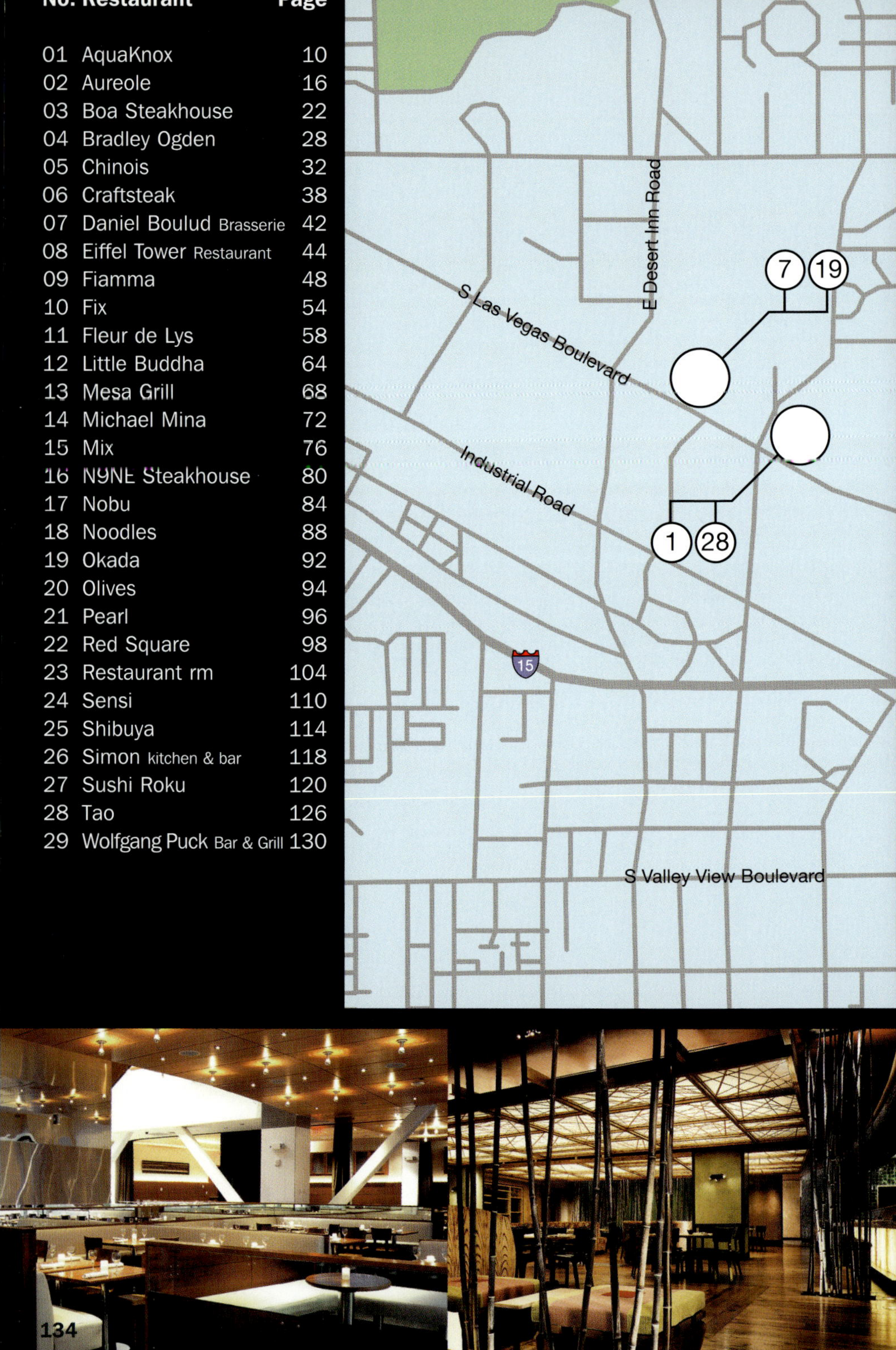

E Desert Inn Road
S Las Vegas Boulevard
Industrial Road
7
19
1
28
15
S Valley View Boulevard

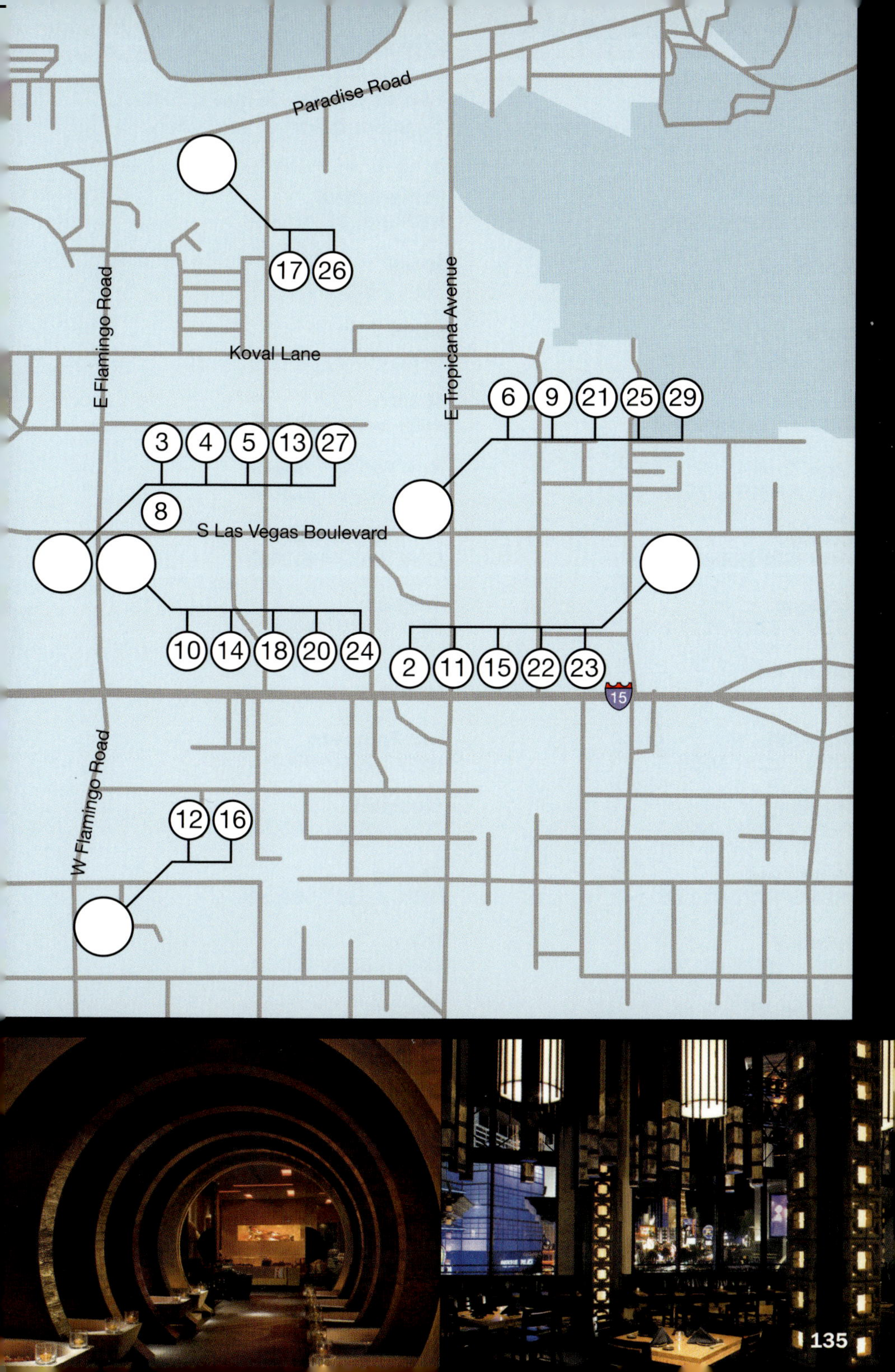

Paradise Road
E Flamingo Road
Koval Lane
E Tropicana Avenue
17 26
6 9 21 25 29
3 4 5 13 27
8
S Las Vegas Boulevard
10 14 18 20 24
2 11 15 22 23
15
W Flamingo Road
12 16